Windows™
for Non-Geeks

Jim Boyce
Rob Tidrow

NRP
NEW RIDERS
PUBLISHING

New Riders Publishing, Carmel, Indiana

Windows for Non-Nerds

By Jim Boyce and Rob Tidrow

Published by
New Riders Publishing
11711 N. College Ave., Suite 140
Carmel, IN 46032 USA

Copyright © 1993 by New Riders Publishing

Printed in the United States of America   3 4 5 6 7 8 9 0

Library of Congress Cataloging-in-Publication Data

```
Boyce, Jim, 1958-
   Windows for non-nerds / Jim Boyce, Rob Tidrow.
      p.   cm.
   Includes index.
   ISBN 1-56205-152-0 : $18.95
   1. Windows (Computer programs) 2. Microsoft Windows (Computer
file)   I. Tidrow, Rob.   II. Title.
QA76.W56B686      1993
005.4'3--dc20                                    93-9563
                                                    CIP
```

Publisher
David P. Ewing

Associate Publisher
Tim Huddleston

Managing Editor
Cheri Robinson

Acquisitions Editor
John Pont

Marketing Manager
Brad Koch

Product Director
Rob Tidrow

Production Editors
Cheri Robinson
Rob Tidrow

Objective Reader
John Pont

Editors
Patrice Hartmann
Katherine Murray
Nancy Sixsmith
Lisa Wagner

Technical Editor
Jonathon Ort

Book Design and Production
Amy Peppler-Adams
Katy Bodenmiller
Roger Morgan
Matthew Morrill
Juli Pavey
Angela M. Pozdol
Susan Shepard
Mary Beth Wakefield
Alyssa Yesh

Proofreaders
Carla Hall-Batton
Howard Jones
John Kane
Sean Medlock
Tim Montgomery
Angie Trzepacz

Indexed by
Tina Trettin
Joelyn Gifford

About the Authors

Jim Boyce

Jim Boyce is what some people call a *computer guru*. Jim prefers the title "Bonehead Who Knows A Lot About Computers." An ex-boss once called him a "likeable computer know-it-all," so at least Jim isn't one of those obnoxious computer nerds who knows everything and is smug about it. He just knows everything.

Jim has been using Windows since before fire was invented. He is a Contributing Editor to *Windows Magazine*, and a regular contributor to *CADENCE Magazine* and other computer publications. His book *Maximizing Windows* has been a best seller for the past two years. Jim has been a computer user, system administrator, programmer, and college instructor during his years in the computer field. When he hasn't been busy saving the Universe from destruction, Jim has had time to author and co-author the following books:

- *Maximizing Windows 3.1*
- *Inside Windows for Workgroups*
- *Inside Windows 3.1*
- *Windows 3.1 Networking*
- *Maximizing Windows 3.0*
- *Maximizing MS-DOS 5.0*
- *AutoCAD for Beginners*
- *Inside AutoCAD for Windows*
- *Inside AutoCAD Release 12*
- *Maximizing AutoCAD Volume 1*

Jim is a transplanted Texan living in Minnesota with his family. If you are a CompuServe kind of person, you can contact Jim via his CompuServe ID, 76516,3403.

Rob Tidrow

Rob Tidrow is a Product Director at New Riders Publishing who specializes in operating systems and dabbles in graphics- and CAD-related topics. After studying English literature at Indiana University, Rob needed a job so he wandered off the streets and into New Riders Publishing. Unlike Jim, he is **NOT** a computer guru, but considers himself "lucky to have a job."

As an editor at New Riders, Rob edited several popular NRP titles, including *Inside Novell NetWare*, *Inside Windows 3.1*, *Maximizing Windows 3.1*, *Inside AutoCAD*, and *Inside Microsoft Access*. Now as a developer, Rob finds himself awash in titles such as *Technology Edge: A Guide to Field Computing*, *The Fonts Coach*, and *The Modem Coach*, as well as developing *Windows for Non-Nerds*. Rob also is co-author of *AutoCAD Student Workbook*, which is published by New Riders Publishing.

Rob has created technical documentation and instructional programs for use in a variety of industrial settings. He resides in Indianapolis with his wife, Tammy, and their two boys, Adam and Wesley.

Dedication

"This book is dedicated with love to my dad, who knows a lot of stuff about a lot of stuff and is the best cook in the Known Universe. But, he needed this book six months ago." — Jim

"The beauty of a loving family is that it tames the beast within you. Thanks Tammy, Adam, and Wesley." — Rob

Acknowledgments

A lot of people helped put this book together in one way or another. I offer my wholehearted thanks to

Rob Tidrow, for all of his efforts in developing the book, editing, and writing while his wife was busy having a baby. Really, Rob, she did all the work. Congratulations to you both!

Cheri Robinson, for spending long hours editing while her mind was really on shooting down to Cancun for some R and R.

John Pont, for his help in getting the project up and running.

John Schmitt, who didn't have anything to do with this book. I forgot to send him a copy of my last book, so this will make up for it.

Rob would like to thank the following New Riders staff members and Prentice Hall Computer Publishing Production staff who made this book happen:

Dave Ewing, for accepting the challenge to take on this series of books.

Tim Huddleston, for working out the details for the crossword puzzle, word search, and the beer.

Lisa Wagner, Patrice Hartmann, Nancy Sixsmith, and Katherine Murray, for their editing.

Mathew Morrill, Amy Peppler-Adams, and Mary Beth Wakefield, for taking the material at the last possible moment and turning yet another miracle.

PHCP Production staff for putting up with all our changes and idiosyncrasies.

PHCP proofreading and indexing staff, guided by Joelynn Gifford, for their fantastic and timely work.

Jared Lee, Chris Rozzi, and Talmage ("Tal") Burdine, for the illustrations and cartoons.

The puzzles in this book were designed by Terry Hall. Mr. Hall is the owner of Media Ministries, in Wheaton, IL, and has been a professional puzzle designer for several years. Mr. Hall uses computers in most of his design work, and has published several complete books of crossword puzzles, word searches, and other puzzles. His most recent puzzle books--*Tyndale Crossword Puzzles, Volume I and II*--were published by Tyndale House Publisher, Inc.

Trademark Acknowledgments

New Riders Publishing has made every attempt to supply trademark information about company names, products, and services mentioned in this book. Trademarks indicated below were derived from various sources. New Riders Publishing cannot attest to the accuracy of this information.

Microsoft Windows and MS-DOS are registered trademarks of Microsoft Corporation.

WordPerfect is a registered trademark of WordPerfect Corporation.

Trademarks of other products mentioned in this book are held by the companies producing them.

Warning and Disclaimer

This book is designed to provide information about the Windows 3.1 computer program. Every effort has been made to make this book as complete and as accurate as possible, but no warranty or fitness is implied.

The information is provided on an "as is" basis. The author and New Riders Publishing shall have neither liability nor responsibility to any person or entity with respect to any loss or damages arising from the information contained in this book or from the use of the disks or programs that may accompany it.

Contents at a Glance

Contents

Stuff that nobody ever reads, but it's always the best part...

You're probably reading this book for one of two reasons. The first reason may be that you're remodeling your house and thought you had picked up a book that explained stuff like low-E glass, oak extension jambs, weather-stripping, and all the other things you heard Norm talk about on *This Old House*.

Sorry, but you blew it.

You're not remodeling your house? That must mean that you have Microsoft Windows on a computer, either at home or at the office, and you feel like a complete idiot about it.

Just push the button, okay?

Relax, you're in good company. I know a lot of doctors, lawyers, and elephant tamers who feel the same way. (Okay, I only know a *few* lawyers.) They'd rather use the computer for a doorstop than face the fact that they're all thumbs when it comes to Windows and computers. After all, Windows is supposed to make computers *easy* to use, right?

What do all of these people have in common? Basically, they don't know which buttons to push. That's what *Windows for Non-Nerds* is for—to show you which buttons to push and when to push them. You learn a little of the *why* about each topic also, but in everyday terms that make sense. You won't find a lot of technical jargon or explanations of things that don't really matter—just simple answers to all of those things the manual expected you to already know.

NERDY DETAILS

If you really have nothing better to do, there are even some sections scattered here and there that give you some nerdy, technical stuff so that you can impress your friends and intimidate your enemies. When you see this type of formatting in the book, don't read it unless you're wearing your pocket protector.

Wait! Don't press *that* button!

If you're worried about doing something stupid and melting down your computer, stop worrying. This book won't get you into anything you can't easily get out of, and you won't do any *real* damage along the way. Just don't throw the computer at anyone, and never panic...

STOP!

Seriously, there is really very little you can do that will actually damage the computer. In fact, short of the obvious things like hitting it with a hammer or putting it through the spin cycle in your washer, there's really *nothing* you can do to damage the computer just by using Windows or your programs. If I get into areas in which you might find some trouble, you'll see sections like this that tell you when to STOP! and watch out.

More instructions...

Another thing that we show you in this book is what you need to type at the keyboard if it's not a button you have to press. When you see text that is in boldface, such as **EAT**, you know you have to type that word on your keyboard.

If you see something in a special `typeface`, you know that this is what you might see on your computer screen. You don't need to type it unless it also is boldface. If you see text that is both boldface and in a special typeface, you need to type it, such as:

EAT AT JOE'S

What About the Manuals?

Read the manual? Hah! Sometimes you need a manual to explain the things in the manual. Computer hardware and software manuals generally are not written for the novice. A few are excellent, and are great for any level of user. Unfortunately, these are the exception rather than the rule.

 That isn't to say that the manuals that came with your computer and software are useless. Quite the opposite is true. Most are filled with useful information. The problem is that you have to understand the program and how to use it before the manual makes much sense.

 Besides, it's *unnatural* to read the manual first—you never read the directions that fell out of the box marked "Some Assembly Required," did you?

SAVE THE DAY!

Most software or computer manuals don't give you little hints or tips on how you can "save the day" in case you experience a computer catastrophe. These Save the Day notes are intended to help you get out of dire situations, such as when you need to find a file that you just erased or you need to reset the computer's clock.

Don't throw away those manuals. Proudly place them on your bookshelf to make everyone think you're a computer expert. After you've spent a few weeks with *Windows for Non-Nerds*, you'll be using Windows like a wizard, and everyone will *really* think you're an expert.

What You Got for Your Money

This book doesn't cover everything there is to know about Windows 3.1. You'll have to buy a couple of other books to get that far (try *Inside Windows 3.1* or *Maximizing Windows 3.1*, also from New Riders Publishing). The mission of *Windows for Non-Nerds* is to cover enough of the basics of Microsoft Windows to make you comfortable using it, like the following points:

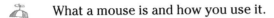 What a mouse is and how you use it.

How to work with all those colorful boxes and pretty pictures in Windows.

How to start programs.

What kinds of programs you got for free with Windows.

Why your printer won't work.

How to get help when you feel overwhelmed.

TRICKS

You also get these free Tricks thrown in when the authors have some pretty useful or neat things to tell. These tricks are designed to give you some Windows "magic" to simplify your life or make your computer do something real cool.

Ready, Set...

You're no doubt ready for some help in using Windows, or you wouldn't be reading this book (unless you're still trying to figure out that low-E glass thing...).

This book is not intended to be read from start to finish (you can do this if you really want to, but we don't suggest it). If you are looking for a particular section or chapter to read, take a look at the following breakdown of each Part to see where you need to go.

Part 1 is your quick start to Windows

Part 1, *Real Basic Windows Stuff*, has you using Windows right from the get-go. Chapter 0 (that's right, Chapter *0*) throws you into the Windows driver's seat, showing you how to play a game of Solitaire and how to write a letter using Windows. The rest of Part 1 covers the essentials all Windows users need to know, from what Windows is to the equipment you need to use Windows, to putting (*installing*) Windows on your system.

Part 2 is where you really get into it

Part 2 is a good place to start if you want to get into the heart of Windows. Called *Make Windows Earn Its Keep*, Part 2 shows you how to start a REAL Windows session, how to do things in Windows, what all that mouse stuff does, and what all those boxes and menus mean in Windows. Go there right now if you already know the type of computer equipment you have, as well as knowing that you have Windows already installed on your computer.

Part 3 is where you tell Windows what to do

Okay, so you already know what Windows does when you start it, you know what to use your mouse for, and you are comfortable with a lot of the Windows jargon. Go to Part 3.

Here we show you how you can tell Windows what to do. You need to set up a new program in Windows? Turn to Chapter 7. You want to organize your files, perhaps. Then turn to Chapter 9. You desperately need to print that financial statement? Hurry, turn to Chapter 11. Part 3 also shows you how to use Windows' built-in help system, as well as how to recycle information from one document to another. This part is worth its weight in icons.

See Part 4 to learn about running programs

The nice thing about Windows is that you can run several programs at once. Part 4 is intended to help you with those little problems you might encounter when you run programs in Windows. You also are given some ideas on how to make your DOS programs work properly under Windows. By the way, if you are unfamiliar with DOS, try to stay that way. You don't really need to know too much about it, but see Chapter 1 if you want a nice introduction to it.

Part 5 might sound scary, but...

Sooner or later (usually sooner than later) you'll want to change the way Windows is set up. That's no problem. In fact, that's why Windows gives you ultimate control over the way your computer area looks. That's also why we offer you Part 5, called *You Mean I Have To Set Up More Stuff?* We are confident that you will want (and need) to change a few things about Windows, increase Windows performance for your particular system, or set up a new printer. This is not really advanced stuff, but you should be comfortable with Windows before moving to this part (maybe after the second day or something).

Part 6 will help you. I promise...

Do you feel really stupid and lost? Try a new religion. No, seriously, turn to Part 6, called *I Really Need Help*, and find out how you can be saved from those nagging problems that you have with Windows. Chapter 18 gives you some hands-on advice that you can use to try to get you out of your mess. Chapter 19, "Some Words You Should Know," provides help with those bothersome technical terms you need to know.

NERDY
DETAILS

When you buy windows that use low-E glass, it usually means that the dead space between the inside and outside panes is filled with argon or another type of gas. The gas helps the window pass heat less easily, keeping warm air inside the house in the winter and warm air out in the summer (and cool air in). You didn't really want to know that, did you?

So, without much to do about nothing, throw on your swimsuit, flip to Chapter 0, and start using Windows!

PART 1

Real Basic Windows Stuff

CHAPTER

0

Get Your Feet Wet

How often do you fast-forward through the opening previews and credits of a video tape to get to the actual movie? Have you ever driven through the corner gas station to bypass a red light? Do you ever turn to the last page of a book and read the ending?

If you're like me, you probably do the first two actions, but never the last one (unless you forgot to read your assignment in Lit 101). Likewise, do you ever skip over the first two or three chapters of a textbook, bypassing all the publisher hype and miscellaneous information that doesn't really help you?

This chapter is your fast-forward approach to using Windows 3.1. After you complete this chapter, you will recognize the following items in Windows:

- The pretty colors in Windows

- A Windows version of Solitaire

- A neat little program that helps you write letters to your mother

What To Know Before You Play

The easiest ways to learn something often is simply to do it. You might not learn everything you need to know, but you do learn some valuable lessons from that initial experience. The same is true with using Windows: the only way to learn it is to use it.

You don't need to know the history of Windows (or computers) to start, run, and use it productively (or even non-productively). The only thing you need to know is whether Windows is on your computer.

Right now, turn on your computer. (By the way, if you don't have a computer, you can't run Windows. Just thought I'd tell you that.) Depending on your equipment, you might have to turn on your *monitor*, which is the thing that looks like a TV set only smaller, separately from your computer.

NERDY
DETAILS

Without confusing you too much right now, I am calling the big, heavy, boxy-looking thing the *computer*. It really is called the system unit, but you'll learn that in Chapter 2. I guess technically your entire setup, including the keyboard (that typewriter-looking thingy), monitor, and system unit, is the computer. But for now, you just need to turn it on. You don't need to know what it's called.

When your computer finally comes on (which takes a few moments of beeping and grinding), you will see one of several different things. One, you might get lucky and see a colorful screen with the words "Program Manager" written atop a box, like the one shown in figure 0.1. If so, you're already in Windows and you can skip all the following garbage and go straight to the section called "Now That You're in Windows."

Figure 0.1

If it's your lucky day, you see a screen something like this one when you turn on your computer.

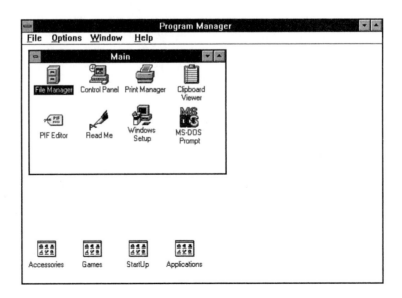

But I don't see Program Manager on my screen!

If you don't see the words "Program Manager" on your screen, but the screen is very colorful with lots of boxes, you still might be in Windows. If this is the case, you might be in some weird place in Windows and you need to see Chapter 18 right now. It might help you get "unlost."

Another screen that you might see is rather daunting looking: the DOS prompt. The DOS prompt is just a black screen with some unintelligible code on it like the one shown in figure 0.2. (Ironically, "DOS" happens to rhyme with "boss," which is appropriate—I usually find them equally demanding and unintelligible.)

```
c:\>
```

Figure 0.2

If you're not lucky, you will see this ugly thing called the DOS prompt.

If you're at this screen, just type three magic letters, **WIN**, and then press the Enter key on your keyboard to start Windows. If all goes well, your screen flickers and a colorful advertisement for Windows 3.1 momentarily appears on your screen. You then see more color, a picture of an hourglass, and then (hopefully) you see the words "Program Manager" at the top of your screen (see fig. 0.1), indicating that you are in Windows.

STOP!

If your screen doesn't look like the one shown in figure 0.1, you might have a problem with the way Windows is set up on your computer. Don't panic, just yell at the stupid geek that told you that everything was okay in the first place. If that person isn't around, there must be a "Star Trek" convention going on, so turn to Chapter 18—it might help you.

Now That You're in Windows...

Ah! The air is fresh, the skies are blue, your life is finally in order...

Think again, buddy. You still have to figure out how to use Windows because the boss is standing behind you, waiting for you to prove that you really do "just have to have" this computer to really do the job right.

For right now, though, let's just play a game.

Playing the Hand You're Dealt

One way to fake out the boss is to turn your computer around so that the boss can't see the screen, then play a game of Solitaire. You might be just messing around, but you certainly look like you're being productive!

TRICKS

Okay, so you don't want to play games with your expensive computer. Think of this game of Solitaire as "training." The neat thing about Windows is that you need to learn only a handful of actions (not a bunch of techie mumbo-jumbo) to get most of your jobs done with the computer. After you complete a game of Solitaire, you will be acquainted with several basic Windows actions that you use every day with every Windows program, whether it is another game, a word processor, or a more complicated spreadsheet program.

Finding the Solitaire game

When you look at your screen, you should see a large box that has several smaller boxes in it. Don't worry about what these are officially called; you learn that in Chapters 5 and 6. For now, just try to find the box named "Games" like the one shown in figure 0.3 If yours looks like this, jump over the following few paragraphs to the section called "Now For the Fun Part!"

If the word "Games" is at the bottom of the screen beneath a tiny little picture (called an *icon*) like the one shown in figure 0.4, you need to perform some magic before you can actually start Solitaire.

Figure 0.3

A box called Games,
with Solitaire waiting to
be started.

Figure 0.4

A tiny picture called
Games.

Without me really telling you what you're doing, follow these steps. You'll be amazed at what happens:

1. Grab your mouse and move it around a little. (Read Chapter 2 for more information on the mouse.) Be sure to keep it on the desk as you roll it around. Some people actually pick up the mouse and point it at the screen like a remote control for a TV. Don't get caught doing this. You will never live it down. But then, I know you're no dummy, or you would've bought that book that was written for dummies, right?

2. As you move the mouse on your desk, you will see an arrow move around on your screen. This is called the *pointer*. Go ahead and remember that term. I use it a lot in this chapter.

3. Move the pointer (um...that is, move the mouse, which moves the little arrow on your screen) so that it points to the little picture (called an *icon*) above the word Solitaire.

4. Now comes the wild and wacky stuff. With your index figure, press the left button on your mouse two times real fast. This action might feel strange at first, but you'll get used to it. Actually, you can master this action, called *double-clicking*, in about two minutes.

5. If you do step 4 correctly, your tiny picture called Games should enlarge to a box called Games that contains the icon shown in figure 0.3. If you don't do step 4 correctly, keep trying. You'll either get the hang of this "double-clicking" thing, or your finger will start cramping. Just remember, you're going to play a game in a few minutes.

Now for the fun part!

Even if you've never played Solitaire, go ahead and start the game now.
Windows won't let you cheat, but it will give you help if you need it.

TRICKS

You might see another game in the Games box called Minesweeper. I think this game is boring, but if you want more
information on playing this game, see the manual that came
with Windows or contact Peter Kuhns at New Riders Publishing. He's a real pro at this game. (My wife's pretty good at
Solitaire, by the way.)

Double-click on the Solitaire icon (the tiny picture of a pack of cards above
the word Solitaire). After Solitaire starts, your screen should look something
like the one shown in figure 0.5. Check out those cool-looking cards!

Figure 0.5

SOLITAIRE!

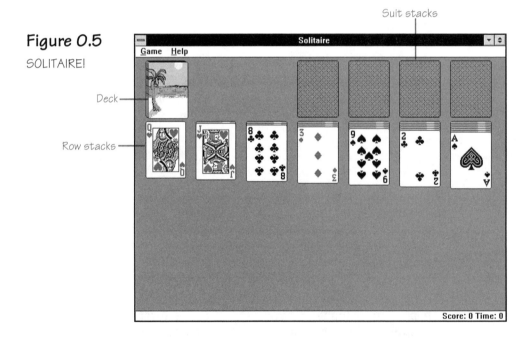

Make sure you have seven stacks (strangely dubbed "row stacks" by some-
body at Microsoft) of cards across the screen. If you don't, don't panic. Just

click on the little up arrow in the top right corner of the Solitaire screen, and your solitaire screen will grow—I mean GROW—until it covers your entire screen. You should see all seven stacks now.

NERDY DETAILS

This "growing" spurt is called *maximizing* in Windowsese. You learn that term in Chapter 6—but don't turn there now. Go ahead and play a game or two of Solitaire first.

The playing field

Before you actually begin playing the game, read over these points to see what Microsoft calls the stacks of cards on the screen:

 Deck. This is in the top left corner of the screen (see fig. 0.5).

 Suit stacks. This is where your same-suit cards go, starting with the Ace and going from low card to high card.

 Row stacks. This is the "main" playing field, where you stack cards from high to low, alternating between black and red cards.

TRICKS

If you don't know how to play Solitaire, you can always buy a Hoyle's book, or ask some people that you go to lunch with. They might know how to play.

More Windows stuff

Okay, you know how to play Solitaire, or at least you have enough bravery to start playing (kind of like when you wouldn't admit that you didn't know how to ski, but your gorgeous date wanted to hit the slopes anyway). You won't break your neck here or your ego, but you might learn a few Windows actions. That's pain enough.

Remember the rules of the game: you have to move cards around and turn over decks of cards, but you have to do this by using that mouse thing again.

STOP!

Don't try putting your hand through your screen to move the cards, because all you'll wind up doing is putting your finger-prints on your screen. You'll get plenty of those when you try to pinpoint some column with a billion numbers in a spread-sheet that the boss wants you to analyze around midnight.

Moving cards around

Use these steps if you want to know how to move some cards around:

1. When you find a card that you can play (like the 2 of Clubs in figure 0.5), move your mouse until the pointer on your screen is on top of it. Press the left button on the mouse and hold it down. Keep holding the button down, and don't let go until I tell you to.

TRICKS

Of course, you might not necessarily have a red 3 or black 2 on your screen that you can move, but you should have some-thing; maybe a black 5 and a red 6, or a red Queen and a black King. Just keep telling yourself "Higher to lower, red-black-red or black-red-black..."

2. With your finger holding down the button, move the mouse. The black 2 moves with it as if it is magnetized to the pointer. You can move that black 2 anyplace in the playing area. Try it. It's pretty cool, actually.

3. When you get tired of moving the black 2 around, find the red 3 and move the mouse so that the black 2 is over that 3. Let go of the mouse button NOW. The black 2 falls off your cursor on top of the red 3. WOW! You just made your first move in what will become a long string of Solitaire games.

NERDY
DETAILS

Because this chapter should introduce some Windows terms to you, I might as well tell you that the action you did in Step 3 is called drag-and-drop in Windows lingo.

When you start a new Solitaire game, the deck of cards is face-down. You will need to use these cards, so you need to turn the cards right-side up. Move your mouse so that the pointer on your screen is over the deck of cards. Press the left button on the mouse once. The top three cards in the deck turn over, exposing the third card in the deck. If you can play this card (that is, if you have someplace to put it), move it as you did the black 2 in the preceding steps.

Recycling the deck

Keep clicking on the deck of cards until all the cards are face-up, playing them as you can. Remember, just like in regular Solitaire, when you move one card, you need to survey the entire Solitaire playing area to make any more moves. Sometimes you can make several things "happen" just by turning over one card. Other times, you can go through the deck twenty times and not make one move.

When all the cards are face-up, cycle through them again, and again, and again.... To do this, double-click on the top card in the deck and the cards return to the face-down pile so you can turn them over again. You might do this several times in a game before you win or before you can't make any more moves.

TRICKS

If you uncover an Ace in the deck or in the row stacks, double-click on it. The Ace moves to the suit stacks automatically. You then can start building the suit stacks in ascending order (low to high) and double-click on any card that you can move to the suit stacks. If you have an Ace of Diamonds in the suit stack, for example, and you have a Two of Diamonds that you can move, double-click on the Two of Diamonds and it will automatically jump on top of the Ace of Diamonds.

As you play the game, row stacks will need to be turned over when the top card is face-down. Just double-click on the top card to turn it over.

 Row stacks also become empty during the game. Remember to fill these empty places with Kings (Windows won't let you put anything but Kings in an empty row).

 As a matter of fact, Windows will not let you make any illegal moves. Try it. You can't. Windows snaps that card right back to where it came from.

 You can move more than one card at a time if they are in the same stack. Let's say you have a row stack that goes from 10 to 6. That's five cards in one stack. Now let's say you can move those cards so that the 10 lays on top of a Jack. Grab the whole stack by moving the mouse to the 10, then press (and hold) the left mouse button. Then move the cards to the Jack and drop the cards there. It looks like a train moving across the screen.

You know enough now to keep playing. A neat little trick in the next section tells you how to "hide" your solitaire game if you see the boss coming so that you can resume the same game after the boss passes by.

Keep playing until you can't move

Solitaire is fun, but it is frustrating because you don't win every game. At least I don't. (I wonder if my wife has any Solitaire secrets?) Sooner or later you have to give up and quit turning over those stupid cards. Just look near the top of the Solitaire screen for the word **G**ame and move your mouse until the pointer is on top of it. Double-click on it. This opens a thing called the **G**ames menu.

 To start a new game of Solitaire, which you will want to do (unless it's quittin' time), just move the mouse until the pointer is over the word **D**eal and double-click on it. Windows deals a new game and you are off and running.

To end the game completely so that you can go to lunch and tell your colleagues that you are working on "a difficult Windows tutorial," move your mouse until the pointer is over the word E**x**it and click on it. This command tells Windows to turn off Solitaire so that you can do something more productive.

 Remember, you need to move all the cards to the suit stacks in the upper right of the Solitaire screen to win. When you do this, you will see only four Kings on top of these stacks—nothing else will be on the playing area. If you get lucky and you win, a really cool thing happens on your screen: the cards start falling off the suit stack and bounce across your screen. That's right—that's all you get for winning the game. (You don't even get to enter your initials for high score or shortest time or anything!) When you get tired of following the bouncing cards, press any key to make it stop.

SAVE THE DAY!

If you hear the boss coming down the hall, you can quickly hide your Solitaire game (or any other Windows program) by pointing your mouse to the down arrow in the top right corner of the Solitaire screen (see fig. 0.6). This reduces the big screen of Solitaire to a tiny picture of a deck of cards at the bottom of your screen. essentially hiding it from the watchful eyes of the boss. (This really should be called a "Save Your Job" note.) You'll use this action quite a bit in Windows, but not necessarily to hide Solitaire.

After the boss leaves, you can quickly return to your game by double-clicking on the Solitaire icon again. (This action is known as *maximizing*.) You can quit your game entirely by clicking on the **F**ile menu, then clicking on E**x**it. This should return you to the Program Manager screen.

Figure 0.6

Press here to hide your
game of Solitaire.

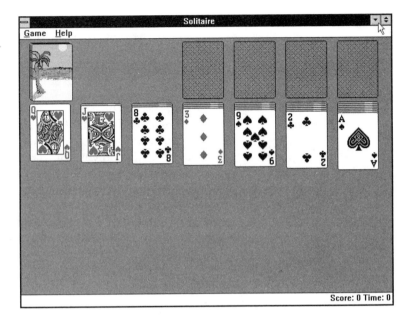

But I Don't Always Want
To Waste Time...

As far I am concerned, after you learn to play Solitaire in Windows, you have
learned all the basic actions that you need to survive in the Windows wilder-
ness. Table 0.1 shows you these actions.

Table 0.1
You Mean I Learned All This?

What you did...	What a nerd calls it
Typed **WIN**	Starting Windows
Moved the mouse	Moving the mouse (gee, what a surprise!)
Pressed the left mouse button	Clicking
Moved cards on top of each other	Dragging-and-dropping

What you did...	What a nerd calls it
Called Peter Kuhns	Winning at Minesweeper
Made your Solitaire game bigger	Maximizing a window
Hid your Solitaire game	Minimizing a window or saving your job
Ended your game	Quitting or exiting a program

On the other hand, you might decide you want to actually get something done, like write a business report or a letter to your mom. I'm not going to show you how to create a sophisticated business report—you probably already know how to do that without using Windows. I will, however, show you how to start a word processor that you get free with Windows, write a short letter to your mom, and then print it out. You don't need any more skills than your reading skills to get through this exercise. Remember, this is Chapter 0, so it doesn't count on the final exam. It only prepares you to take it!

Dear Mom,...

You should have enough control to stop your Solitaire game and start something more practical. Or, you might have used my last tip in the preceding directions when the boss came in and now you need something to do. Easy enough. Just make sure the words Program Manager appear on top of your screen again, then look for a box with the word Accessories at the top of it, or an icon called Accessories.

Move the mouse until the pointer is on top of the Accessories icon, and then double-click to make the icon turn into a window. The word Accessories should appear at the top of the box.

NERDY
DETAILS

> When I say "box" in this chapter, I usually mean *window*, but I don't want to confuse you right now. When I first started using Windows, I was confused by the term "Windows," meaning the Microsoft product called Windows, and "windows," which are the boxes that display on your screen. I'll try to call them boxes, but I might start calling them *windows* if I forget. Either way, Chapter 5 tells you what a window is in Windows.

Find the word Write below an icon of a fountain pen and double-click on it. This action starts another program that Windows gives you for free (see fig. 0.7). This program is called Write and it is a word processor.

Figure 0.7

Write, the Windows
built-in word processor.

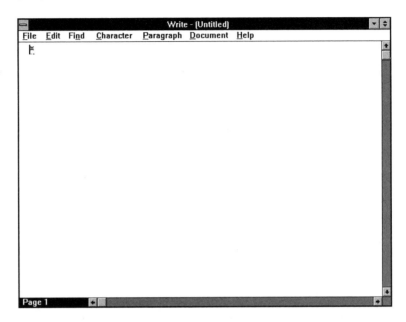

NERDY
DETAILS

This isn't really a technical note, but more of a definition. Word processors help you create memos, letters, and documents for your home, business, and recreational needs. In everyday language, that means that word processors replace your typewriter.

Typing your letter

The top of the screen says Write - (Untitled). You can start writing a letter right now by placing your fingers on the keys of your keyboard and typing. You might want to type something goofy, such as the following:

```
Dear Mom,

How are you? I am fine. I hope that you and dad have finally rented out
my bedroom like you said you were going to do while I lived with you for
ten years after my college graduation.

Sincerely,

Your Son
```

Press Enter on your keyboard when you want to start a new paragraph. The letter shown in figure 0.8 shows where you need to press the Enter key.

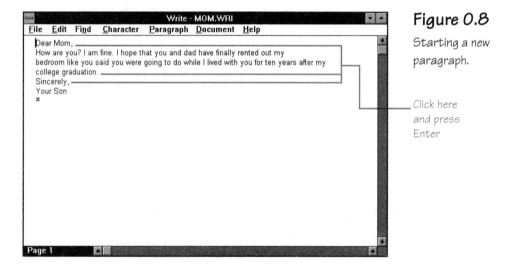

Figure 0.8

Starting a new paragraph.

Click here and press Enter

Notice that you do not need to press Enter at the end of every line, only when you want to start a new paragraph. Within a paragraph, the word processor automatically kicks the words to the next line if they don't fit on one line. This feature, called *word wrapping*, is another great feature of a word processor.

TRICKS

Although I told you not to worry about doing anything fancy yet, you might want to dress up your letter a little by putting more space between your greeting ("Dear Mom,") and salutation ("Sincerely, Your Son") and the rest of the letter. To do this, just press Enter two or three times where it shows you to press Enter in figure 0.8.

Storing your letter

The letter you just wrote needs to be stored away so that you can use it again. I usually shove the letters I write into a junk drawer in my desk because I'm too lazy to buy stamps and mail them, but you can save your letters in the computer by just using these steps:

1.   Move the mouse until the pointer is over the word **F**ile in the upper left corner of the screen, then click on it.

2.   Press the left button on the mouse once so that a rectangular box appears on the screen. This is called the **F**ile menu, but don't worry about that right now.

3.   Move the mouse until the pointer is over the word **S**ave, then press the left mouse button. Another box appears on your screen (see fig. 0.9), but it's closer to the middle of your screen. This thing is called a *dialog box*, which you'll learn more about in Chapter 4.

Figure 0.9

The Save As dialog box, in which you tell the computer what you want to name your letter.

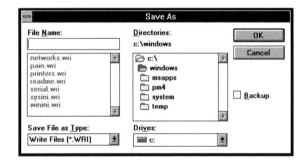

4.   You can now type the name that you want to call your letter. You can call it anything you want (sort of), but for now, just type **MOM**. Windows takes care of the rest. Oh yea. Press Enter, too.

NERDY
DETAILS

You can name your letters anything you want as long as the name is not longer than eight letters long (actually, eight characters long), but you will learn more about that in Chapter 9. For now, just type **MOM**. It's short and sweet, and it will help you find your letter later when you are looking for it.

Signing your letter

After you write your letter and save it for posterity, you will want to send it to your mom so she can either tape it to the refrigerator or throw it away. Unlike a typewriter, a word processor does not spit out your letter from the top of the screen, ready for you to fold and slip into an envelope. You need to tell the computer to give you a copy of your letter on a piece of real paper. This is called *printing*.

Move the mouse until the pointer is over the word **F**ile in the upper left corner of the screen (this is the same **F**ile menu that you used to store your letter in the preceding section) and click on it. Press the left mouse button. Now move the mouse until the pointer is over the word **P**rint and press the left button on the mouse. Another box, called the Print dialog box, comes on your screen (see fig. 0.10).

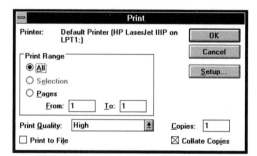

Figure 0.10

The Print dialog box, in which you tell the computer to print out a copy of your letter.

Ready, set, print

The Print dialog box might look rather busy, but don't worry about all that stuff right now. All you need to do is press Enter to tell the computer to tell the printer to give you a piece of paper that has your letter written on it. So go ahead and do it. Press Enter right now.

If you actually do have a printer attached to your computer, in a few moments your letter will be printed on a real piece of paper, ready for your grubby little hands to grab it.

STOP!

> You might not have a printer hooked to your computer, or you might actually get some scary-looking message on your screen telling you that the computer or printer is not working right. If this happens, you need to see Chapter 11, which is all about printing in Windows. If this does happen, I'm really sorry that I screwed up your day.

Licking the stamp

Of course, you will now want to send your letter to your mom, so get an envelope, address it using a real ink pen, and then put your letter in it. Make sure you seal the envelope and put a stamp on it. Otherwise the Post Office gets real mad and won't deliver the letter to your mom.

That's All For Now...

If you are not completely bored yet or you want to leave your computer on, just turn to Chapter 1 to learn more about Windows.

If you want to turn off your computer now and mail that letter to your mom, you have to do a few things first so that Windows doesn't freak out too much when you turn it off. Just do the following steps:

1. Move the mouse until the pointer is over the **F**ile menu and click on it.

2. Now move the mouse until the pointer is over the word E**x**it and click again.

The Write word processor vanishes from your screen. Don't worry, it's still on your computer. You have just "exited" your program, telling Windows that you want to stop working in it. You tell Windows goodbye the same way: click on **F**ile in the upper left-hand corner of the screen. Then do this:

1. Click on the E**x**it option. Your computer will start making noise. Don't worry. It's just putting everything back where it is supposed to go. Wouldn't you like your kids to put away their toys like this when they are done playing with them?

2. A message-in-a-box that says `This will end your Windows sessions` appears on your screen. Just press Enter and your computer again makes a bunch of noises and the pretty colors that were once on your screen now become that ugly black screen I showed you at the start of the chapter (the DOS prompt).

Dat's all, folks!

Windows, the Universe, and Everything

Let's say that you know a little about the way your computer works, and you have an idea of what Windows is. If you want to use Windows to do some real work *right now*, jump to Chapter 4. If you don't have Windows installed on your computer yet, make a side trip to Chapter 3.

If you're not too sure what Windows is, or why it's on your computer, or you don't know much about your computer in general, start here. Here are some of the questions that this chapter answers:

- What are programs?
- What is Windows?
- Is Windows necessary?
- Is Windows useful?
- What will Windows do for me?
- What is DOS, and what does it have to do with Windows?
- Do I need both DOS *and* Windows?
- What types of programs can I run with Windows?

Just a Little Bit About Programs and Data

Programs let you perform certain tasks with your computer. Here are some common tasks that people like you and me use computer programs to do:

- Write memos, letters, reports, and any other things that we used to create with a typewriter or pen and paper. Use a *word processing* program for these tasks.

- Keep track of lots of numbers, such as sales figures, income and expenses, tax stuff (yuck), test results, and just about anything else that requires fiddling with lots of numbers. Use a *spreadsheet* program for these jobs.

- Draw neat engineering drawings, graphs, and charts; make up fancy slides for overhead presentations; or keep the kids entertained with a doodling program. Use *graphics* programs for these tasks.

- Keep track of information and sort the information in a way that makes sense. You can keep track of names and addresses, inventory, recipes, or all the promises your candidate made in the last election.

- Connect your phone to your computer and call another computer to look up stock prices, airline schedules, the price of yak milk in Tibet, or send messages to people. Use a *communications* program for these jobs.

- Games. 'Nuf said.

- None of the above. Tons of special-purpose programs that let you program your mouse buttons, crunch lots of big files into one little file, and do all sorts of special purpose functions. These are *utility* programs.

A little about data

Data is the name of the android that's the Chief Science Officer on the Starship Enterprise. *Data* also is information that you type and store on your computer system. If you keep memos, letters, drawings, a list of your favorite polka bands, or any other kind of information on your computer, that's your *data*. You view, change, print, and store data by using programs. Usually, you store data in *files* on your computer's disks. Files are often called *documents* in Windows.

Running programs

You have two common ways to run programs on your computer. (Really, you have a choice of five ways, but I won't confuse you with the other three right now.) These two methods are DOS and Windows. These set up an electronic *environment* on your computer in which programs can run.

GEEK

NERDY DETAILS

Okay, maybe I will confuse you. There are five popular operating environments for the PC. They include various versions of DOS, Windows, UNIX (pronounced eu-nix), OS/2 (pronounced oh-es-two), and Windows NT. All offer differing capabilities when it comes to running programs. Other operating environments, such as the X Windows System, also are available for the PC. By far the most common operating environments, however, are DOS and Windows.

You can run programs in DOS, or you can run programs in Windows. In fact, with Windows, you get to do both (run DOS programs and Windows programs). Now you're probably asking "what the heck are DOS and Windows?" Let's start with Windows.

Windows?

You may already have Windows on your computer and not know what to do with it. Or, your friend, the obnoxious computer know-it-all, told you that you "absolutely gotta have the latest version of Windows" on your computer. (These people call themselves *experts*; other people call them *gurus*; the generic term is *computer nerd.*)

In either case, your first reaction probably was "Huh?" I could tell you about Windows until I'm blue in the face (or is it until I get carpel tunnel syndrome from too much typing?). But, it's easier to show you. So, here goes.

Tada!

What does Windows do?

Windows isn't all that complicated. To put it simply, Windows is a collection of computer programs that do these three things:

Make your computer much easier to use

 Let you do a lot of things on the computer at once

 Let you use stuff you create in one program somewhere else, even in a different program

Figure 1.1

Here's Windows!

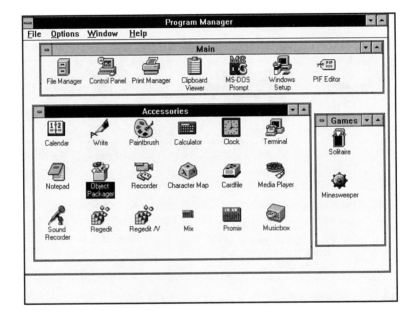

Why Use Windows?

What Windows can do for you depends on what you *need* it to do and on how you want to make use of your computer. To give you an idea of some of the things Windows can do for you, I'll tell you what it does for *me*.

A built-in secretary

As I'm sitting here writing this chapter, for example, I decide I need to call the editor to discuss something about the book, such as "when do I get my first check?" I open up an address-book program, find the phone entry for the editor, and push a button. The computer dials the number as I continue to write. When the editor answers, we talk while I keep writing. I want to make a note of the editor's suggestion, so I open another program, type the note, then save it for later.

Doing a bunch of things at once

After we hang up, I decide to call another computer (an information service called CompuServe) and copy some stuff down the phone line to my computer. The problem is that it will take half an hour to transfer the files. I have a ridiculous deadline to meet; I can't afford to give up control of the computer for that long. Windows comes to the rescue! Without closing my word processing program, I open up a data communications program, call CompuServe, and start moving the files to my computer. While that's going on, I switch back to my word processing program and keep writing. Windows is letting me do two things at once.

NERDY DETAILS

CompuServe is one of many information services you can access with your computer. CompuServe enables you to send electronic mail (email) to other computer users, send faxes (even if you don't have a fax machine), check stock prices, and find information on thousands of different topics. To access an information service such as CompuServe, you need a modem. The modem connects your computer to your phone line.

Rest and relaxation

Now I'm bored. I need some soothing music to keep the keys clicking. I pop a Bob Marley CD into the computer's CD-ROM player, start another program running, and a few seconds later I've got vintage Reggae music bouncing off the walls. Ah, now I can *really* do some damage.

Get more productive

I look at the time on the clock program that's running at the bottom of my computer screen. Federal Express will be here in about an hour to pick up some printouts that I'm sending to the editor. The problem is, I haven't printed them yet. I don't want to stop working on this chapter to print them, and with Windows, I don't have to. I open another program, start the printer, and go back to writing. I've got tunes coming out of my speakers, files coming down the phone line, pages coming out of the printer, and words going into a chapter (see fig. 1.2). Is there no end to my ingenuity? I'm so productive, I could spit!

Figure 1.2

Windows lets you do a
lot of things at once.

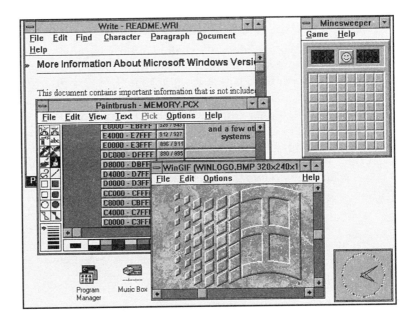

Copy those files

Now to top it off, I need to copy some files from my hard disk onto a floppy
disk to send along with the printouts. Windows comes to the rescue again—
I open up File Manager (a Windows program), graphically select all of the
files with just a few clicks of a button, then drag a picture of the files onto a
picture of a floppy disk drive. Within a few seconds, all the files are going
right where I want them. In this case, I needed a quicker and easier way to
copy the files. Windows provided that way.

Okay, maybe you don't need to listen to sunny island tunes as you do four
things at once on the computer. Maybe you just can't figure out those stupid
DOS COPY and ERASE commands, and need an easier way to communicate
with the computer. So what is Windows going to do for you? First, it gives
you an escape from those dreaded DOS commands.

Escape from DOS

What's DOS? Basically, it's a throwback from about 10 years ago that gives
you a bunch of commands to do things on your computer. You can do a lot
of neat stuff with DOS commands. That's the good part. The bad part is that
DOS is a real bear to use if you don't use it a lot. It's hard to remember all
those cryptic commands, and many of those commands don't always make

a whole lot of sense. Figure 1.3 shows you what you see if you're unlucky enough to end up at a DOS prompt.

```
c:\>
```

Figure 1.3

This is what the typical DOS command line prompt looks like. Pretty boring, huh?

After the DOS prompt, you're supposed to type some commands. Although you may use only a few of the many DOS commands, you must remember the right way to type the command, what other information you have to type on the command line, and when to hit that big Enter key. Jeez! All you wanted to do was pull a new disk out of the box and start storing some of your work on it for safekeeping. Why does it take so many bizarre commands?

Figure 1.4 shows the commands you must type to prepare a new blank disk so that you can store information on it. Just the stuff on the line following the C:\> is what you type; DOS spits back all the lines after that.

What are all those slash marks and letters at the end of the FORMAT command? What's that LABEL command for again? Hmm, this could be confusing...that's just two out of about 75 DOS commands you can use. Maybe computers aren't going to be as much fun as you thought. Maybe you're thinking you should have bought that Macintosh.

Figure 1.4

These are typical commands for formatting and labeling a disk in DOS.

```
C:\>FORMAT B: /U /F:720 /S
Insert new diskette for drive B:
and press ENTER when ready...

Formatting 720K
Format complete.
System transferred

Volume label (11 characters, ENTER for none)? A New Disk

    730112 bytes total disk space
    133120 bytes used by system
    596992 bytes available on disk

      1024 bytes in each allocation unit.
       583 allocation units available on disk.

Volume Serial Number is 3425-17D7

Format another (Y/N)?n


C:\>
```

SAVE
THE DAY!

Windows comes to the rescue by providing a graphical user interface (called a GUI and pronounced gooey) that offers alternatives to the many DOS commands. Rather than remembering the way to use the FORMAT and LABEL commands, for example, you open a Windows program called File Manager and use a menu of simple choices to format and label the disk (see fig. 1.5). Maybe there are a few more steps involved, but you don't have to dig in the closet to find the DOS manual either. In the long run, you get the task done quicker in Windows because you don't spend as much time scratching your head for an answer.

Replacing arcane DOS commands with simple menus and pictures is just part of the way Windows shields you from the DOS prompt. When you want to run a program from DOS, you generally type some commands to get to the place on the disk where the program lives. Then you type the name of the program's main file, often followed by some optional stuff to get the program to work the way you want it to. Hmm, more weird stuff to remember that doesn't make a lot of sense...

Figure 1.5

The Windows alternative for formatting a disk in File Manager.

In Windows, programs are represented by pictures, called *icons*. When you want to run a program, you just find its icon on the screen and press a button on the mouse or keyboard. The program starts up with no fuss. Figure 1.6 shows some program icons in Windows, with the arrow cursor pointing to one that's about to be started.

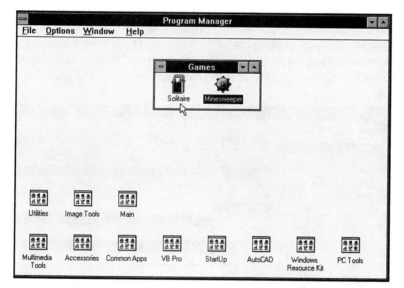

Figure 1.6

A program icon for a program that's about to be started in Windows.

NERDY
DETAILS

Even though Windows is often easier to use than DOS, you still need DOS on your computer. DOS forms a basic set of services that your computer couldn't function without. Windows is just a program that runs on top of DOS. (If you're confused, it's okay—this is all explained in the next chapter.) Remember those toe-clips you put on your bicycle pedals? The clips made it easier to pedal the bike, but they didn't replace the pedals. The same can be said of Windows. It supplements DOS.

Programs are easier to use

If you use a specific program all the time, you become very comfortable with it. You know that if you want to do *that*, you press *this* button or choose *this* command. What if you only use that program once a week? What if you use six different programs to do six different things, and use each of the six only once a week? Hmm, again. It might get pretty tough to keep them sorted out. After all, none of them look alike or work alike.

You might push *this* button because it does what you want in one program, only to find that it implodes the galaxy and melts the wax in your ears when you do it in another program. That could ruin your whole day. Windows programs, however, *do* look alike. What's more, they *work* the same way, at least in terms of how you make them do things.

In Windows, the commands to open a file *are* the same from program to program. Each program has a list of menu options you can choose, one of which is **F**ile. Lo-and-behold, the **F**ile menu includes an **O**pen command. Let's see...**F**ile **O**pen...that makes sense. Best of all, every Windows program that uses files has that **F**ile **O**pen command! Don't believe me? Look at figure 1.7!

Figure 1.7

The same **F**ile **O**pen command shows up in lots of different Windows programs. You always know how to open a file in Windows.

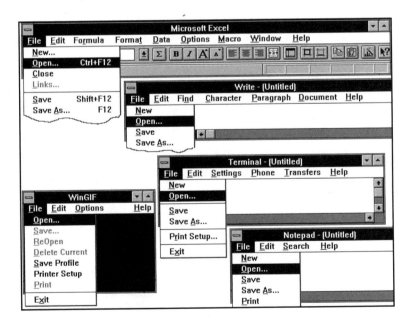

Opening a file is just one of the functions for which Windows programs share a common command. If you need help using a program, you can always choose the **H**elp menu. Need to delete something from a document you're working on? You'll find the command you need in the **E**dit menu, regardless of what program you're using.

TRICKS

Where's the catch? They probably hide the menus in different places in each program, right? Not! **F**ile is always at the far left, **E**dit is always second, and **H**elp is always over on the right. Some of the stuff in between changes from program to program, but the basic stuff is always where you expect to find it.

You can recycle your data

Suppose that you just spent two hours entering some data into a program. Now, you realize you'd also like to use it in another program. Do you want to sit there for another two hours and enter that stuff again? No, really, it'll be fun...you'll probably make some mistakes and have to go back through it to check and make sure the two sets of data match each other. You don't have anything better to do, do you?

Of course you have something better to do! Star Trek is going to be on in 20 minutes, and Picard is going to get Borged again! But what if the data you want to copy is a picture or something else you *can't* re-create yourself? Again, it's Windows to the rescue.

Windows includes something called the Clipboard. The Clipboard is similar to a real clipboard. You can copy something from one program and put it on the Clipboard. Then you carry it over to the other program, pull it off of the Clipboard, and place it in the second program. In a few seconds, you have copied the data you want from one program to another. You never had to worry about whether you had what it takes to re-create from scratch. Figure 1.8 shows the Clipboard being used to copy a picture from one program to another.

That's a simple type of copy operation that you can perform in Windows.

Figure 1.8

You can copy stuff, like a picture, from one program to another using Windows.

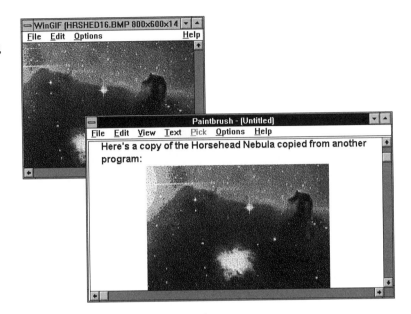

You also can have data change automatically in one program when you change it in another. Change a picture *here*, and have it also change *there* automatically. Want to take a file, wad it up into a ball, and stick it on a letter you are sending to someone so they can use the file, too? Windows lets you do that, as well. It's called OLE (pronounced *olay*), and it's covered in Chapter 13.

CHAPTER
2

Basic Stuff About Your Computer

A lthough many of the parts of your computer are really complicated in the way they *work*, they are really simple for you to *use*. And contrary to what you may think, there's really nothing you can do to actually damage the computer just by using it. Make as many mistakes as you want...you're not going to implode your computer into a molten pool of goo.

To help you get familiar with your computer, this chapter explains basic stuff about your computer, such as:

- What's hardware?
- What's software?
- What's the difference?
- What's all them computer parts for?
- What's an operating system?
- What are applications and programs?
- What are Windows programs and DOS programs, and what's the difference?

Hardware

Computer systems include two basic parts—*hardware* and *software*. The hardware is the easy part to understand. It's the keyboard, the mouse, the computer box, the monitor (screen), and all the other gadgets and doodads that might be hooked up to or are inside the computer. It's like all the metal, plastic, glass, and rubber that make up your car.

The system unit (the box)

The main part of your computer is known as the *system unit*. That's the large box that either sits underneath your monitor (the video screen) or stands beside your desk. System units that sit on top of a desk are called *desktop* systems. System units that stand on the floor and stick up vertically are called *tower* systems.

Inside the system unit are the computer's motherboard, floppy drives, hard disk, a power supply, maybe a CD player, and some other hardware items. What's all that stuff? You learn about them in this chapter. The items that aren't covered are things you never get to touch, things you don't want to touch, and things only nerds want to touch.

The CPU...now for the numbers

Inside the computer is a *microprocessor*. For us non-nerds, that's a *chip*. This chip is called a *central processing unit*, or CPU for short. The CPU is about 1 1/2 inches square and about 1/8 of an inch thick.

The CPU is where all of the computing in your computer takes place. That's why it is commonly referred to as the "brain" of the computer. The CPU has a number that identifies its type, such as 8088, 8086, 80286, 80386, and 80486.

Table 2.1
CPU Numbers and Letters

Computer	CPU Numbers	So What?
PC	8088	Obsolete. Now used as doorstops. Designed to run older versions of Windows, but it wasn't a pretty sight.
XT	8088 and 8086	Doorstop with a hard disk.
AT	286 (drop the 80)	Runs Windows, but why bother? It's really slow compared to the next two types. If you have a 286, give it to charity and buy a 386 or 486.
386	386DX 386SX 386SL	These systems are good for the average user. The DX is better than the SX. The SL is a low-power version for laptop notebook PCs.
486	486SL 486DX 486SX 486DX2	If you do heavy stuff, get a 486. Don't get a 486SX—that's a marketing gimmick. Get a DX2 if you want to scream and blow your socks off, too. Again, the SL is for notebooks and laptops.

 Now to really confuse you. Each chip comes in different *clock speeds*. The higher the speed number, the faster the chip is and the faster the computer runs.

 The 486 is a couple of times faster than a 386 that's running at the same clock speed. This is because the 486 can handle more things at once than the 386 can—but you probably already guessed that. The 486 also has a built-in circuit called a *math coprocessor*, that lets it do math operations very quickly (the 486SX doesn't have this).

GEEK

NERDY
DETAILS

The 386 doesn't have this circuit built into it, but you can buy a math chip that does the same thing. The 386 and earlier chips can still do math fast enough to blow your socks off, but just not as fast as the 486.

continues

continued

Windows itself doesn't use a math chip even if one is there. Some Windows programs, however, can perform better if there is a math coprocessor in the system. Check your program manual or call the people who wrote the software to find out if it is worth putting a math coprocessor in your system.

A motherboard?

The CPU needs somewhere to live. You can't just toss it inside the box and expect it to work. So, inside the system unit is a large circuit board called a *motherboard*. This circuit board looks kind of like the one inside the transistor radio you took apart when you were a kid. The CPU plugs into a socket on the motherboard. The motherboard also contains a lot of support circuits and other chips that help the CPU do its thing.

Memory

The motherboard also is where your computer's *memory* lives. This memory is a set of chips that are mounted in sockets on the motherboard or on another circuit card that plugs into the motherboard. This memory is called *RAM* (Random Access Memory).

Your computer uses this memory to store programs and data while it runs. This isn't the same thing as disk storage space. Think of it this way: the computer's memory is where the computer stores information while it is turned on and using the information; the disks are where the computer stores information while it is off or while it doesn't need the information.

Disk drives

In addition to the motherboard, the system unit also holds other equipment that helps the computer work. Although they are on the inside of the computer, these other devices are called *peripherals*. Usually, one or two floppy disk drives are mounted in the case.

In most cases, the system unit also contains a hard drive. The hard drive is like a floppy drive on really severe steroids. It holds a lot more information and works a lot faster than the floppy disks do. You can't take them out, so the drive unit is mounted inside the case.

Adapter cards

Also inside the system unit are some *adapter cards*. These adapter cards are circuit boards that plug into sockets in the motherboard. The *video adapter* generates all the images you see on the screen. The *hard disk controller* connects the hard disk to the computer. The hard disk controller makes it possible for you to store and retrieve information from the disk drive.

Another adapter inside the computer is the *floppy controller.* It controls the floppy disk drives (imagine that). Sometimes the floppy controller is part of the hard disk controller—the circuits for both are on the same adapter card.

NERDY DETAILS

Depending on the type of computer you have, you also might have some other adapter cards that are used to connect the mouse, printer, and other devices to the computer. These are called I/O cards (pronounced "eye-oh," as in "ee-eye-ee-eye-oh"), because they are used for I/O, which stands for Input/Output.

The monitor

The computer also relies on some *external peripherals* to work. They are external to the computer but are connected to the back of the computer case by cables. One of these peripherals is the computer's monitor.

The *monitor* is the thing that looks like a small TV set. The size is measured just like a TV set. A 14" monitor is roughly 14" diagonally from the upper left corner to lower right corner of the screen.

NERDY DETAILS

Images on your computer monitor are made up of really small dots. The more dots the monitor can display, the better the image quality will be. Think of the number of dots a monitor can display as its resolution. That's not 100 percent correct, but who cares? The important thing to remember is that the monitor has to support a resolution that is equal to or better than what the video adapter (next section) can put out.

The video adapter

The monitor doesn't actually create the images you see when you work with your computer. A card called a *video adapter* is inside the system unit. This card takes information from the computer and turns it into something the monitor can display and you can see. Then the monitor puts the picture on the screen.

Table 2.2 lists some common video adapter designations, from worst (read: cheapest) to best (read: most expensive). I left off a few types because you can't use them with Windows.

Table 2.2
Monitor Types and Resolution

Monitor Type	Resolution	So what?
EGA	640x350	This is the absolute least resolution you'd want for Windows (and really, you'll *want* better).
VGA	640x480	This is the most common resolution today, and is what comes with most PCs. Consider VGA the starting point for Windows.
SuperVGA	800x600	This is what I prefer.
SuperVGA	1024x768	Unless you have a 17" or larger monitor, everything is too small on the screen to read comfortably.
SuperVGA	1280x1024	Wow. You really need a 19" monitor or better, which will cost major bucks.

Higher resolution is good up to a point. If you have a small monitor, however, resolution over 800x600 can be really hard to read.

TRICKS

The keyboard

Ah, something that makes sense! Basically, the *keyboard* is like a typewriter keyboard with a calculator keypad and some other keys built in. This is pretty much a no-brainer. When you press keys, letters or numbers appear on your screen. But, this *is* a computer, so there has to be some nonsense involved:

- The keyboard has special keys called *function keys* labeled F1 through F10 or F12, located at the left or top of the keyboard. (Fancy models have them in both places.) Function keys are usually used as shortcuts for commands in a program.

- The keyboard has a numeric keypad, which is like the keypad on a calculator. You can use this keypad to enter numbers.

- Some of the numbers on the numeric keypad have arrows on them. These are called *cursor keys*. Use these to move the cursor around. (The *cursor* is the flashing block or line that stays one letter ahead of everything you type.) When the Num Lock key is on (and the Num Lock light is on), pressing the 2, 4, 6, or 8 key on the numeric keypad gives you a number. When Num Lock is off, these keys move the cursor. (Again, fancier models have cursor keys separate from the number keypad.)

NERDY
DETAILS

> You also can use the keyboard to select commands (like in case your mouse dies). Chapter 6 tells you about that.

Eeek! A mouse!

The *mouse* is the gadget with buttons on it that sits beside your keyboard. You use it to select commands in Windows and in your Windows programs. (I know I just told you about keys that do this; a mouse does it, *too*.) You also use the mouse to move stuff like windows and icons around on the screen.

Using the mouse is easy; getting comfortable with it may take a little while (maybe 5–10 minutes if you're a real klutz like me). After you're comfortable with it, you'll probably only use the keyboard to type text and enter numbers; you'll use the mouse to select commands and move objects.

Here are some pearls of wisdom about mice:

 Some mice hook up to one of your computer's *serial* ports. Other types of mice require a special adapter card (these are called *bus mice*). But it doesn't matter which kind you get. They work the same.

 A *trackball* is an alternative to a mouse. A trackball is a ball that sticks up out of a cup; the cup is surrounded by a platform that has buttons just like the mouse. The platform stays in one place and you roll the ball around with your thumb or finger to move the cursor. It's kind of like turning your mouse upside down and using it backwards.

Basic mouse actions

Here's how to use the mouse:

 String the cord (the mouse's "tail") toward the back of your desk. If your mouse is cordless, aim the end with the buttons toward the back of the desk.

 You use the mouse buttons to issue commands and select things. Sometimes you'll press a button once, and sometimes you'll have to press it twice in quick succession (I'll tell you when). One click is called a *click*. Two clicks in quick succession is called a *double-click*.

STOP!

> The mouse stays flat on your desk, or on top of a mouse pad that sits flat on the desk. If you pick the mouse up off of the desk and point it at the monitor, it won't do anything except make you look like a complete idiot.

Now, something useful about the disk drives

I told you earlier that disk drives are used to store data and programs long-term. If you want to save something you have created on the computer, you'll have to put it on a disk somewhere.

First, your hard disk

Usually, there are two types of disk drives in the computer. The first is the *hard disk* drive. The hard disk is usually where you store all of your programs. Windows lives there, too. The hard disk is where you will probably put all of your data for safekeeping while the computer is turned off. It can store a lot of data and programs, and it can save and retrieve information from the disk very quickly.

SAVE THE DAY!

When you want to save something, you should put it on your hard disk. For your everyday work, store your data on the hard disk. Use the floppy disk to make an extra copy (a backup) of your data in case something happens to the hard disk.

Second, your floppy disks

The other type of disk drive in your system is the *floppy disk* drive. You might have one, or you might have two. These drives have slots on the front of the system unit so that you can insert *floppy disks* into them. Floppy disk drives let you store information on floppy disks. Here are some tidbits about floppy disks and floppy disk drives:

 Floppy disks come in two common sizes. Some are 5 1/4 inches and come in a flexible plastic case (don't bend them unless you want to screw them up); others are 3 1/2 inches in a rigid plastic case. The 3 1/2-inch disks are best. They're small enough to stick in your pocket (unless you wear a pocket protector), and you can toss them around without hurting them.

 Floppy disks can't store as much data as a hard disk, but you can use as many floppy disks as you want. When one fills up, you can use a new one. More on this in a minute.

 Because you can save stuff on them and then remove the floppy disk from the floppy disk drive, you can use floppy disks to give copies of your data (like memos, reports, letters, and doctored pictures of Uncle Ned in a nightgown) to someone else.

STOP!

Magnetic fields can screw up the way that floppy disks work. Keep disks away from your monitor, telephone, and other electronic gizmos. Don't stick them to your refrigerator with refrigerator magnets.

How to use your disks

Now you probably want to know how to use the disk drives. Each of the drives has a letter associated with it, which is called a *drive letter* (duh...). The first floppy disk drive is assigned letter A. It's the one on top if there are two floppy disk drives. The second floppy disk drive, if you have one, is drive B. (Elementary, Mr. Watson.)

Drive letters need a colon (:) after them. For example, if you want to specify drive A, you type **A:**.

Using the hard disk

The hard disk starts at letter C. If you have more than one hard disk, or your one hard disk has been set up to look like more than one hard disk, you might also see drive letters D, E, and so on, up to letter Z.

When you're working in Windows, your disk drives show up in lists in *dialog boxes*, or as icons (little pictures on your screen). When you want to read information from a disk, you select it from the list by its drive letter. Figure 2.1 illustrates a typical dialog box that shows drive letters.

Figure 2.1

Drive letters help you figure out which disk is which.

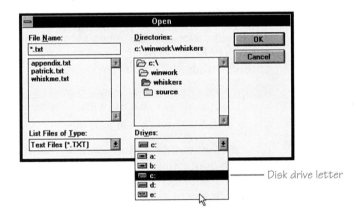

Disk drive letter

Using a floppy disk

Floppy disks require a little fiddling when you use them. When you want to use something from a floppy disk or store something on it, you have to insert the floppy disk in the right-sized drive. Most 5 1/4-inch floppy disk drives have a lever that you turn from horizontal to vertical to close the drive after you put a disk in. To take the disk out, turn the lever from vertical back to horizontal. The disk pops out a little so you can grab it.

For 3 1/2-inch disk drives, you just push the disk in until it disappears into the drive. A button under the disk slot pops out a little when you insert the disk. When you want to take out the disk, push the button.

And something useful about memory

The more memory your computer has in it, the better.

- More memory means faster performance in Windows. It also means you can run more programs at once, or use really large amounts of data. Speed is the most important consideration for Windows users.

- Memory is measured in megabytes. Most systems today have between 1M and 4M. You need at least 2M to run Windows, but it's really slow. You should really have 4M as a minimum. Get 8M if you can afford it.

- You can add memory to the computer yourself. I'm not going to tell you how to do it. It's in your computer manual. If you don't like fiddling inside your computer, have a nerd do it for you. You can buy extra memory for about $50 per megabyte, but you'll probably get charged a few bucks to put it in if the nerd does it for you.

What's Software?

Your computer is a lifeless piece of junk until you turn it on. Yes, I know; sometimes it seems like a lifeless piece of junk *after* you turn it on. The point is that the computer doesn't do anything by itself. It's a bunch of chips and other components that *just sit there*. It's like your car—if you don't put gas in it and get behind the wheel, it will just sit in your driveway (your car, that is, not your computer).

Software makes it go

Just like your car needs gas before it will start, the computer needs *software* before it can run. Without software, a computer is about as intelligent as a doorknob, and even less useful. Software isn't all that mysterious. It's just a set of step-by-step electronic instructions (written by someone who has a lot more patience than I do) that tell the computer to act and react in a certain way. You type a command or click a button; some software tells the computer what to do to carry out the command. One nice difference between cars and computers: your computer gets *much* better mileage!

What's an operating system?

When you turn on the computer, some of the system's software automatically loads into the computer's memory. This software is part of the computer's *operating system*. It is what enables the computer to accept commands from you and to load other programs.

On PCs, the operating system is generically called *DOS*, which rhymes with "boss" and stands for disk operating system. Since it gets loaded automatically, you really don't need to worry about how it gets there unless you're one of those people who wonders about things like why clock hands don't spin the *other* direction or why birds can't fly upside down.

NERDY
DETAILS

When you turn on the computer, some instructions contained in one of the computer's chips make the computer automatically test its memory and other systems. Then, some additional instructions make the computer look for an operating system to load. It looks first at the disk in floppy drive A; if there is no disk in drive A, it looks on the system's hard disk for an operating system. When it finds an operating system, the computer begins copying it from the disk into memory. After DOS is loaded, your computer is ready to do something other than collect dust.

DOS is software

DOS, which you also might see referred to as MS-DOS, PC-DOS, DR-DOS, and a lot of other names that aren't fit to print, is a set of programs that perform very basic functions. Programs are software, so DOS is software.

These basic functions enable programs to run on the computer and to use and control the computer's hardware. They also enable you and your programs to save information on a disk, read that information, print it, and perform just about every other task there is to perform on the computer.

SAVE
THE DAY!

I could go on about DOS for a long time, but you're using Windows. So, you probably don't need to know all that much about DOS. If you *do* want to know more about DOS, pick up a copy of *DOS for Non-Nerds*. I didn't write it, but it's a good book anyway.

Windows! (Yeah, it's software, too)

Microsoft Windows, which everyone generally refers to as just *Windows*, is an *operating environment*. An operating environment is a lot like an operating system, but it can't work all by itself. Windows needs DOS to run.

Windows is a group of programs, so Windows is software, too. When you start your computer, DOS starts so that the computer can function. Then, you have to start Windows.

Applications are just programs with an attitude

You've been reading about programs in this chapter. You've probably seen the word "applications" used a lot somewhere else. Maybe you're asking yourself, "Self, what the heck is the difference between an application and a program?" Well, there really isn't any difference at all. Software companies call programs *applications* just because it sounds more impressive.

While there isn't any difference between a program and an application, there are differences between the types of applications you'll run across on your computer. Some are specially written for Windows, and some are written just for DOS.

Windows programs

Windows programs all look a lot alike, at least in general terms. Almost all appear as a rectangular window, have a menu of command choices at the top of the window, and use many of the same commands. Figure 2.2 shows some typical Windows programs.

Obviously, because different Windows programs are designed to do different jobs, each will have unique commands and special features that other programs don't have. But for the most part, they are all very similar. That's good news, because it means that once you learn how to use one Windows program, it won't take much effort to learn to use another.

Figure 2.2

Some typical Windows programs.

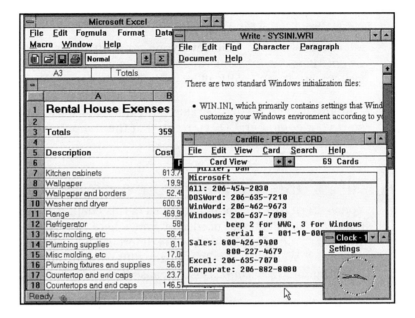

Windows has other benefits:

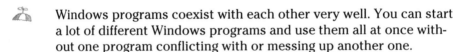

Windows programs coexist with each other very well. You can start a lot of different Windows programs and use them all at once without one program conflicting with or messing up another one.

Windows programs can share data. You can create a picture, some text, or just about any other type of document in one program, and copy it into almost any other Windows program.

DOS programs

DOS programs are designed just for the DOS operating system. They don't have any special instructions that let them make use of the Windows operating environment. DOS programs have been around as long as DOS has (over ten years), and there are a lot of them around. Many of them are very useful and powerful programs. But they do have some drawbacks.

Disadvantages of using DOS include:

 Dos programs are all different. A word processor uses one type of command menu and set of commands, while a spreadsheet program uses an entirely different set of commands. Usually, not only are the commands different, but they appear in different places. The more DOS programs you use, however, the harder it is to remember how to use each program because they are so different.

 The other problem is that DOS was designed to be a *single-tasking* operating system. That means that normally only one program can run at a time. You usually have to stop one program before you can start another. This means you can't start printing in one program and switch to another one to work while the first one prints. As soon as you switch away from the first one, it stops printing.

DOS programs in Windows

If you've been using DOS programs for a long time and just don't want to give them up, Windows is going to make those DOS programs even more useful. Although you can't run more than one DOS program at a time with just DOS, you *can* run more than one program in Windows. This is called *multitasking*.

Windows lets you run more than one DOS program at a time. You can switch from one to another without stopping or exiting from any of them. You can open a DOS word processing program and start it printing, for example, then jump into another one to do something else, just like you can with Windows programs.

You also can run your DOS programs in a window. Figure 2.3 shows Word for DOS running in a window alongside a Windows application.

NERDY
DETAILS

Most of these DOS program benefits rely on the capability of your computer's hardware. You need a 386 or 486 system to run DOS programs in a window and run more than one at the same time.

Figure 2.3

Word for DOS and a
Windows application in
peaceful coexistence.

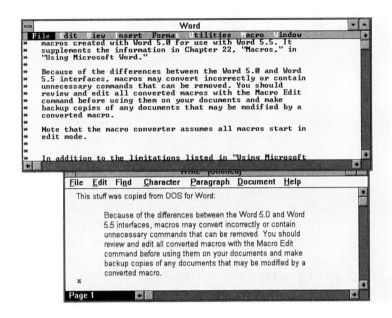

**NERDY
DETAILS**

If you're one of those people who *really* wants to learn everything there is to know about your hardware, buy *The Winn L.
Rosch Hardware Bible*. It's over 1000 pages of nothing but how
hardware works. It's not published by New Riders Publishing, so
the editors will probably erase this paragraph in disgust. But,
Winn wrote one heck of a good book. I have one. You should, too,
if you want to know *how* the parts of your computer work.

What If I Have To Install Windows?

*O*kay, so you don't have Windows on your computer. No big deal. You can put it on there in just a couple of minutes without much fanfare or major problems. All you have to do is follow the steps in this chapter, paying attention to the directions Microsoft gives you during the installation procedure.

This chapter tells all you need to know to get Windows onto your computer, without going into great detail about special or customized setups. You can learn about that stuff in Chapters 16 and 17. For right now, you will learn the following points:

- Turning on your computer
- Finding the DOS prompt
- Starting the Setup program
- Telling Windows which printers you have
- Running a Windows tutorial

How Do I Turn On This Piece of Junk?

To install Windows, you have to turn on your computer. (Sorry, there's no way around this problem.) If this is the first time you've turned it on, keep reading—you might need to know some of this stuff. If, on the other hand, you've already found the on/off switch on your own, go ahead and skip over the next section and move to the section called "Where Do I Put Windows?" (If you played a game of Solitaire in Chapter 0, you can skip this chapter entirely because you already have Windows installed.)

Starting the computer

The first thing you need to do is find the computer's on/off switch. Sometimes it's in the back of the system unit (which most people just call the "computer"), in the front of the unit, or on the side. Sometimes it's a big push button or a big flip switch.

 Don't worry too much about your computer making noises—they are natural. You should, however, listen to the computer and become aware of any weird noises it might make later in its life. These are noises you might have to tell technical support people if you think your computer is malfunctioning.

 Some systems let you plug your monitor's power cord into the back of the system unit. That way, your monitor will come on automatically when you turn on the computer.

TRICKS

> If you know that your system unit is on, but you don't see anything on your screen, make sure your monitor is turned on. The switch for the monitor is either on the back of the monitor case, in front, in front but underneath (kind of like where your fuse box is in your car), or on the side. Just run your hand around the monitor until you feel a button or switch. That might be the power switch (or that fuzzy weasel Jim keeps talking about).

Some people (a lot of Mac users do this) leave their computers on all day and all night. I leave mine on during the day (or through the night if I'm working on it all night), but I usually turn it off when I quit work for the day. You can safely turn it off when you are finished for the day, but you probably should go ahead and leave it on when you are just taking a break or eating lunch.

STOP!

Don't turn off your computer when you are using Windows or any other program. You might lose your information (such as that business proposal you've been working on for the last six days), or you might even damage your programs.

Where Do I Put Windows?

You really don't need to know where Windows goes on your computer to safely install it. When you run the Microsoft Windows Setup program, it will suggest a place for it—called the WINDOWS directory. (*Directories* are places where you store things on your computer, sort of like an office file cabinet, only electronic.) Unless you already have a copy of Windows on your hard drive, you can just place Windows where the Setup program suggests.

Where's the DOS Prompt?

When your computer starts, you are in one of three places: the DOS prompt, a program, or a menu. To install Windows, you need to be at the DOS prompt, which looks like the following creature:

```
C:\>
```

If this is what you see on your screen, turn to the section called "Installing Windows," and don't worry about the next few sections.

What if I don't see the DOS prompt?

You might not see the DOS prompt when you first turn on the computer. Instead, you may see a list of options, which is called a *menu*. Computer menus are similar to menus in restaurants. The restaurant menu tells you your choices. A computer menu is the same. (Pick the duck with plum sauce.)

If you see this type of animal on your screen (not the duck), look for an option that says something like "Return to DOS" or "Exit to DOS". If you can't find this option, go ask the nicest looking person you work with how you can find the DOS prompt. Then ask them if they have time to help you install Windows.

What if I'm in a program?

Again, if your computer starts and you are in a program right away, such as WordPerfect or Lotus 1-2-3, you need to leave that program and get back to the DOS prompt. If you routinely use this program to get your work done during the day, which you probably do since that is how your computer is set up, just press the keys you normally do to exit that program.

NERDY
DETAILS

Because of the number of computer programs you might have on your computer, this discussion cannot show you how to exit or leave all of them. Some of the most popular ones, however, use menus, function keys, special keystrokes, or a combination of these elements to exit a program. If you are not sure how to get back to the DOS prompt, ask someone in your office.

If you are left in Windows (see fig. 3.1), you probably have an older version of Windows installed, such as Windows 3.0.

Figure 3.1

What Windows looks like, if you didn't already know.

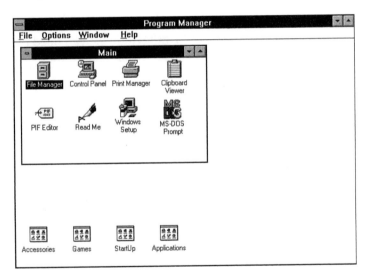

You need to get out of this mess by doing the following:

1. Find the Alt key on your keyboard (it's usually next to your spacebar), and hold it down.

2. Then find the key on your keyboard labeled F4 (it's usually at the far left or at the top of your keyboard), and press it once. This tells Windows that you are ready to leave.

3. When it asks if you are ready to leave, press the Enter key or click on the OK button with your mouse. Your screen goes black for a few seconds, and you are left stranded at the DOS prompt, ready to install your new version of Windows.

Installing Windows

It's pretty easy to load Windows onto your computer. You don't need to read instructions that have been translated from a foreign language three times, or look at a picture that has hundreds of different-size screws you have to secure to make your child's tricycle work. Windows makes it simple (well, about as simple as can be expected).

TRICKS

You might want to make a backup copy of the important files on your system before installing any programs. If you want to do this, use the DOS COPY command or go out and buy a hard disk backup program. While you're at it, pick up *DOS for Non-Nerds*, by Michael Groh. It's published by New Riders Publishing and is a pretty neat book.

You'll be asked if you want to customize Windows as you set it up, or just let Windows do its thing. When you install Windows for the first time, you should just let Windows do its thing and worry about customizing later.

NERDY DETAILS

Windows requires a certain amount of space before you can install it. When you are in the Setup program, it snoops around your hard drive and determines whether you have enough room for it to fit. If you don't, you need to clean out some of the stuff you have stored there. To do this, you need to use a few DOS commands, such as DIR, DEL, and COPY. You should consult that DOS book I just told you about to learn more about these commands, or just ask that nice-looking person who helped you find your DOS prompt in the first place.

The quick and easy setup

If you are not comfortable making setup decisions, follow these steps to get Windows installed on your computer right now:

1. Find the Windows floppy disk labeled Disk 1 and put it into the appropriate disk drive.

SAVE THE DAY!

> If you bought the wrong size disks for your computer, take them back to the store or send them back to the company from which you bought them. If you have only one floppy disk drive, or if you have two drives and they are the same size (such as 5 1/4-inch), you need to make sure you buy the correct size disks to load your copy of Windows. This is a hassle, but you have to do it.

2. Tell the computer to look at the stuff on the disk in whichever disk drive you placed the disk in step 1. If you put the disk in drive A, for example, type **A:** and press Enter; if you put the disk in drive B, type **B:** and press Enter.

    Your computer screen will look like the following one, depending on whether you typed **A:** or **B:** and pressed Enter (this example shows what your screen looks like if you typed **A:** and pressed Enter):

    A:\>

3. You now can tell Windows to start loading itself by typing **SETUP** and pressing Enter.

    SETUP is the "secret" code word that tells the Windows disks to start setting up Windows for you. When you press Enter, your disk drives start making noise, and the Setup program shows you a neat little Welcome screen on your monitor. This screen tells you that you are installing Windows, and that you did everything correctly up to this point.

4. Press Enter to tell Windows to keep installing itself.

NERDY
DETAILS

GEEK

The installation process takes a few minutes, and you have to
answer a few more questions and supply the computer with
the Windows floppy disks, so don't plan on going anywhere just
yet. If you go to the bathroom or to lunch, don't expect
Windows to be installed when you get back. It will just be
sitting there waiting for you to answer a question or to feed it
another disk.

5. Windows asks if you want to use the Express Setup or the Custom
Setup. Just press Enter right now to choose the Express Setup. You
can use the Custom Setup the next time you need to set up Windows.

The Express Setup copies over any older version of Windows you
might have already on your system. When windows installs over an
older version, it does not delete anything that you had set up in that
version, it just adds some new features and enhancements to your
system.

TRICKS

If you don't want to install your new copy of Windows over an
existing version on your system, go ahead and install your new
version of Windows in a new directory (such as WIN31 or
something like that), and then use Windows 3.1 for awhile. You
then can erase the old version of Windows from your computer.
If you do this, make sure you delete the Windows 3.0 PATH
setting in your AUTOEXEC.BAT file. (Consult your *DOS User's
Guide* if you really want to know what this means.) If you want
some real advice, however, just go ahead and set up your new
version of Windows over your older version.

6. You now need to tell the program what your name is and what your
company name is. Just type in your name and press the Tab key
on your keyboard. Then type in your company's name and press
Enter. Windows displays a screen, showing you what you just typed.
Read it over carefully and make sure it's correct before continuing.
Change any typos and tell Windows to proceed with the installation.

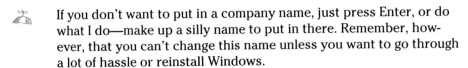 If you don't want to put in a company name, just press Enter, or do what I do—make up a silly name to put in there. Remember, however, that you can't change this name unless you want to go through a lot of hassle or reinstall Windows.

After you enter your name and company name, the Setup program starts setting up Windows on your hard drive. During the setup program, you are asked to insert the Setup disks. Just follow the procedure that Windows tells you and you'll be okay.

Telling Windows what kind of printer you have

When the Setup program displays a box with the words "Printer Installation" at the top of it, you know it's time to set up your printer(s). This box is called a *dialog box* (you learn more about these types of animals in Chapter 5).

You can set up more than one printer, or you can set up none. You should, however, tell Windows to set up at least one printer.

1. To select the printer(s) you want to install, use the arrow keys to view the printer list and stop when the black highlight bar is on your printer name, such as Agfa Compugraphic 400PS.

SAVE
THE DAY!

If your printer is not listed in the list of printers, you need to select a printer that yours *emulates*; that is, one that acts like your printer. To find out what type of printer your printer emulates, dig out all that paperwork you got with your printer and read through it. It should tell you.

Laser printers usually emulate Hewlett Packard LaserJetII or PostScript laser printers, so you can choose one or both of these. Then, when you are using your printer, try one and then the other one to see which works. If you know neither one of these options will work, select the No Printer Attached option, which is the first option in the list. Windows will let you set up your printer later.

2. After you highlight a printer, press Enter, and the Setup program starts looking for the correct printer driver from the installation disks.

    Drivers are instructions that tell programs how to handle certain pieces of hardware (such as printers). The Setup program also may ask you to insert another disk into the floppy disk drive so that the program can find the correct driver.

3. When the printer driver is found, you then are confronted with a pretty serious-sounding question: which port is your printer connected to? In most cases, you can select the first choice, which is LPT1:. Don't worry, you can change this selection if you need to later. In fact, Chapter 11 discusses how to do this.

Windows Sets Up Your Programs

After you have your printers set up, Windows starts automatically setting up the programs that you already have on your computer. Setup searches your hard drive looking for all the programs you have on your computer and assigns them *icons* (those tiny pictures that Chapter 0 told you to double-click on) to display when Windows starts up.

Unless you have been running an older version of Windows, you shouldn't have any Windows programs installed on your hard drive. Actually, you can't install a Windows program without being in Windows, but that's a different topic.

You may have a program that Windows cannot identify. If this happens, Windows asks you what it is and gives you choices. Windows might, for example, ask you if the application name for "C:\WORD\WORD.EXE" is Microsoft Word 5.5 or another type of word processor. Say what!?! If you know the answer, use the arrow keys to move the highlight bar until it is on the correct answer and press Enter.

If none of the names match what you think is the correct name of the program, select the None of the above option and press Enter. Once Windows starts and you don't find a program you once had, you can set up that program as an icon using the instructions you find in Chapter 7.

Taking a Tutorial

When Windows finally gets all your programs set up, it then displays a Windows Setup dialog box. This dialog box asks if you want to take a tutorial of Windows or whether you just want to skip it. You should take the tutorial if you have the time and if you want some more information on mouse movements and Windows actions. It's not really exciting, but you can learn a few things from it.

When you get tired of taking the tutorial (and you probably will), press the Esc key on your keyboard. This quits the tutorial and takes you back to the installation.

TRICKS

You can start the tutorial again by clicking on the <u>H</u>elp menu in Program Manager and then clicking on <u>W</u>indows Tutorial (see fig. 3.2). You then can press Esc again to stop it.

Do this as many times as you want. Sooner or later, you'll make it through the entire tutorial. (I actually haven't, but you might have more patience than I do.)

Figure 3.2

To take the Windows tutorial after you install Windows, select this option.

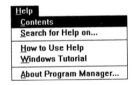

It's About Time...

After you finish the tutorial (or end it early or not take it all), the Setup program does some stuff, and then gives you a multiple-choice question. I will give you the answer: pick **R**eboot. This option lets Windows use all its options when your computer restarts.

STOP!

After you select **R**eboot, you need to remove your floppy disk from drive A. This way, your computer doesn't give you some silly non-system disk error warning when it restarts. If you leave a disk in drive A, and you see an error message like this, just remove the floppy disk and press Enter. Everything will be fine. Just wipe those little beads of sweat from your temples and carry on.

PART 2

Make Windows Earn Its Keep

Starting a Real Windows Session

W ay back in Chapter 0 you started Windows and played a little Solitaire. Now, it's time to start getting some real work done. Do you remember how to start Windows? (Do you remember what day it is? I've had days like that.) No problem—starting Windows is easy.

When you finish reading this chapter, you will know the following:

- At least one way to start Windows
- What Program Manager is
- What icons and group windows are
- How to switch between programs
- SlimeyGreenFrogs=1

Here's How To Start Windows

After you turn on your computer and it's finished beeping and whirring, does Windows magically appear on your monitor? If so, great! Your computer has been set up to start Windows automatically.

But *yours* doesn't? It just sits there with something like the little C:> DOS prompt blinking stupidly at you? No problem, just type **WIN** and press Enter.

What now?

After you type WIN and press enter, your computer will go black for a few seconds until the words "Microsoft Windows" pop up on your screen. Your screen then goes black again and a screen called Program Manager appears. This is your starting place in Windows.

NERDY DETAILS

Windows is a bunch of programs that all work together. When you start Windows, Windows has to get all of its programs running. It also has to test some of your computer's hardware to make sure it really wants to run on your computer. Be patient. Take a deep breath and prepare yourself for another glorious day at the office. Think only happy thoughts.

When You're Finally in Windows

When Windows starts, you should see a screen like the one in figure 4.1.

If the screen in figure 4.1 doesn't look familiar, maybe you'll have better luck recognizing the one shown in figure 4.2. If it looks like figure 4.2, do this:

1. Move the mouse until the arrow cursor is in the middle of the small picture with the words Program Manager under it (the picture is called an *icon*).

2. Now press and release the select mouse button once (usually, that's the left button) to select the Program Manager icon.

3. Press the Enter key.

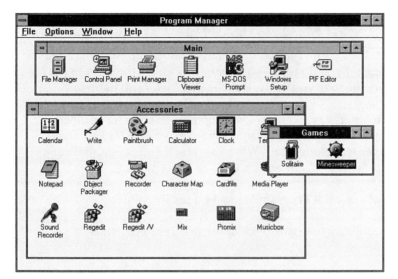

Figure 4.1

This is one of the ways Windows might look after you first start it.

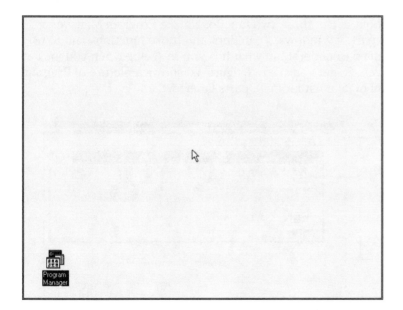

Figure 4.2

This is the other way Windows might look when you first start it.

Now, your screen should look something like figure 4.1. What is it you're looking at? It's not really Windows, it's a Windows *program* called Program Manager.

What Is Program Manager?

You can't just talk to your computer and have things happen. Okay, maybe things *will* happen if you do that—someone will call for the guys in the clean white coats to come take you away. But nothing *useful* will happen.

You need some other way to control your computer and start programs. Program Manager is a Windows program that lets you do these things. Program Manager is included with Windows, and it starts automatically whenever Windows starts, either as a window or as an icon.

Here's a rundown of what Program Manager does for you:

 Provides a way to organize all of the different programs on your computer.

 Gives you an easy way to start programs.

Really, that's about it. But those two functions make Program Manager a very important part of Windows. To understand those functions and to use Windows, you need to understand what it is you're seeing when you look at Program Manager. To get you started, figure 4.3 shows a picture of Program Manager with all of its most intimate parts labeled.

Figure 4.3

Program Manager's parts laid bare for all the world to see.

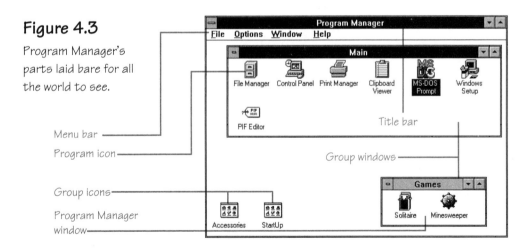

Here are some basic facts to know about Program Manager:

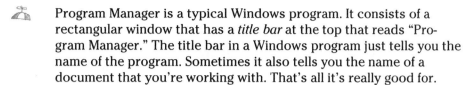

Program Manager is a typical Windows program. It consists of a rectangular window that has a *title bar* at the top that reads "Program Manager." The title bar in a Windows program just tells you the name of the program. Sometimes it also tells you the name of a document that you're working with. That's all it's really good for.

Just below the title bar is a *menu bar* displaying the menu options <u>F</u>ile, <u>O</u>ptions, <u>W</u>indow, and <u>H</u>elp. These menus are where Program Manager's commands live. Don't bother them now.

Program Manager has some other rectangular windows inside its main window. These are called *group windows*.

Behind the Program Manager window is a blank area called the *desktop*. The desktop is just a background on which program windows appear. The desktop doesn't have anything to do with Program Manager. It's just a part of what Windows looks like.

NERDY
DETAILS

If you want to get technical (you wouldn't be reading this if you didn't), the Windows desktop *is* Windows. At least, the desktop is what Windows *looks* like. Everything else that shows up on the desktop belongs to a Windows program, a DOS program, or some other entity besides Windows itself. Does any of that really matter? No.

What Are Those Little Pictures?

If you took the time to look at figure 4.3, you'd know those little pictures that are just about everywhere in Program Manager are called *icons*. When you're talking Windows with someone else, don't call them *little pictures*. That's like calling the steering wheel of your car "that round thing where the airbag lives."

Icons represent things in Windows. The main thing to remember is that icons are just pictures that are associated with something on your computer. They aren't the thing itself. If you somehow delete a program icon, you haven't deleted the program—it's still on your disk somewhere. All you did was delete the picture that represented the program.

Here are some things icons can represent in Program Manager:

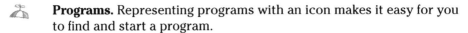 **Programs.** Representing programs with an icon makes it easy for you to find and start a program.

Group. This is a *group* of program icons. It's kind of like a folder—the folder contains other things. In this case, a *group icon* contains individual *program icons*.

Documents. Documents include things like letters, memos, drawings, pictures, spreadsheets, and even sounds that you or someone else creates.

Hardware. Sometimes, Windows uses icons to represent parts of your computer's hardware. It's a lot easier to choose a printer by selecting a picture of a printer than it is to hunt through a list of printer names or descriptions.

Icon do that!

Icons are pretty simple. Here are some interesting things to remember about icons:

You'll see icons outside of Program Manager. Usually, these icons represent programs that are running on your computer at the time. They usually show up on the desktop at the bottom of the screen.

You can move icons around in Program Manager, but only from one group to another.

And What About Those Other Boxes?

Inside the main Program Manager window you'll see some other windows. These are called *group windows*. Figure 4.3 shows what group windows are.

Group windows let you organize program and document icons. The free programs that come with Windows are organized into different groups called Main, Accessories, Games, and Startup. Here are some knowledge-nuggets about program groups:

- Program groups can appear either in a window or as an icon. In either case, groups always stay inside the main Program Manager window.

- You can't change the type of icon Windows uses for groups. All program groups in Program Manager have the same boring icon, no matter what.

- Program group icons sometimes hide behind other group windows or behind a program window. If you can't find one of your program group icons, it's probably hiding behind a window or past the edge of the main Program Manager window.

Starting Programs in Windows

You've slogged through almost four chapters now, and maybe you're wondering when you get to start using all the really cool programs on your computer. Just remember the old saying, "You have to learn how to crawl before you can walk, and you have to learn how to walk before you can trip over your own two feet and fall flat on your face." Well, it's something like that.

Remember all of those program icons you read about a few minutes ago? Those represent programs that are on your computer. When you want to run a program in Windows, there are two ways to start the program.

Starting programs with a double-click

Find a program you want to run. We'll use Windows Write for the example. You're going to start the Write program by double-clicking on its icon.

1. If the Accessories group is not open in a window in Program Manager, find its icon on the screen somewhere. It'll say "Accessories" underneath the icon. If your Accessories group is already open in a window, skip to step 3.

2. Double-click on the Accessories icon. To double-click, just click the left mouse button twice quickly. This opens it to a window.

NERDY
DETAILS

Some people find it tough to get used to a mouse. If you have problems getting your screen pointer to go where you want it or have problems clicking the button fast enough to do a double-click, you can change the way the mouse works. You do that by double-clicking on the Mouse icon in the Windows Control Panel and changing some settings. You learn how to do this in Chapter 16.

3. Find the Write program icon in the Accessories group. If you absolutely can't find the Write icon anywhere, press the down-arrow cursor key on the keyboard a few times. Write may be hiding past the edge of the window.

4. When you find the Write icon, double-click on it. After a second or two, Write should appear in a window on your screen.

TRICKS

If you just can't get the hang of the double-click, just single-click on the icon, and then press Enter. Pressing Enter starts the program that belongs to whatever icon is selected.

Starting programs the other way

What if you don't have a mouse or your mouse just packed its bags and moved to Jamaica? You're not sunk, but you're taking on water and the boneheaded first mate just torpedoed the only lifeboat. You can use the keyboard to move around in Windows and start programs, but it's not much fun. If you really want to use the keyboard instead of the mouse, you'll have to wait until Chapter 6 to learn how.

Where's Program Manager?

When you started Write, Program Manager did one of two things: It either jumped into the background and Write opened in front of it, or Program Manager became an icon at the bottom of the desktop. Both behaviors are normal.

NERDY
DETAILS

Having Program Manager zap down to an icon when you start a program helps keep your Windows desktop clear and uncluttered. But it doesn't change the way any of your programs work. It's just a matter of personal preference. See Chapter 7 for more stuff on Program Manager.

I Want To Use This *Other* Program

One of the best things about Windows is that you can run more than one program at a time. You don't have to stop one program before you start another. And, when you are working with one program, you can press a few keys or click a few mouse buttons, and *switch* to another program that is running.

What does switching programs mean? First, you need to understand what *active program* means. It's really simple, and I've thoughtfully summarized it for you in the following list. When a program is active:

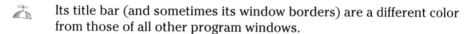 Its title bar (and sometimes its window borders) are a different color from those of all other program windows.

Its window usually shows up on top of the stack of all other program windows on the desktop.

Its icon label is highlighted if the program is running as an icon instead of in a window.

Right! Now, what does it mean to switch programs? It just means you change which program is active. Say you're working on a letter in Write (which means it's the active program), and you want to switch over to Cardfile to look up an address. Assuming both Write and Cardfile are running, you *switch* from Write to Cardfile, find the address, and then *switch* back to Write again.

"Great. Thrilling. I'm beside myself with anticipation. Now just tell me how to do it."

If you can see both windows, just click anywhere inside the one that you want to make active. The one you click becomes active.

If the program you want is running as an icon at the bottom of your desktop, just double-click on the icon.

But what if you can't see the other window? What if it's behind the active window? Or, what if the icon you need is hiding behind another program window? You can use the Task List.

What's a task, and what's the Task List?

To Windows, each of the programs running on your computer is a *task*. If you made a list of all the programs that are running under Windows, you'd have a *task list* (see fig. 4.4). Hah! That's how Windows decides which program to call up next when you press Alt-Tab. It looks through a list of all of the programs that are running and selects the next one down on the list. Don't you wish you could do that?

Figure 4.4

The Task List.

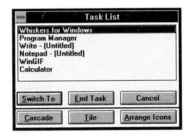

Finding the Task List

Before you can use or see the Task List, you have to tell Windows to display it. Here are three different ways to make the Task List appear:

 Press Ctrl-Esc. That means hold the Ctrl key down, press the Esc key, and then release both keys. That's all there is to it.

 Find a program window (any one will do, but it has to be a program window). Look for a small square box in the upper-left corner of the program window that has a horizontal bar in the middle of it. Click on it. Click on the words Switch To.

 Double-click anywhere on a blank area of the desktop. Remember, the desktop is that blank wall that's *behind* everything else on the screen.

Pressing Ctrl-Esc is the easiest way to display the Task List if you're a keyboard kind of person. Double-clicking on the empty desktop is the easiest way if you are a mouse kind of person.

Using the Task List

When you have a bunch of programs running and want to switch to a different one, bring up the Task List. Then do one of these two things to switch to a program that is displayed in the Task List:

- Just double-click on the program name in the list. That program then becomes active.

- Click on the program name (that's a single-click), and then click on the words **S**witch To.

What are all those other things at the bottom of the Task Manager that look suspiciously like commands? They're command *buttons*. Here's what the top three do when you click on them:

- **S**witch To. Switches to whichever program is selected in the Task List.

- **E**nd Task. Closes (exits) whichever program is selected in the Task List. The program goes adios.

- **Cancel.** Closes the Task List without doing anything at all.

"Come on," you say. "There has to be an easier way to switch programs. Give me that 'nobody-but-me-knows-this' tip." Well, everyone knows this one:

Just press Alt-Tab

That's almost all there is to it. Just press and hold down the Alt key; then press the Tab key; and then release both keys. Windows switches from the currently active program to the next one in the Task List.

Try it. Press Alt-Tab a couple of times and see what happens. Assuming that you have only Write and Program Manager running, you switch back and forth between the two. Here are some of the reactions you might see after pressing Alt-Tab:

Even if there are more than two programs in the Task List, pressing Alt-Tab usually just cycles between the first two programs in the list.

If a program is running as an icon, it doesn't usually pop up in a window, no matter how many times you press Alt-Tab.

If a program running as an icon is the only *other* program running, it pops up in a window when you press Alt-Tab.

If a program is the *only* program running, and it's running as an icon, it pops up in a window when you press Alt-Tab.

Give me a break! What is CoolSwitch?

What if you have a bunch of programs running and you don't want one of the first two in the Task List? How can you select a specific program with Alt-Tab? You use CoolSwitch.

Here's how to use CoolSwitch:

1. Press and hold the Alt key. Don't let it up. Press the Tab key and release it, but don't let up the Alt key. Keep the Alt key down.

2. A little rectangular window containing an icon appears in the middle of the display. This is the icon for the program that will become active *if you let up that silly Alt key.*

3. Without letting up the Alt key, press and release Tab again. The icon changes to show the program that is next on the Task List.

4. Just keep the Alt key down and keep pressing Tab until you see the icon for the program you want. Then, let the Alt key up. Your program becomes active.

NERDY
DETAILS

Why is it called *CoolSwitch?* Deep in the bowels of Windows there are switches that control just about everything. These switches are just words to which a value has been assigned, like Rudabagas=True, or SlimeyGreenFrogs=1. CoolSwitch is the name of the switch that controls whether or not Windows puts that little icon window on the display when you press Alt-Tab and hold down the Alt key. Programmers have a sense of humor. They just don't show it very often.

You can cycle all the way through the Task List this way. When you get to the bottom of the list, it starts over at the top of the list.

TRICKS

How can you get CoolSwitch to work on your system? It should work already. If it doesn't, you'll have to go into the Control Panel and double-click on the Desktop icon. Look for something that reads Fast Alt-Tab Switching. Click on it if there is an empty box beside it. Leave it alone if there is an X in the box.

Starting another program

You've started a program and switched to a different program. What do you do if you suddenly decide you want to start the Solitaire program and play a couple of hands?

Just switch to Program Manager by using one of the many forgettable ways you just read about. Then find the icon for the program you want. (It will be in one of your Program Manager group windows.) When you find the icon that represents the program you want, double-click on the icon. That's it!

I Want Out of This Program Now!

Now you should have Write running in a window on your desktop. Let's say you're through using it, and you want to close it (that is, quit using the program and get it off of your screen).

Exiting (or closing) a program

There are at least four ways to close a program in Windows. ("Oh, no," you're thinking, "not another list!") Okay, I'll tell you about just one method for now. When the program is active, press Alt-F4. That means hold down the Alt key, press the F4 function key, and then release both keys.

If you haven't created any new documents or changed an old one, the program closes. If you opened a document and made changes but haven't saved it yet, the program pops up a message like the one shown in figure 4.5.

Figure 4.5

When you close a program in Windows, but haven't saved the changes you've made to a document, you see something like this message.

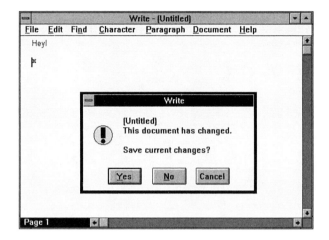

The message is asking whether you want to save the document changes before you exit the program. If you want to throw away any changes you've made, click on **N**o. If you want to save the changes, click on **Y**es. If you're not sure, click on **C**ancel. That will cancel the command and let you back into the program so you can look it over and decide.

STOP!

When you close Program Manager, you will exit Windows. If you want to shut off your computer, for instance, you need to exit Windows first. By pressing Alt-F4 when you are in Program Manager, you will exit Windows. A dialog box displays asking you if you are ready to leave Windows. Click OK if you are; click Cancel if you are not.

CHAPTER 5

How To Do Things in Windows

L et's face it: What you see in Windows is *different*. If you've been working with DOS for a while and just became a Windows convert, there's nothing much about Windows that's familiar. If you're new to computers, you're probably better off. You don't know what to expect. Just how are you supposed to use this thing, anyway?

Using Windows is what this chapter is all about. It shows you how to get things done in Windows. Here's what you'll find here:

- What good is a mouse in Windows?

- How do you select things on the screen and why?

- Why does that $%@$#&! arrow pointer keep changing to something else?

- What the heck is a window, anyway?

- What are all of those gadgets and gizmos stuck all over those windows?

- Are those words lined up across the top of the window for anything?

- This *box* just popped up on the screen—what are all of *these* gadgets for?

Hello Mouse!

Getting things done in Windows usually means using the mouse. Yes, you can use Windows without a mouse, but you don't want to try unless you have to. It's a real pain. Working without a mouse takes four times as long to get most things done. So, the mouse is important. That's why you're reading about it now.

NERDY
DETAILS

As you read in Chapter 2, there are different types of mice and mouse-like computer creatures. The most common type of mouse has a cord that connects it to the back of the computer, and either two or three buttons on top. Other mice don't have cords. They use infrared to communicate with the computer.

There also are *trackballs*. These are kind of like upside-down mice. The ball is on the top, and you rotate the ball with your thumb, finger, or hairy palm instead of sliding the whole unit around. Trackballs often are used with notebook and laptop computers.

Regardless of what type of mouse you have, the general concept is the same:

 You move the mouse or rotate the ball on the trackball, and a *screen pointer* of some kind moves on the screen. Usually, the screen pointer looks like an arrow pointing up and to the left (like northwest). Sometimes the screen pointer looks different. Let your mind think that the mouse is connected to the screen pointer. It's a Zen sort of thing.

 Something happens when you click the mouse buttons. What happens? It depends on what the screen pointer is sitting on at the time. It also depends on how you click the buttons.

Something new to do with your mouse!

Two wonderful mouse actions, click and double-click, were covered in Chapter 4. Here's a new action word to learn: *drag*.

This means to put the screen pointer on something (such as an icon), press and hold the mouse select button (usually the left mouse button), and move the mouse.

Whatever was under the screen pointer is *dragged* across the screen by the screen pointer. When you release the mouse button, dragging stops.

Selecting things on your screen

A big part of using Windows involves selecting things on the screen. That means moving the mouse so that the screen pointer is sitting on top of something, then clicking some mouse buttons. Sometimes it also means moving the mouse while you hold a mouse button down.

Selecting things on the screen includes selecting a program, highlighting some text, selecting part of a picture, choosing a command from a menu, and doing all sorts of other things you might not understand yet.

What's Hooked to the Mouse?

The thing that moves on the screen when you move the mouse is the *screen pointer*. I already told you that, but I tend to repeat myself.

Windows changes the screen pointer to tell you that the action you can perform with the mouse has changed. Windows might change the familiar arrow pointer, for example, to a circle with a slash through it. That's the same thing you see on No Parking signs. By changing the pointer, Windows is telling you that whatever you are trying to do with the mouse is *verboten*. That means it's forbidden. You can't do it.

Arrow pointer

This is the most common screen pointer. It looks like any plain old arrow. You see this when you can select icons, windows, buttons, commands, and other items in Windows. Use this when you want to say "I want to use *this* thing now," or "I want to select *this*" or "I want *this* to be active."

Hourglass

If you see an hourglass pop up on your screen, Windows is telling you "wait a minute...I'm busy." This is the one you'll come to hate. You'll just have to wait until the hourglass is replaced by a different pointer.

STOP!

If the hourglass never goes away, Windows has died. If the hourglass doesn't go away within a few minutes, press Ctrl-Alt-Del. This probably will reboot ("restart") your computer, so you may lose some work if you have a document open that you haven't saved lately. Make the habit of saving your work frequently.

Sizing pointers

When you put the screen pointer on top of a window border (those are the lines around the outside of a window), the screen pointer changes to a horizontal, vertical, or diagonal pointer. Which sizing pointer you get depends on where on the window you put the pointer. You can *resize* the window in the directions indicated by the screen pointer.

I-beam

Whenever you're inside a window or a box where there's text, you see a pointer that looks like an uppercase "I" on steroids. This is called an "I-beam pointer."

GEEK

NERDY
DETAILS

If you're writing a letter in Write, for example, you'll see the I-beam pointer when the screen pointer is inside of the Write window. Use this pointer to select sections of text or put the cursor in a particular spot to begin typing. (The cursor is the flashing line where your text appears when you type on the keyboard.)

Hand

When you see a little, tiny hand appear on your screen, don't freak out. Usually, this pointer is used just like the arrow pointer. Instead of using the tip of the arrow to select something, you use the tip of the finger on the hand pointer. How cute.

Four-sided arrow

You almost never see a four-sided arrow unless you're using the keyboard instead of the mouse. When you move the arrow keys on the keyboard, the active window will move in the same direction.

Prevent pointer

When you see a prevent pointer, it means you can't do what you're trying to do. Look at the front cover of this book. See the big international "Non-Nerds" sign? That's what a prevent pointer looks like, only without the words "Non-Nerds" on it.

- You might, for example, see this when you drag an icon from Program Manager outside of a group window.

- Program icons in Program Manager can't live outside a group window. Move the icon into any group window, and the prevent pointer goes away.

Crosshair pointer

You usually see a crosshair pointer with programs that let you draw pictures on the computer, like Paintbrush. A crosshair pointer looks like a plus sign (+) that is on steroids.

Use this pointer to select part of a picture (kind of like stretching a rectangular rubber band to enclose something).

By the Way, What Is a Window?

This may have been a good question to ask way back in Chapter 0. Basically, a window is a rectangular area with border lines around it. Inside the window is usually a program.

- Usually, you can stretch the window out to any size you want, shrink it to an icon, or expand it to fill the whole screen.

- Take a look at figure 5.1. This shows a typical program window and labels a few of its various parts.

Figure 5.1

This figure shows a program window on the desktop. A window consists of a rectangular box with various items inside the window.

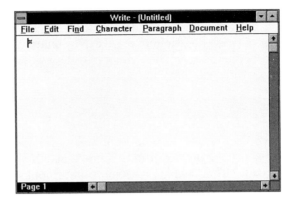

Run to the borders

Borders are the lines that go all around the outside of the window. It's the rectangular box that forms the window. It's also called the window's *frame*. It's actually made up of two lines that are really close together.

Title bar

The title bar shows you the title of the program that lives in the window. If you're working on a document, like writing a letter in Write, the title bar might change to show the name of the program *and* the name of the document you are working with. That's about all a title bar is good for. (All right, it's also good for moving and resizing the window, but that's for a later chapter.)

Menu bar

The *menu bar* is where most of a program's commands gather to wile away the hours after work. Actually, this is where you can find many of the commands for a program.

 In the menu bar are words called *menus*. Usually, clicking on a menu will make a list of commands drop down from the menu bar.

 You then can select a command from the list by clicking on it. These things that show up on a menu are called *menu items*.

TRICKS

Sometimes commands also appear in the menu bar along with menus. These commands usually have an exclamation mark (!) as the last character to tell you that they are commands and not menus. Clicking on one of these executes the command instead of dropping down a menu.

Scroll bars

These show up at the right side and bottom of a window. They're harder to explain. Sometimes they don't show up at all. Sometimes you'll have one scroll bar but not the other. Sometimes the window will have both.

- A scroll bar indicates there is some information past the edge of the window. You can click on either of the arrows on the scroll bar to move the view in that direction.

- The rectangle inside the scroll bar is called a *thumbtrack*. The vertical scroll bar represents the entire length of the document; the horizontal scroll bar represents the width of the document.

- Remember how to *drag* stuff with the mouse? To drag a thumbtrack along the scroll bar, put the screen pointer on the thumbtrack, press and hold the mouse select button, then move the mouse. When you have the thumbtrack where you want it, release the button.

- You can click the pointer in the area above or below the thumbtrack (or on either side of the thumbtrack in a horizontal scroll bar). This action is the same as pressing the page down or page up keys on the keyboard.

Buttons? Give Me a Break!

Windows makes its programs look like you can actually touch them and fiddle with them. Why? Because we're like the chimpanzees at the zoo—we love to pick things up, push things around, and play with them.

Take buttons, for example. When you have a piece of high-tech equipment, like uncle Jimmy's juicer machine, there are push buttons all over it. Well, Windows includes buttons, too.

NERDY
DETAILS

Buttons in Windows are rectangular or square things on the screen that usually look like, well, buttons. There are two basic types of buttons: those that have commands on them and those that don't. The minimize and maximize buttons are two examples of buttons that don't have commands on them. Take a look at figure 5.2.

Figure 5.2

These Windows buttons don't have any command words on them. Clicking on them is like "pushing" a button.

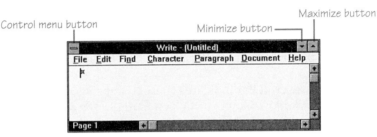

Control menu button

Minimize button

Maximize button

Maximize me, baby!

The up and down arrow buttons at the upper-right corner control a program's window.

 The down-arrow button is the *minimize button*. When you click on it, the window *minimizes* to an icon.

 The up-arrow button is the *maximize button*. When you click on it, the program window *maximizes* to fill the entire screen. This is great when you want to concentrate just on one program.

 When a window is maximized, the maximize button changes to a double up-down arrow. This is the *restore* button. Clicking on this button reduces the maximized window to a normal window with borders.

Control menu button

Figure 5.2 showed a control menu button. Nearly all program windows have a *control menu button*.

Press Alt-Spacebar to open up a control menu with just the keyboard.

TRICKS

Click on a control menu button to open a program's *control menu*. Figure 5.3 shows a control menu.

Double-clicking on a control menu button is the same as choosing the **C**lose command from the control menu.

Control menu

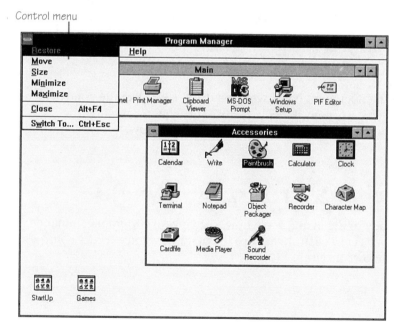

Figure 5.3

The Control menu lets you close the program, minimize and maximize the window, and do a few other standard actions.

NERDY
DETAILS

The main thing to remember about the control menu button is that almost all programs have them—even DOS programs that you run inside a window. They also show up in most dialog boxes, which is something you haven't heard about yet. Be patient.

Baby window buttons

See figure 5.3 for these. Okay, these are not really called baby window buttons. They're *document control buttons*, and they have to do with something called MDI.

NERDY
DETAILS

MDI stands for Multiple Document Interface. That doesn't really tell you much. Remember how Program Manager has other smaller group windows inside its main window? These group windows are called *child windows*. Program Manager is the *parent window*.

So what does the document control button do? It's just like the control menu button for a parent window. It lets you close the window, minimize it, maximize it, and so on. But it only does it for that window, not for the whole program.

Working with a Program—Menus

Now you're ready to dig in and learn how to give your program commands to carry out your every wish. *Menus* are the main way you execute commands in a Windows program.

Menus? I'll have the duck and plum sauce, please

No, it's not that kind of a menu. You can't order one from column A and two from column B and get an egg roll on the side. You just get a list of commands.

Remember the menu bar and the menus listed on it? Click on a menu in the menu bar and a list of commands (called *menu items*) drops down. You then can click on one of the commands to execute it (carry it out). Figure 5.4 shows some commands in a menu.

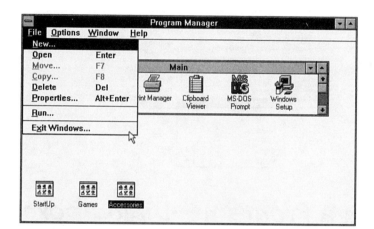

Figure 5.4

These are the commands in Program Manager's File menu. When you click on one of these commands, the action associated with it is carried out.

Remember this stuff

Here are some key points about menu commands:

- If the command word doesn't have anything after it, clicking on it will execute the command.

- If the command is followed by an ellipsis (that's three dots, like **Boo...**), it means you'll be asked some questions before the command is carried out. Usually, this means the command needs some information from you before it can actually do its thing.

- If the command has a check mark beside it, it's a *toggle* command that you can flip on and off. The check mark means it's on. No check mark means it's off.

- If the command has an arrow at the right side of the command name, it will open up yet another menu of choices. This other menu is called a *cascading menu*.

Cascading menus

When a command in a menu has an arrow beside it, clicking on it opens a *cascading menu* of additional choices. Sometimes, you can go two or three levels deep in a cascading menu. Figure 5.5 shows a typical cascading menu:

Figure 5.5

This is an example of a typical cascading menu. Picking the first one opens another one beside it.

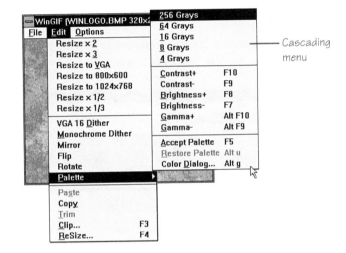

Cascading menu

Controlling a Program—Dialog Boxes

A menu is just one gadget you can use to control a program and issue commands. The dialog box is another. Programs use dialog boxes to let you set options for how the program works and to issue commands. Figure 5.6 shows a typical dialog with its parts labeled. All the things you see in a dialog box are called *controls*.

Command buttons

Command buttons are rectangular areas in a dialog box that look like buttons that you can push. When you click on a command button, it even "depresses," just like a real button.

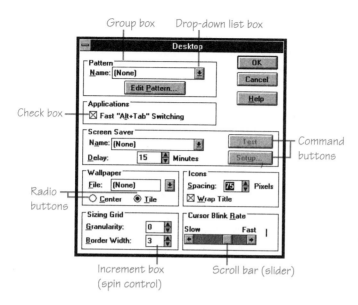

Figure 5.6

A dialog box that includes all of the basic controls you might find in any Windows dialog box.

Group boxes

This is just a box around a bunch of other controls. It helps group them into some kind of logical order. It doesn't do anything else.

Text boxes

This is a rectangular box in which you can type some text. Sometimes they start out with text in them. Sometimes they're empty.

 The screen pointer changes to an I-beam pointer when positioned over a text box. Place the I-beam pointer at the point where you want to start typing and click the left mouse button.

 Just click in the text box to start typing in it.

 To select all the text in the text box and replace it with some new text, double-click in the text box, then start typing.

TRICKS

List boxes

A list box is a box with a list of things in it. You can click on an item in the list to select it. A list box will have a scroll bar beside it if there are too many items in the list to fit inside the box.

You also can select items in a list box by using the cursor keys. Just press Tab until you get into the list box. Then, press the up or down cursor keys to select the item you want.

TRICKS

Sometimes, you can select more than one thing in a list box. If you want to select some items here and there in the list, hold down the Ctrl key as you click on the different items. Each one will be highlighted when you click on it.

If you hold down the Shift key instead, all of the items between the last selected item and the next one you click on will be selected.

If you want to cancel a bunch of items that are selected and select only one item, just click on the one you want (don't hold down the Shift or Ctrl keys when you do it).

Drop-down list boxes

These look like text boxes with an underlined down-arrow beside them. If you click inside the text area or click on the down-arrow, the list drops down below the text box. When you select an item from the list, the list disappears again.

Check-boxes

Check boxes are little square boxes that either have an X inside them or they're blank. It's just like an election ballot. If there's an X in the box, you have selected that option. If there is no X (it's cleared), the option is not selected. Click inside the check box or on top of the option word beside it to toggle the X on and off.

Radio buttons

These are circles that are either empty or have a solid dot inside them. Think of them as push-buttons.

When there is a dot inside the radio button, they are "pushed in" and that function is "turned on" or selected. When they are clear (no dot), the option is not selected.

Radio buttons come in groups—when you click one radio button in a group, it turns off any other one that might be selected.

More scroll bars? Argh!

You also will see scroll bars in a dialog box. These are like slider controls. In fact, they're also called *slider controls*. Usually, they are used to set options that vary according to some scale. It's like sliding a lever over to turn up the heat. Just scroll the button one way or the other.

Spin controls (increment boxes)

These have a small text box at the left and dual up-down arrows at the right. They usually are used to select sequential numbers or letters. You can click in the text box part and enter a value directly, or click either of the arrows. Clicking the up arrow increases the setting. Clicking the down arrow decreases the setting.

CHAPTER
6

Moving Things Around in Windows

A large part of using Windows is the use of the mouse to move and resize things on the screen. That's what this chapter is about. This list shows the things you learn about in this chapter:

- Why you need to move and resize things on the screen

- How to make a window larger or smaller, or turn it into an icon

- How to turn an icon into a window

- How to organize the Windows desktop by neatly arranging all those windows

- What to do when your mouse dies and you feel really sunk

- How to use the keyboard rather than the mouse to move and resize things

¿Bueno? Bueno, sí!

Why Move or Resize a Window?

That's a good question. It's easier to show you than to tell you. What if you want to see and use both Write and Cardfile at the same time? Look at figure 6.1. To be able to see and use both program windows at the same time, you must be able to move and resize their windows.

Figure 6.1

Both Write and Cardfile are running at the same time.

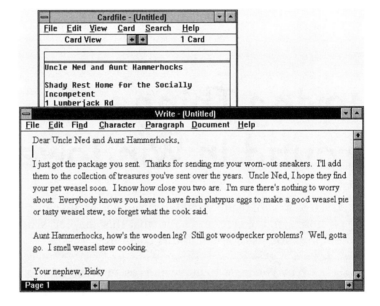

You organize your desktop by moving and resizing windows. This list shows the reasons for organizing your desktop:

 When you run more than one program at a time, at least one program is hidden behind another one. You have to be able to move and resize the windows so that you can see everything.

 Sometimes you will want to work with just one program. You can resize the window to fill the entire screen so that you can concentrate on only that one window.

 When you don't want to use a program for a while, you can shrink its window to an icon. When you need it again, you can change it from an icon back to a window.

Sometimes you will want to move a dialog box out of the way to read something that's hiding behind it.

 Maybe you just don't have anything better to do.

Dragging, Dropping, and Resizing Stuff

You're going to need your mouse again. Sorry, but you just have to get the hang of it. It's the easiest way to drag-and-drop and resize things in Windows. What's drag-and-drop? It's what you do when you move or resize something with your mouse. This list shows some examples of what you can do:

 Drag a window border to make the window smaller or larger.

 Move an icon from one place to another.

 Move a window from one place to another.

 Drag a document to an icon to open or print the document.

Resize a window with the mouse

Resizing a window is relatively easy:

 When you want to make a window wider or narrower, you place the screen pointer on top of the left or right border of the window. The pointer changes to a horizontal resizing arrow. Click and hold down the mouse button, and then move the mouse left or right to resize the window. Let the button up when the window is the size you want. You just *dragged* the window border.

 To stretch or shrink a window vertically, place the screen pointer on the top or bottom window border. The pointer changes to a vertical resizing arrow. Then drag the window to resize it.

 To stretch a window vertically and horizontally at the same time, place the screen pointer on a corner of the window. The pointer changes to a diagonal resizing arrow. Drag the window to resize it.

NERDY
DETAILS

If your window borders are very narrow, it can be tough to grab hold of a border to resize the window. You might want to make your window borders thicker to make them easier to grab. To do this, use the **B**order Width setting in Control Panel's Desktop program.

Resize a window with the cursor keys

It's possible to resize a window if your mouse dies (do it a couple of times, and then rush out and buy a new mouse):

 Press Alt-spacebar to open the active program's control menu.

 Press S or the down-arrow cursor key to select the **S**ize command. The screen pointer changes to a four-way sizing arrow.

 Press one of the arrow keys to "grab" the corresponding window border. Press the up-arrow key, for example, to grab the top border.

 Move the arrow keys to resize the window.

 To grab a window corner, first grab a border and then press the arrow key that points toward the corner you want to grab. After you grab the corner, resize the window with the arrow keys.

I have only one thing to say about resizing windows with the keyboard: El yucko grande!

Move a window with the mouse

Don't you wish that you could grab a window or a dialog box with the mouse and move it a little to see something behind it? Of course, you do—and you can. This section shows you how to move a window with the mouse:

1. Place the tip of the arrow pointer in the window's title bar. If it's a dialog box, place the arrow pointer on the title bar of the dialog box.

2. Drag the window. That means that you press the mouse button, hold it down, and move the mouse. The window moves along with the screen pointer. Pretty cool, huh?

3. When the window frame is where you want it, release the mouse button to drop the window. Crash! Watch your toes.

As you drag the window, Windows shows a "ghost" window border being dragged by the pointer. The original window stays where it is until you release the mouse button. Then it jumps to its new location.

TRICKS

> To move a window with the keyboard, open the active window's control menu and select **M**ove. Press the arrow keys until you have the window where you want it. Press Enter.

Fill the screen with a window

Suppose that you want to fill the screen with one program window so that you can concentrate on that one window. You can do it in two ways:

 Click the maximize button. It's the arrow that points upward in the upper right corner of the window.

 Open the window's control menu by clicking on it with the mouse or by pressing Alt-spacebar. Then choose the Ma**x**imize command.

Figure 6.2 shows a maximized window. The maximize button has changed to show a dual up-and-down arrow, called the *restore button* (explained in the following section).

Shrink the window back down (restore it)

Now suppose that you want to shrink a window you have maximized back to a normal window. You want to *restore* the window. You might do that because you want to see something else on the screen while you work with a program. Here are two ways to do it:

 Click the restore button. It's an up-down arrow button in the upper right corner of the window, where the maximize button used to be.

 Open the window's control menu and choose the **R**estore command.

Figure 6.2

The maximize button in
this window has
changed to a restore
button.

Restore Button

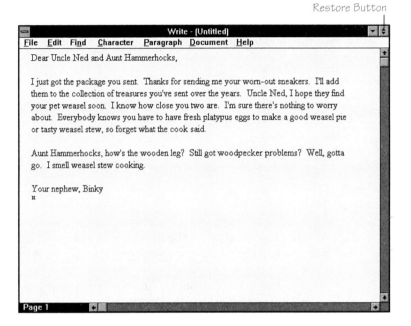

Change a window into an icon

When you finish working with a program for a while, you might want to
remove its window from the screen. You're going to use the program again
in a few minutes, though, and you don't want to close the program completely. You can shrink the window to an icon, or *minimize* it, in two ways
(the icon appears at the bottom of the desktop):

 Click the minimize button. It's the down-arrow button in the upper
right corner of the window.

 Open the window's control menu and choose the Mi**n**imize command.

NERDY
DETAILS

GEEK

When you minimize a Windows Program, it continues to work
even though it is running as an icon. The program name usually
appears under the icon. If the program has a document open,
the name of the document probably will also appear under the
icon—the program decides.

Change an icon into a window

Now that you have all those programs running as icons at the bottom of your desktop, how do you change them back to normal windows so that you can work with them again? You either *restore* them to their normal window state or you *maximize* them.

 Double-click on the icon to restore it to a window.

 Or, click on the icon (with a single click). This method opens the icon's control menu. Then choose the **R**estore or Ma**x**imize command.

Uncluttering Your Desktop

I'm usually not a neat person. Papers, books, and computer parts litter my office like nuclear fallout. It looks similar to Andy Rooney's office. My Windows desktop, in contrast, *is* neat. The reason is that it's much easier to keep it tidy than it is to risk opening that closet door again to look for an empty nook or cranny.

One way to organize your windows is to minimize the ones you're not using now. You also can perform two other basic actions on your windows to keep the desktop organized: tile and cascade.

Tiling windows

When you tile windows, they fit themselves together neatly like tiles on the floor. Figure 6.3 shows some program windows that are tiled.

The first way to tile windows is to click the **T**ile command button in the Task Manager.

 Double-click on the blank desktop. When the Task Manager dialog box appears, click the **T**ile button.

 Or, open any of the programs' control menus, choose the S**w**itch To command, and then click the **T**ile button.

 Or, press Ctrl-Esc to open the Task Manager and then click the **T**ile button.

Figure 6.3

Tiling windows arranges them edge-to-edge so that you can see all of them at the same time.

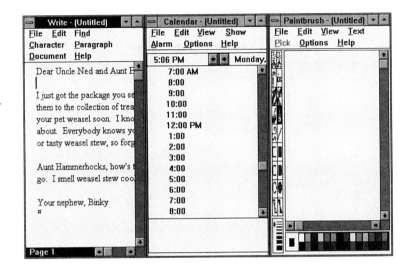

TRICKS

When you use the **T**ile command, the Task Manager tiles all program windows on the desktop. To tile just the document windows inside a program window, you must use a different method. Usually, you must choose the program's **W**indow menu and then choose the **T**ile command from the menu.

Cascading windows

Cascading is the other option you have for organizing windows. When you *cascade* windows, the windows line up on top of one another so that you can see a little of each one. Figure 6.4 shows windows in a cascade arrangement.

 To cascade all your program windows, open the Task Manager and click the **C**ascade button.

TRICKS

With programs that use multiple document windows, such as Program Manager's group windows, you can cascade the document windows inside the main program window.

Select the program's **W**indow menu and then choose **C**ascade from the menu.

Try it with Program Manager to practice moving and resizing windows.

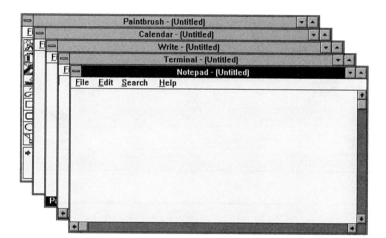

Figure 6.4

These windows have been cascaded—each one overlaps the last one in the stack so that you still can see the one underneath.

Put those program icons back!

When you have programs running as icons, they usually show up at the bottom of the desktop. But, you can move them anywhere on the desktop. Just drag them wherever you want them and then drop them. Take a gander at figure 6.5. Looks like I need some organization.

Arranging all the program icons scattered all over the desktop is something the Task Manager does well.

 To arrange program icons in a neat little row at the bottom of the desktop, open the Task Manager and click the **A**rrange Icons button. (See fig. 6.6.)

NERDY
DETAILS

GEEK

The **A**rrange Icons button in Task Manager doesn't affect icons that are tucked safely in their group windows in Program Manager. Arranging those icons is for another chapter.

Figure 6.5

Honestly, could you find anything in this mess? I need to arrange those icons.

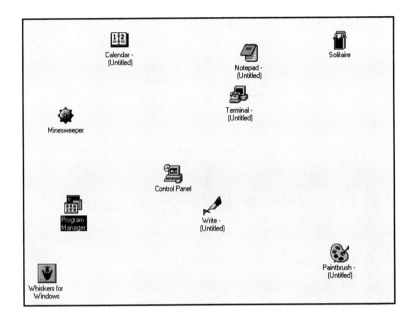

Figure 6.6

That's much better. Just open the Task Manager and click the **A**rrange Icons button to put your icons in order.

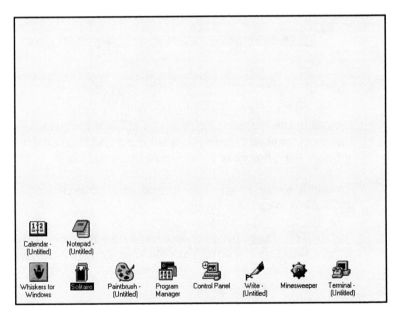

Keeping things where you put them

Program and document windows usually don't resize or move by themselves. When you maximize a program window and then restore it to normal, it returns to both the same location and the size it was before you maximized it. So, you don't have to do anything to keep things where you put them—*just don't move them yourself!*

What To Do When Your Mouse Dies

It happens. Your mouse gets tired of being scooted all over your desk all day. I mean, how would *you* feel? You can use the keyboard rather than the mouse until you get a new one, but you should make sure that the problem isn't something simple you can fix.

SAVE THE DAY!

Check out the things in this list if your mouse quits working and you haven't done anything to make it mad:

- Make sure that your pet weasel didn't yank the mouse cord out of the back of your computer.

- Look at the bottom of the mouse. Did it pick up a bunch of gunk from the desk? Gross! Clean it off and try it again.

- Take the little ball out of the mouse (look on the bottom) and see whether any hairballs or dust bunnies have been living with the ball. Clean them out. Rub the ball on some cloth to clean it off. Try the mouse again.

Is it still *quebrado?* You will have to use the keyboard.

Moving around in Windows with the keyboard

You can do almost anything in Windows with just the keyboard. It just takes much longer. You can use a zillion different key combinations in Windows. Table 6.1 shows some keystrokes you can use in Program Manager.

Table 6.1
Program Manager Keystrokes

What You Press	What Happens
←, →, ↑, ↓	Selects a different program icon within the current group
Alt-hyphen	Opens a group window's control menu
Ctrl-F6	Selects the next group window
Ctrl-Tab	Selects the next group window (same thing as Ctrl-F6)
Ctrl-F4	Closes a group window (minimizes it to an icon)
Enter	When a program icon is selected, starts the selected program; when a group icon is selected, opens the group window
Alt-Enter	When a program icon is selected, displays the icon's properties; when a group icon is selected, displays the group's properties

Table 6.2 lists some standard keystrokes that control Windows in general.

Table 6.2
General Windows Keystrokes

What You Press	What Happens
Alt-spacebar	Opens the control menu of the active program
Alt-hyphen	Opens the control menu of the active document window
Alt-F4	Closes the active window
Alt-Esc	Cycles through application windows and icons, but doesn't restore icons to windows
Alt-Tab	Cycles through application windows and icons and restores icons to windows
Alt-Enter	Switches DOS application between full-screen and windowed modes
←, →, ↑, ↓	Moves and resizes windows after you select the **M**ove or **S**ize commands from the window's control menu

What You Press	What Happens
Ctrl-Tab	Cycles through document windows and document icons within a program window
Ctrl-Esc	Opens the Task Manager
Print Screen	Copies the entire screen to the Clipboard
Alt-Print Screen	Copies the active window to the Clipboard
Ctrl-F4	Closes the active document window
F1	Opens the Help Contents page for the active program
Shift-F1	Opens a program's Help file to explain the command or action that is active in the program

Now, how about menus? Table 6.3 shows some special menu keys.

Table 6.3
Menu Keystrokes

What You Press	What Happens
Alt or F10	Selects the first menu in the menu bar
Alt-x	Opens the menu with an underlined letter that matches the x
x	Selects the menu or menu item (command) that matches the x
← or →	Moves between menus in the menu bar
↑ or ↓	Moves between items in a menu
Enter	Selects the highlighted menu or menu item
Esc	Cancels the selected menu

Last, but not least, are special keys for moving around in a dialog box and using its controls. Table 6.4 lists the keys.

Table 6.4
Keystrokes for Dialog Boxes

What You Press	What Happens
Tab	Moves to the next control
Shift-Tab	Moves to the previous control
Alt-x	Selects the control whose title has an underlined letter that matches x
↑, ←, ↓, →	Moves between different options in a group box. Moves the cursor up and down in a list box. Moves the cursor in a text box
Home	Moves to first character in text box or to first item in list box
End	Moves to last character in text box or to last item in list box
Page Up or Page Down	Scrolls up or down one boxful of items in a list
Alt-↓	Opens a drop-down list box
↑ or ↓	Moves the selector through the items in a list box
Spacebar	Selects an item or cancels selection of an item in a list box or check box
Ctrl-/	Selects all the items in a list box
Ctrl-\	Cancels all selections in a list box
Shift-↑ or Shift-↓	Extends selection to multiple items in a list box
Shift-Home	Extends text selection in text box to first character in text box
Shift-End	Extends text selection in text box to last character in text box
Backspace	Moves to the left to delete one character at a time
Enter	Selects active item and executes the selected command button
Esc or Alt-F4	Cancels or closes the dialog box

Hotkeys! (keyboard accelerators)

Open a menu. Almost any menu will do. Do you see some letters that are underlined? No? Try a different menu.

The underlined letters that show up in menu items, in dialog box controls, and on command buttons are called *keyboard accelerators*. Normal people call them *hotkeys* or *shortcut keys*. What are they for? Shortcuts, of course!

If you use the keyboard to select menu items, dialog box controls, or command buttons, just hold down the Alt key and press whichever letter is underlined in the item you want. Then release the Alt key. It selects the item for you.

PART 3

Now For the Real Stuff

CHAPTER
7

All About
Program Manager

W hen you start Windows, what do you see? Windows? No, you see Pro
gram Manager. Program Manager is what most people think of when
you say "Windows." It is one of the most important aspects of the way you
use Windows. This chapter expands on the material you learned about in
Chapter 4 and, specifically, shows you how to do the following tasks:

- Start programs from Program Manager.
- Install new programs in Program Manager.
- Create program groups and program items.
- Move program icons between groups.
- Delete program items and groups.
- Customize the way Program Manager works.
- Make Program Manager more useful.

What Is Program Manager, Anyway?

This one's simple. The Program Manager is not the person who hands out
programs at the opera, or the guy who runs NBC, or the person at the radio
station who decides whether Rush Limbaugh is going to get on the air. So,
what is Program Manager? It's a Windows program. It's the main method you
use to organize and access your programs in Windows.

You Start Programs from Program Manager

You know how to do this already if you have read Chapter 4 (there I go again). Each icon that appears in a Program Manager group window represents either a program or a document.

Here's a quick review of the main ways to start programs in Program Manager:

 Double-click on an icon in one of Program Manager's group windows.

 Single-click on an icon in a group window or select it with the keyboard and then press Enter. Or, select **O**pen from Program Manager's **F**ile menu rather than press Enter.

 From Program Manager's **F**ile menu, choose **R**un. This method opens a dialog box you can use to specify the name of the program you want to run and its location on your computer (see fig. 7.1).

Figure 7.1

The Run dialog box lets you type the name of the program you want to run. You also can hunt for it by clicking the Browse button.

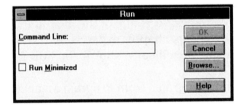

TRICKS

You must know what a file is to use the Run dialog box, because you start programs by entering the name of the program's file in the **C**ommand Line box. Notepad's program file is NOTEPAD.EXE, for example. If you're not sure what a file is, read Chapter 9. Usually, files you can run have EXE, COM, BAT, or PIF as the last three letters of their names.

Create Your Own Program Groups

Program Manager comes with four standard groups: Main, Accessories, Games, and Startup. The Main, Accessories, and Games groups contain many useful programs included with Windows for free.

NERDY
DETAILS

The Startup group usually does not have anything in it. This special group lets you start programs automatically as soon as Windows starts. This chapter presents more information about the Startup group later.

Create a group

You also can create your own program groups, to help you organize your programs the way you want. To create a new program group, follow these steps:

1. Select Program Manager's **F**ile menu and then choose **N**ew.

2. A dialog box called New Program Object pops up. Click the Program **G**roup radio button and then click OK. A different dialog box called Program Group Properties pops up (see fig. 7.2).

Figure 7.2

Use the Program Group Properties dialog box to create a new group.

3. Type a description, such as Useless Stuff, for the new group in the **D**escription box. This is the text that appears under the group icon and in the group's window title bar.

4.   You can type a file name for the group in the **G**roup File box, or you can leave it blank. If you leave it blank, Program Manager assigns a file name to the group automatically. It's OK to let it do that.

5.   Click OK to create the group.

Nothing is the new group yet—you put icons in it. You read about that in a minute.

TRICKS

> You can create as many groups as you want, but don't go crazy making groups. Every group uses a little bit of memory, so the more groups you have, the more memory you use.

Delete program groups

Suppose that you don't want a certain program group anymore. Maybe you never use the Games group and want to get rid of it. No problem—you can zap it out of existence by minimizing the group window to an icon, then pressing the Del key. You also can select **F**ile and then **D**elete in Program Manager.

SAVE
THE DAY!

> The programs that are represented by icons in a group you create are not deleted when you delete the group. The programs are still on your disk.

Put Some Icons in Your Groups

An empty group box is as useful as a screen door on a submarine—it's great for catching fish but not for keeping the H_2 out of the O. Windows comes supplied with program items in each of its standard groups, but you can create your own program items, in either the standard groups or in your own groups.

Create a program item

A program item is more than just an icon, but—for now—think of it as just a small picture that represents a program or a document. Here's how to create your own program item:

1. Open the group window where you want the new item to be, and make sure that the group is active (you can click inside it or on its title bar to make it active).

2. From Program Manager's **F**ile menu, choose **N**ew. The New Program Object dialog box pops up (see fig. 7.3).

3. Click the Program **I**tem radio button and then click OK. The Program Item Properties dialog box pops up.

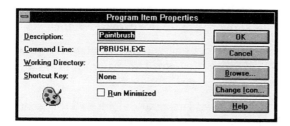

Figure 7.3

Use this Program Item Properties dialog box to create a new program item.

4. Click in the **D**escription box and enter a name for the item. This name appears under its icon in the group box.

5. Click in the **C**ommand Line box (or press Tab) and type the name of the program's file. Include the full path to the file. (You don't know about files? Read Chapter 9 and then come back.) Here's an example: **C:\WINDOWS\NOTEPAD.EXE**.

6. You can ignore all the other text boxes and such for now. Click OK to create the program item.

TRICKS

You can use EXE, COM, BAT, and PIF files in the **C**ommand Line box. You also can use the name of a document file. When you use a document file to create a program item, it usually takes on the icon of the program with which it is associated. See Chapter 10 for an explanation of file associations.

If you are not sure about the name of the program's file, you can click the **B**rowse button in step 5 and use the dialog box Program Manager displays to hunt for the file.

Delete program items

You say that you never use the Object Packager or the Media Player and you want them out of your Accessories group? You want to get rid of that Bart Simpson icon your three-year-old somehow put in the Main group? No problem. Deleting a program item is even easier than deleting a group:

1. Click on the program item to make it active (or select it from the keyboard).

2. Press the Del key or choose **D**elete from Program Manager's **F**ile menu.

Most of the same things that apply to deleting program items apply to deleting groups, with a few exceptions:

-   You can't undo the deletion. If you realize that you didn't want to delete an item, you must re-create the program item.

-   When you delete a program item, you don't delete the program or document associated with the icon. The program or document still is on your disk. (Whew! Aren't you glad?)

-   If you somehow blow a head gasket and delete all the items in one of the standard groups, you can use Setup to bring them back automatically. Check out Chapter 18 for help with that.

Move a program item to another group

Suppose that you don't like the way the items are organized in groups. Or, maybe you have a special group for all your main programs and you want to put Notepad in it rather than in the Accessories group. It's easy to move an item from one group to another. To use the mouse for moving an item, follow these steps:

1. Open the group where the icon *is*, and open also the group where you want the icon to *go*.

2. Position the two group windows so that you can see both of them.

3. Drag the icon from where it is to where you want it to be. (Click on the icon, hold down the mouse button, and move the mouse.)

To use the keyboard for moving an item, follow these steps:

1. Select the icon you want to move to another group.

2. In Program Manager's <u>F</u>ile menu, choose <u>M</u>ove (or press the F8 key). This step opens the Move Program Item dialog box.

3. In the <u>T</u>o Group drop-down list box, press the up- and down-arrow keys to select the group where you want the icon to be. After you select it, press Enter.

TRICKS

> Do you want a program to be in two or three groups? No problem—you can copy it.
>
> To copy an icon using the mouse, open the two group windows so that you can see both of them. Next, hold down the Ctrl key and drag the icon from one group to the other. Release the icon in the second group and then release the Ctrl key.
>
> If you want to use the keyboard, follow these steps:
>
> 1. Select the icon you want to copy to the other group.
>
> 2. From Program Manager's <u>F</u>ile menu, choose <u>C</u>opy (or press F7). This step opens the Copy Program Item dialog box.
>
> 3. In the <u>T</u>o Group drop-down list box, use the up- and down-arrow keys to select the group where you want the icon to be. After you select it, press Enter.

Make Programs Start Automatically

Do you have some programs you want to start automatically as soon as Windows starts? Maybe you want the program you use most often to start automatically or you want Notepad to open at the bottom of your desktop so that it's handy when you need it.

To set up a program to start automatically in Windows, you only have to place its icon in the Startup group. If the item doesn't exist in another group, just create it in the Startup group. If it *does* exist in another group, use the method described in the preceding section to copy the icon from the original group to the Startup group.

NERDY
DETAILS

If you are using Windows 3.0 rather than Windows 3.1, you can't use the Startup group. It doesn't exist for you. You must manually edit the WIN.INI file and add some settings to it. WIN.INI is in the Windows directory. You can edit it with Notepad.

Look for the lines **Run=** and **Load=** near the top of the WIN.INI document. Programs listed on the **Run=** line run in a window as soon as Windows starts. Programs listed in the **Load=** line start up as icons. Put on the appropriate line the names of the programs you want to run, as in this example:

Load=C:\EXCEL\EXCEL.EXE

Change How Icons Work or Look

It's easy to change the way an item looks or the way it starts a program. You just have to change the item's properties.

Every item has properties

The properties are those things you saw in the New Program Item dialog box. Figure 7.4 should jog those gray cells.

Figure 7.4

The Program Item Properties dialog box, which helps you change the way a program item looks or works.

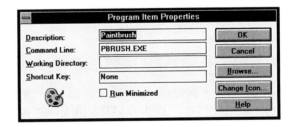

You can change the way icons work

To change the way the icon works, follow these steps:

1. Click on or select the icon you want to change.

2. Press Alt-Enter to open the Program Item Properties dialog box (or from Program Manager's **F**ile menu, choose **P**roperties).

3. Click in the **C**ommand Line entry or **W**orking Directory entry to change either, depending on what you want to change.

4. Change the status of the **R**un Minimized check box to change whether the program runs in a window or is minimized when you start it.

Change the way icons look

Okay, *now* you can change the icon. Windows programs usually include one or more icons in their program file. But where do icons come from?

 Program Manager's file, PROGMAN.EXE, contains more than 40 icons you can assign to a program item.

Other Windows programs usually include at least one icon you can use to assign to the program.

A file in your Windows directory called MORICONS.DLL contains more than 100 icons you can assign to different program items.

> If you have the correct type of program, called an *icon editor*, you can draw your own icon files and save them in a file on disk. You can then assign them to a program item.

TRICKS

Great! Maybe you're not clear on what a file is yet, but you know that a bunch of icons are hiding on your computer system in some files. Here's how to use those icons for a program item:

1. Click on or select the item you want to change.

2. Press Alt-Enter to open the item's Program Item Properties dialog box.

3. Click the Change **I**con button. This step opens the Change Icon dialog box. Make sense?

    The name of the file the item's icon is coming from shows up in the **F**ile Name text box. The icons in the file show up in the **C**urrent Icon box. If more than one icon is in the file, you can use the scroll bar in the dialog box to view all of them.

4. To use a different icon from the same file, just find it with the scroll bar and click on it. Then click OK. To look at the icons in a different file, click in the **F**ile Name edit box and type the name of the file. Change it to read MORICONS.DLL, for example, and then press Enter. You will see a new set of icons to choose from.

Change the Way Program Manager Works

You can use three options to change the way Program Manager works. These wonderful options are in Program Manager's **O**ptions menu.

Organize icons automatically

If the **A**uto Arrange command in Program Manager's **O**ptions menu is checked (has a check mark by it), icons in a group window will do the following:

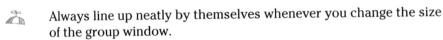 Always line up neatly by themselves whenever you change the size of the group window.

Realign themselves to fill in the gap if you delete a program item, drag an icon into the group from another group, or if you move an icon from one place to another inside the group window.

Program Manager, get lost!

The **M**inimize on Use command in Program Manager's **O**ptions menu controls the way Program Manager behaves when you start a program from one of the program items.

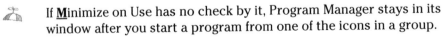 If **M**inimize on Use has no check by it, Program Manager stays in its window after you start a program from one of the icons in a group.

If **M**inimize on Use is checked, Program Manager automatically shrinks to an icon after you start a program. This gets Program Manager out of the way so that you can work. Just select the**A**uto Arrange command to toggle this box on or off.

Keep those changes for next time!

After you move group windows, and open some and close others, you probably want to save the arrangement for the next time you run Windows. The **S**ave Settings on Exit command controls that arrangement.

STOP!

The **S**ave Settings on Exit command does not save the icons in each group or the arrangement of the icons in each group. They are stored in each group's file. If you clear the **S**ave Settings on Exit command, it doesn't bring back an icon you have deleted. Sorry, Charlie.

 If **S**ave Settings on Exit is checked, the location, size, and state (whether it's an icon or a window) of all group windows is saved. The next time you start Windows, the arrangement appears just as it is now.

 If **S**ave Settings on Exit is clear (no check), any changes you made in the current Windows session to the position, size, or state of the group windows is not saved. The next time you start Windows, everything comes back the way it was before you made the changes.

SAVE
THE DAY!

To save the arrangement of your group windows *right now* without leaving Windows to do it, follow these steps:

1. Choose **F**ile.

2. Hold down the Shift key and select E**x**it Windows.

3. Release the Shift key.

These steps don't make you exit from Windows—I promise. They just save the arrangement of your group windows.

Organize Your Desktop

Keeping your Windows desktop organized is one of the best things you can do to make Windows more useful. You won't spend ten minutes scratching your head and looking for the icon that "used to be here somewhere." Here are some tips for keeping Program Manager nice and tidy.

Too Many Groups, Too Many Icons. If you create too many program groups or icons, you spend too much time hunting for the group icon you want or trying to find one group window in a sea of others.

Use a Common Group. Create a group in which to keep all the programs you use regularly.

Keep Those Groups Closed! If you don't use a group very often, keep it closed (leave it as an icon). This way you save memory and your desktop is less confusing to look at.

Argh! I Lost Everything!

Did you start up Windows and get the shocking surprise that all your groups are gone? Or, maybe all the items in your standard program groups have suddenly disappeared? Not a good feeling, is it? Here is how you can recover from that major screw-up:

1. Select Program Manager's **F**ile menu and then choose **R**un.

2. In the **C**ommand Line edit box, type **SETUP /P**. Then press Enter or click OK.

3. Setup runs and then automatically re-creates your four standard program groups and puts all the items back into them.

4. If any of the four groups had items in them before you ran Setup, you may have to delete a few duplicates. But, you should be able to do that, right? After all, you succeeded in wiping everything out.

All Those Programs You Get For Free

O ne of the really neat things about Windows is that you can actually get a lot of work done without going out and buying big, expensive programs. When you buy Windows, you get not only the colorful screens and pretty icons, but you also get some free programs.

These programs give you a way to work with Windows as soon as you install it on your computer. These programs also let you do some pretty neat things, such as write memos, add up a list of numbers, dial your telephone, or draw a pretty picture for your girlfriend or boyfriend. This chapter tells you how to:

- Draw a picture with Paintbrush.
- Dial your telephone with Cardfile.
- Use neat little characters (like smiley faces) in your letters.
- Write a letter using Write.
- Tell the time with Clock.

Getting Something for Nothing

First off, you may be wondering why Windows gives you these programs for free. All I know is that I use a couple of them each day, and some I have used only once or twice since I started using Windows. When you install Windows, these programs usually are set up in the Accessories group, as shown in figure 8.1.

Figure 8.1

Your free programs probably are in the Accessories group.

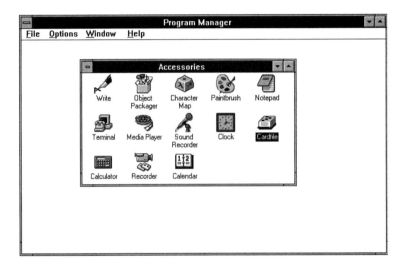

NERDY
DETAILS

You might hear the word *applet* used to describe the programs that come with Windows. This is because they are little applications—like baby applications—and the word "applet" is kind of cute. I'm sure that some nerd would try and tell you that this term is used incorrectly in describing these programs, but so what. You can call them anything you like. They're yours. You also can call nerds anything you like. They're nerds, they won't fight back (unless you steal their Star Trek convention tickets).

Be an Artist with Paintbrush

You can find the Paintbrush program by looking for the icon that looks like a paint palette, like this:

Paintbrush is used to draw pictures, make posters, doodle, and do some fancy graphic stuff. You can start using Paintbrush right away without learning any complex commands or mouse movements—you just draw.

Selecting brushes

When you first start Paintbrush, you are given a paint brush, called oddly enough the *brush tool*, that lets you paint the drawing area by holding down the left mouse button and moving the mouse around. You might think of this tool really as a pencil or pen because it doesn't really make marks on the "canvas" like a regular paint brush does.

NERDY
DETAILS

> Unfortunately you need a steady hand to draw straight lines with the brush tool. That's why Paintbrush gives you several other tools that you can use to create your own masterpieces. These tools live on the *Toolbox*, which is on the far left of the Paintbrush screen.

Do the following steps to make a nice looking hollow box on your screen:

1. Click on the box tool in the Paintbrush Toolbar (that's the thing on the far left side of the screen). The box tool is the sixth tool down on the left side of the Toolbar.

2. Move your mouse until the pointer is somewhere on the painting canvas.

3. Press and hold down the left mouse button to establish the first corner of the rectangle. Make sure that you don't release the mouse button until I tell you to do so.

4. Move your mouse down a little and watch how the box starts forming from the tip of your pointer. Keep moving the mouse until you feel that the box is large enough, and then let go of the left mouse button. You should see a box on your screen. That's how easy it is to draw a box in Paintbrush.

What do all those other tools do?

Table 8.1 tells you about the tools that you can use in Paintbrush. One of the tools, called the *text tool*, lets you add words to your drawing. You can use this tool, for example, to create a sign telling people to leave your computer alone while you're on vacation.

Table 8.1
Artistic Tools in Paintbrush

If you pick this...	You can do this...
	Use the **scissors** tool to cut out a piece of your drawing so that you can remove it from your drawing, copy it someplace else in your drawing, or copy it to another program in Windows.
	Cut out a rectangular piece of your drawing so that you can place it someplace else. Paintbrush refers to this tool as the **pick** tool.
	Paint your picture by using a spray pattern. Microsoft ingeniously calls this the **airbrush** tool.
abc	Add letters or other keyboard characters to your drawing. You can use the **text** tool to add some class to your otherwise silly looking drawing.
	Erase or change the currently selected color in your drawing. The **color eraser** tool is helpful if you want to change a particular color in one area of your drawing.
	Erase EVERYTHING with the **eraser** tool. After you drag this tool over something in your drawing, you are left with only the background color.

If you pick this...	You can do this...
	Fill up a closed area with "paint" (color) by using the **paint roller** tool. If you have a square that you want to fill with blue, for example, just use this tool and click inside the box. The box turns blue.
	Draw objects in freehand by using the **brush** tool.
	Create a curve in your drawing with the **curve** tool. You just draw a straight line, let go of the mouse button, then click on the line and bend the line into a curve. You then can bend it again.
	Draw perfectly straight lines with the **line** tool. If you want to draw horizontal or vertical lines, hold down the Shift key as you draw the line.
	Make hollow or filled boxes with the **box** and **filled box** tools. The filled boxes fill with the color you have selected. Hold down the Shift key to make a perfect hollow or filled square.
	Just like the box tools, but you can make boxes with rounded corners with the **rounded box** and **filled rounded box** tools. Do that Shift thing again to get a perfect hollow or filled rounded square.
	Create circles and ellipses with the **circle/ellipse** and **filled circle/ellipse** tools. (Ellipses is a fancy way of saying "ovals.") Hold down the Shift key to draw a perfect circle or filled circle.
	Draw polygons by using the **polygon** and **filled polygon** tools. A polygon is just an object that has several sides.
	You can change how wide you draw the lines or objects by clicking on one of the lines in the **linesize** box. The best way to see how this feature works is to give it a try.

SAVE
THE DAY!

As you use Paintbrush, you might screw something up, like erase something accidently or draw a circle the wrong size. If this happens, don't panic. You can undo what you just did by clicking on the <u>E</u>dit menu and then selecting the <u>U</u>ndo command.

Paintbrush's color

When you start Paintbrush, you have a basic set of colors to work with: black lines on a white background. To fully use Paintbrush's capabilities, you need to experiment with the color *palette*, which is like a box of crayons.

The palette has a collection of colors from which you can change the foreground and background colors. The *foreground* color is the color you are drawing with. The *background* color is the color you are drawing on.

TRICKS

You also can see pretty colors by looking into the eyes of someone you love.

 Select the color you want to use as the foreground color by clicking on that color with the left mouse button.

 Select the color you want to use as the background color by clicking on the color with the right mouse button.

 You can tell which color is the foreground color by looking at the *selected colors* box. The inside rectangle shows the foreground color; the background color surrounds the foreground color (see fig. 8.2).

TRICKS

If you want to change the color of an object, try using the color eraser tool. The color eraser changes the selected foreground color to the selected background color.

If you want to change your red objects to green objects, for example, click on red with the left mouse button, then click on green with the right mouse button. Next rub the color eraser over the object you want to change, making sure to press and hold down the left mouse button as you do so. The object magically changes from red to green.

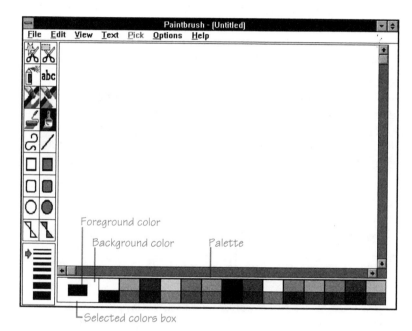

Figure 8.2

You can see the currently selected colors by looking at the selected colors box on the palette.

Write This Way

In Chapter 0, you saw how easy it was to write a short letter to your mother using Write, which is the free word processor program that you get with Windows. Although Write is not very sophisticated (compared to those expensive word processor programs that you have to pay for), it does have more options and features than I let on in that earlier chapter.

Some things you should keep in mind as you use Write:

- When you get to the end of a line, you don't need to press Enter or hit the side of your screen to advance the cursor to the next line. This feature is called *word wrap*.

- Write doesn't come with any of those fancy extra "add-in programs" such as a grammar checker, spell checker, or thesaurus. You do get Write for free, so quit your belly aching.

- You save the letters you write in Write the same way you save stuff in other Windows programs. You select the **F**ile menu and then click on **S**ave. Then just type the name you want to use to store your file. Read Chapter 9 for more information on storing your work in Windows.

- Another cool thing that you can do with Write is to put a picture in your letter. Suppose, for example, that you are away at college and you need money. When you write home to your mom and dad, you can include a picture of a stack of money in your letter as a not-so-subtle hint. Figure 8.3 is an example of some things you can do in Write.

TRICKS

One feature of Write that often is overlooked is the ruler. The ruler is a handy tool that sits at the top of your Write screen that helps you set up your document, including paragraph alignment, spacing, and indentations.

If the ruler is not present after you start Write, open the **D**ocument menu and click on **R**uler On. Don't expect this tool to make your document look pretty—you have to do that. It can, however, *help* you make it look pretty.

Taking Notes with Notepad

Unlike Write, Notepad doesn't give you a bunch of ways to set up your page. But that's OK. Notepad isn't meant for making fancy documents. Notepad is designed to help you make quick notes of things and fiddle around with some of the important "system" files that are on your computer. One great thing about Notepad is that it appears on your screen as soon as you double-click on its icon, which looks like a spiral notepad Jimmy Olsen might carry:

Notepad

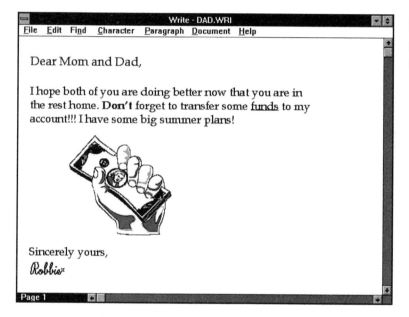

Figure 8.3

For a free program, Write isn't that bad.

Some things to watch out for...

Notepad does have some annoying little traits. As you type text, Notepad seems to travel on forever before it starts a new line. You may go batty because your screen will appear to hop each time you type a character. You then will get really mad when you have to keep scrolling over to read what you have just typed.

SAVE THE DAY!

To remedy this annoying problem, select the **E**dit menu and click on the **W**ord Wrap option. This option makes your lines end at the edge of your view and throws your words to the following lines.

Notepad also is quite strange in that it keeps all the text you type in memory, meaning that you are limited to the size that you make a Notepad file. This size generally is 50,000 characters.

If you want, type a note and count the number of letters, spaces, and any other characters it contains. This count is the approximate number of characters in your document. Then estimate how many pages you can write before Notepad tells you that you have run out of space in memory.

Notepad's funky printing habits

When you print your stuff from Notepad, you might find that it doesn't look exactly the same on paper as it does on-screen. Notepad prints according to the way you have things set up in the Page Setup option. To see this setup, select **F**ile and then Page Se**t**up. Adjust the **L**eft, **T**op, **B**ottom, and **R**ight margin numbers to get the effect you're looking for. If you find the settings that you like, write them down someplace—Notepad won't save them for you. Then you'll know for sure how things will look after you print them.

TRICKS

Just so you don't think Notepad is completely quirky, you can do one pretty cool thing with it. You can stamp each entry with the date and time you created it. You can, for example, pretend that you're on the Starship Enterprise and you're filling in the star log. Yeah right. Get a life.

To stamp your notes, type the word **.LOG** (make sure to include the period and use uppercase letters) in the upper left corner of your file and save the file. Then, each time you open the file, such as to write down ideas you have for book proposals, the date and time appear above your entry. I did this in figure 8.4. Notice how the time changes as I open and close the file to input my book ideas.

Clock Is Just a Clock

Windows gives you a clock so that you can tell what day and time it is. This clock is real handy for those days when you say, "I'm hungry. Is it lunch yet?" Just check out Clock quietly ticking away those painfully slow minutes before chow time.

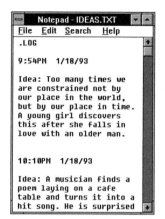

Figure 8.4

Notice .LOG in the upper left corner of my "idea" journal.

If you can't tell which icon Clock is, look right here and I'll show you:

If you can't tell which icon Clock is, look right here and I'll show you:

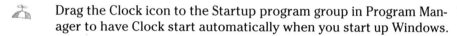
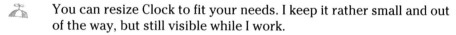

Drag the Clock icon to the Startup program group in Program Manager to have Clock start automatically when you start up Windows.

You can resize Clock to fit your needs. I keep it rather small and out of the way, but still visible while I work.

In Clock's **S**etting menu, select **A**nalog or **D**igital to tell Windows how you want to see Clock displayed. *Analog* means the old fashioned kind of clock; that is, the kind with hour, minute, and second hands. *Digital* means the way your kids learn how to tell time now days.

TRICKS

To get Clock to look larger by not resizing it, click on the **N**o Title option in the **S**ettings menu. This removes the title (all that stuff at the top of the clock window) and enlarges the clock display without enlarging the actual window. To get the title stuff back, just click on the clock face. If you use the analog option and you do this, you lose the date line. But who cares about the date—you just want to know if it's time to eat or go home. Your kids will remind you when it's Saturday.

Get Organized with Calendar

Ok, so you do want to know what day it is. Start the Calendar program, and look at the top of the page. Look for the following icon to start Calendar:

Calendar

If you want to see how today relates to other days in the month, press the F9 key. Regardless of how you want to view today's date, you don't get much from Windows with this program. In fact, Microsoft stuck too closely to the desktop calendar motif when it created the Calendar program.

NERDY
DETAILS

Motif is just a term used by a lot of Windows gurus to explain how Windows emulates a certain task that you usually do with your real desk. In this case, the Calendar program is designed to replace the appointment calendar you have on your desk (or shoved in your desk drawer under those Little Debbies).

One of Calendar's limitations is the inadequate space in which you can log entries for a particular time. If your appointment description gets too long, it scrolls off the right side of the page, like mine did in figure 8.5. To see it, you must use the arrow keys or press the End key on your keyboard. This is inconvenient, but there's no way around it with this program.

SAVE
THE DAY!

Ok, you're sitting there hacking away at your budget so you can get it done before the big 3:00 meeting. You are so involved that you forget what time it is. You look at your watch and it's 3:30! You blew it.

Next time (if there is a next time) be sure to set Calendar so that it gives you a warning alarm prior to your meeting time. Click next to an appointment and press the F5 key. You also can click on the <u>A</u>larm menu, and then select the <u>S</u>et option. You can set the alarm to go off up to ten minutes before your meeting.

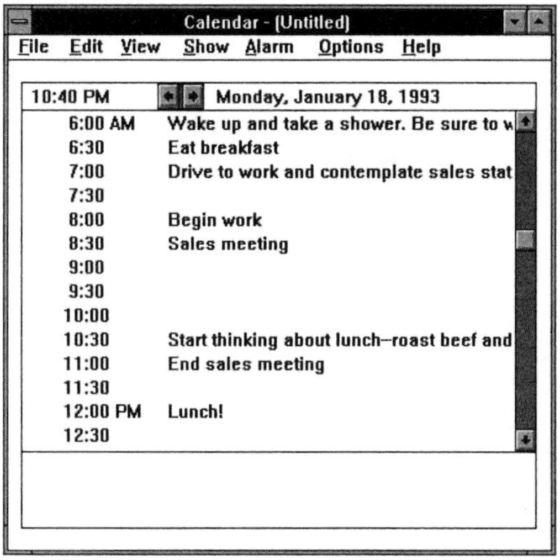

```
 ⊟              Calendar - [Untitled]          ▼ ▲
 File  Edit  View   Show  Alarm   Options  Help
 ┌─────────────────────────────────────────────┐
 │ 10:40 PM      ◄ ►   Monday, January 18, 1993 │
 │      6:00 AM    Wake up and take a shower. Be sure to w ▲│
 │      6:30       Eat breakfast                │
 │      7:00       Drive to work and contemplate sales stat│
 │      7:30                                    │
 │      8:00       Begin work                   │
 │      8:30       Sales meeting                ▒│
 │      9:00                                    │
 │      9:30                                    │
 │     10:00                                    │
 │     10:30       Start thinking about lunch—roast beef and│
 │     11:00       End sales meeting            │
 │     11:30                                    │
 │     12:00 PM    Lunch!                       │
 │     12:30                                    ▼│
 └─────────────────────────────────────────────┘
```

Figure 8.5

I hate it when my schedule scrolls off the Calendar display.

You actually want to use Calendar?

Calendar provides you with two views: daily and monthly. When you start Calendar, it always starts in the day view, regardless of what you do or how you save it. If you like to view calendars the way I do—real big with each day of the month showing, this view is not very helpful. I want to know if I'm getting paid this week, or if there's a holiday coming up, or if my wedding anniversary's coming up. I'm sure you're the same way.

☝ To see a monthly view, press F9 or open the **V**iew menu and click on **M**onth. Press F8 to get back to day view.

☝ To mark a special date (such as paydays or holidays), select the **O**ptions menu and choose **M**ark.

☝ You can print your daily calendar, but you can't print a copy of the monthly view.

Find a Phone Number with Cardfile

Cardfile, another nifty program that comes with Windows, is intended to replace your Rolodex, plus do something that your Rolodex can't do: dial the phone. Look for the icon that looks like a the real card file that you might have sitting on your real desk:

Cardfile

After you start Cardfile, you see a row of cards, with the names and phone numbers running across the top of the cards. Each card can contain the person's name, address, phone number, Social Security number, underwear size, and even a picture of them.

How do I make a new card?

It's really pretty easy to make a contact list by using Cardfile. You can group together a number of cards and save them as a file, a file that contains just one card, or a file that has several cards. You also can have as many files of cards as you have space on your computer.

TRICKS

You might, for example, have one file of cards that is strictly your business contacts. Another file might have your personal contacts. Another file might have numbers that you just write down if you want to harass someone. Don't harass someone over the phone; it's illegal, unless of course you're harassing a telemarketer. Then it's ok.

Follow these steps to fill in a new card:

1. Choose Index from the **E**dit menu or double-click on the Index line (which is the top line of the card).

2. In the Index dialog box, type the text (up to 39 characters) that you want to appear in the Index line, such as last name, first name, and phone number.

3. Click on the OK button or press Enter to enter the text onto a card.

4. Type the text that you want to appear on the card. This function is similar to a word processor, but you just don't have as much space to write in.

It's that simple to create a card. To save the card in a file, select the **F**ile menu and choose **S**ave. Type the name that you want to use for the card file, such as CONTACTS, BUSINESS, or LOVERS.

I need another card, please

To get another card, just select the **C**ard menu and choose **A**dd (or press F7). The Add dialog box appears, which does the same thing as the Index dialog box in step 2.

Looking at a card

It's pretty easy to look at a particular card in Cardfile. Just click on the Index line of the card you want to read, and it jumps to the front of the stack. The stacks are arranged alphabetically by the first character listed on the Index line.

If you save your cards in separate card files, you need to select the **F**ile menu and choose **O**pen to open a particular file that you want to see.

TRICKS

If you have a modem and it's hooked up to your computer, you can have Cardfile dial a phone number for you. Click on the card of the person you want to call, and select Au**t**odial from the **C**ard menu. Check to make sure that the number you want to dial is the correct one in the **N**umber line in the Autodial dialog box. (If you need to use a prefix, such as 9, make sure that you fill in the Pre**f**ix line and click in the **U**se Prefix box.) Click on OK or press Enter, and Windows will tell you when to pick up your phone.

If it doesn't work right away, click on the **S**etup button, and change any settings that aren't correct.

Cheat on Your Math Test with Calculator

If you need to use a calculator a couple times a day or even once a week, you can rely on the Windows Calculator to provide a cheap alternative to an expensive desktop calculator. Start Calculator by clicking on the icon that looks like a tiny calculator:

Calculator

How fast is the Universe expanding?

You can use Calculator to compute simple calculations (like I do) or do advanced scientific and statistical stuff (like Carl Sagan does). If you just need to add some numbers or divide some stuff, use the standard calculator, which is what it opens up to when you first start Calculator. This calculator is pretty safe looking, as is shown in figure 8.6.

Figure 8.6

Even English majors (like me) can use this calculator.

NERDY DETAILS

If you need to calculate some more advanced stuff, such as the rate at which the universe is expanding and contracting, you can use the scientific calculator. In fact, you shouldn't even need a calculator if you are intelligent enough to comprehend that universe stuff. You should just be able to do it all in your head.

To change to the scientific calculator, click on the View menu and then click on the Scientific option. If this setup gives you the heebie-jeebies, click on the View menu again and select Standard.

Use the mouse to click on the on-screen number pad to enter the numbers you want to calculate. You also can use the number keypad on your keyboard if you want to speed up things. Press the Esc key or the C or CE buttons on the calculator to clear the entry.

Add Some Character to Your Letters

Windows lets you insert some cool characters into your letters, memos, and other documents without going through that ANSI stuff I mentioned earlier. If you need to spell out some foreign words that place that little symbol above the word (like voilà) or you want to add a smiley face to your letter (such as ☺), use the Character Map, which looks like this:

Pick a character, any character

The Character Map is pretty simple to use even if you're not sure what you're looking for. Each font (that's just a fancy name for "styles of letters") has its own set of characters from which you can choose. After you start Character Map (see fig. 8.7), look in the **F**ont field to make sure that you have the correct font that you want to use.

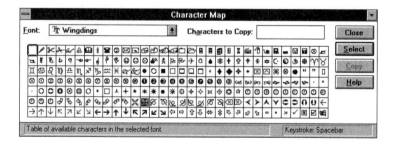

Figure 8.7

Add some character to your memos with the Character Map.

Click on the down arrow to get a list of all the fonts you have installed. Then do these steps:

1. Find the character you want to use and double-click on it. If you take your pointer and gently nudge the character by pressing the mouse button and holding it down, it enlarges so that you can actually see it.

2. Click on the **C**opy button or double-click on the character. The character(s) are copied to the Clipboard for safe keeping.

   You can select more than one character if you want, by double-clicking on the ones you want or selecting them and pressing **C**opy.

3. In the document that you want the character(s) to appear in, click where you want the character(s) to be placed.

4. Press Ctrl-V. The character(s) appears.

TRICKS

After you insert a character, you can change the size of it by increasing or decreasing the point size of the character. The point size is what determines the size of the character. A point size of 10 or 12 is pretty common for typewritten or word-processed documents.

Repeat Your Actions By Using Recorder

Recorder is another free program that you might want to use. Even if you don't end up using it forever, at least try it out. Go ahead and click on its icon:

Recorder

With Recorder, you can record keystrokes and mouse actions to play back at a later time. This is called a *macro*. If you find that you're doing repetitive tasks on your computer, speed up these tasks by creating macros to do the job for you. After you create a macro, you then just punch in the secret code that makes the macro do its thing.

To find out how to record your own macros using Recorder, refer to your Windows manual or pick up a copy of *Inside Windows 3.1*.

TRICKS

What's That Sound Coming from My PC?

Ok, I admit it. I'm just a little jealous of those Mac users who have a cool looking microphone hooked up to their computers. They can use these microphones to record their voices, burping, or other strange noises, and then play them back. You can do this in Windows as well, but you have to go out and buy a few parts to do so; namely a sound card, microphone, and probably some nice speakers.

The Sound Recorder program in Windows lets you play, record, or edit sound on your computer. You can start it by clicking on the icon that looks like a microphone:

Sound
Recorder

If you have all the necessary equipment to use the Sound Recorder, you might be tempted to start recording every sound you can think of. Don't! Doing so hogs the hard disk space on your computer because sound files are really large.

The buttons (see fig. 8.8) on the Sound Recorder are similar to those on a VCR: play, stop, rewind, and forward. The Record button has a picture of a microphone on it.

You have to install special instructions called *drivers* so that Windows knows what kind of equipment you are using. See Chapter 16 for help in putting these drivers on your system.

Figure 8.8

The Sound Recorder
has buttons that look
like the controls on a
VCR.

 To use Sound Recorder, you just select the **F**ile menu and choose the **O**pen option. Pick the sound file you want to play and choose the OK button. Then press the Play button and the sound plays. Press the Stop button and it stops. The sound wave is depicted in the Wave box on the Sound Recorder.

Recording some sounds

You can record a sound by selecting the **N**ew option in the **F**ile menu. Then choose the Record button on the Sound Recorder, and speak into the microphone. Windows lets you record up to one minute of speech. Use the Stop button to end your recording session, and then select Save **A**s in the **F**ile menu. Save the sound file with a descriptive name, such as SINATRA or SNEEZE.

The Sound Recorder lets you add some special effects to your sounds. You can make the sound softer or louder, slow it down or speed it up, reverse the sound (particularly interesting when you want to freak out your neighbors), and add echo to the sound.

What Is the Media Player?

Another program that Windows gives you for free is the Media Player. If you want some advice, click on the icon that looks like a spool of film and press your Del key to delete it from your desktop. All Media Player does is sit there making you feel poor and stupid because you can't afford all that cool video and special effects stuff that you really want to buy. (If you can't find the icon, it looks like this):

Media Player

Media Player lets you play multimedia stuff and compact discs and videodiscs. You can't use Media Player to record anything, but that's why they call it "Media *Player*" and not "Media *Recorder*."

 If you do purchase all that hardware and software, be sure to get a copy of *Technology Edge: A Guide to Multimedia*, published by New Riders Publishing. That book shows you how to use your computer to take advantage of all that really cool stuff you just spent a lot of money on.

NERDY
DETAILS

Another icon that you may see in your Accessories group is the Terminal program. This program is indicated by a telephone and a computer screen and is used to transmit computer data across phone lines. If you want to learn more about using modems, see New Riders Publishing's *The Modem Coach*. This chapter is big enough without talking about this program.

CHAPTER 9

It's on the Computer Someplace!

H ave you heard that one before? "Honest, I stored it on the computer!
It's here somewhere...maybe the computer ate it!" Maybe you've
said it yourself. Maybe you blamed the computer for the fact that you can't
find that letter you were writing to crazy, but filthy rich, Aunt Agnes. You
know...the letter where you ask her if she wants to come live with you in her
golden years and maybe give you her power of attorney.

Well, this chapter is all about storing stuff on your computer. Maybe these
topics will help you find that lost letter to lovable Aunt Agnes:

- How do you store stuff (they're called *files*) on the computer with
  Windows?

- How do you organize files on the computer so that you can find them
  again?

- What are disks and directories?

- What are files?

- What is a *path*?

- Help! I just want to find something I stored on the computer.

Saving Your Stuff On Your Computer

You probably use your computer to write memos and letters, create drawings, create spreadsheets full of numbers, or keep track of some other type of data. The chances are good that after you've gone to the trouble to put this data together and organize it in your program, you'll want to save it for later use. In computer terms, this means saving it in a *file*.

It's where your information lives

A *file* is a collection of data that is stored on some kind of *storage media*, such as a floppy disk or a hard disk. (You also find files on CD and magnetic tape—they're the same thing, just stored on a different type of storage media.)

NERDY
DETAILS

Conceptually, files are not all hard to understand. A file is used when you want to put some data on a disk for safekeeping. If you write a memo or letter on your computer, you can save it in a file. If you create a picture with Paintbrush or some other graphics program, you can save it in a file.

Putting something in a file is like saying, "Take this letter, wad it up into a little ball, call it 'AGNES', and stick it on this disk." Later, when you want to finish that letter to Aunt Agnes, you look for something on the disk called AGNES.

There are different types of files. Programs are stored in *program files*, and data is stored in *data files*. There's really not much difference between the two, except for what's in them. A program file contains the step-by-step instructions that make the program do whatever it is designed to do. The data file just contains data of some kind.

Documents=files (eventually)

In Windows, when you create something with a program, it's called a *document*. It doesn't matter if the data you're creating with a program is a letter, drawing, picture, sound recording, or database—it's still generically called a document. Remember that.

When you store that document on a disk, you've created a *document file*. It's the same thing as a data file—it's just a file that contains some data. *Document* is just a term used by Windows people to describe their data and data files. Everybody has to be different.

What's in a Name...

You've already read that files have names. Remember that letter to Aunt Agnes? It had a name—AGNES. It didn't get the name all by itself; you had to give it the name.

NERDY
DETAILS

Why give a file a name? Because it gives you a way to tell a program that you want a particular file. It also gives you a way to keep track of what's in each file. Most importantly, a name gives the *computer* a way to keep track of your file.

Here's how to come up with a new file name

File names that you create on your computer really have two names: a first name and a last name. The first name is a name that you give it. The last name is called the *file name extension*, and it is determined by the program that you are using. The first name can have up to eight characters, including any letter from A to Z, any number from 0 to 9, and these special symbols:

_ ^ $ ~ ! # % & - { } ( ) @ ' `

STOP!

That's it. Any other characters are off-limits for file names. If you try to use periods and colons and all those other special symbols that aren't on the list, all kinds of weird problems are going to happen. You may even lose your data.

When you need to come up with a new file name for a document, just use something that makes sense to you. Use the name to describe what's in the document (like you could really do that in eight characters...), such as the following file names:

FRED1234

FRED34

BAR-NEY

NOT_NOW

LETTER1

MEMO1292

TRICKS

> Although the preceding list of file names shows names in all uppercase letters, you do not have to worry about this. Windows and DOS do not care if you use lowercase or uppercase letters to name your files. They read the file name the same whether you name it with uppercase, lowercase, or both cases.

What about the last name of a file?

In addition to a first name, a file can have a last name, or an *extension*. A file extension generally is used to identify the type of file; that is, what kind of program created it.

A file extension can be from one to three characters long, and it gets tacked onto the end of the file name. There's a period between the name and the extension. Here are a couple of examples:

WHATNOT.DOC

AGNES.TXT

123HELP.WRI

FRED1234.A

BARNEY.A1

NERDY
DETAILS

GEEK

The computer literati call the period between the first name and last name of a file name a *dot*. (That's really creative, isn't it?)

When you're talking file names with someone (which you will do sooner or later), you can say, "Take a look in config-dot-sys or autoexec-dot-bat." Those are the files CONFIG.SYS and AUTOEXEC.BAT. It's easier than saying "config-period-sys," and the other person will think you're infinitely wise in the ways of files. Beam me up, Scotty.

What programs name their children

Most programs expect their document files to have specific extensions. Table 9.1 shows some of these file extensions and their related programs.

Table 9.1
File name extensions

Extension	What program uses them
WRI	Windows Write
TXT	Notepad
BMP or PCX	Paintbrush
DOC	Word for Windows

If you tell Write to open a file called AGNES, for example, and don't supply any file extension, Write is going to look for a file called AGNES.WRI.

TRICKS

Almost all programs let you specify a different file extension from what they would normally look for. You can specify AGNES.TXT in Write, for example, and Write will look for a file called AGNES.TXT.

Use these tips when you use file extensions:

- When you save a document file that you're working on in a program, you usually don't have to specify a file extension. The program tacks on the right extension.

- When you look for a file in Windows, you usually have a standard dialog box that lists files on the disk. Usually, the dialog box lists the files that have the extension the program is expecting (see fig. 9.1).

- You can click on a file name in the file list box (see fig 9.1), or you can type its name in the **F**ile Name box. You usually don't have to type the extension part of the file name.

How Do I Work with Files in Windows?

The answer to that question depends on what it is you want to do with the file. If you want to save a new document file or open an existing file, you usually do so from the program you used to create the document. If you want to work with a whole bunch of files at once (that were created by you or someone else), such as to erase them from the disk or copy them to a different disk, you can use File Manager.

Figure 9.1

This is the Open dialog box, which pops up in almost all Windows programs whenever you want to open a file that's stored some-where on a disk.

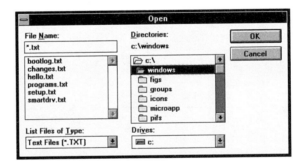

Here's File Manager!

You already know that *Program* Manager is a Windows program that lets you manage your programs. *File* Manager is another Windows program, and it lets you manage your files. File Manager comes with Windows, and it's located in the Main program group. Figure 9.2 shows what File Manager looks like.

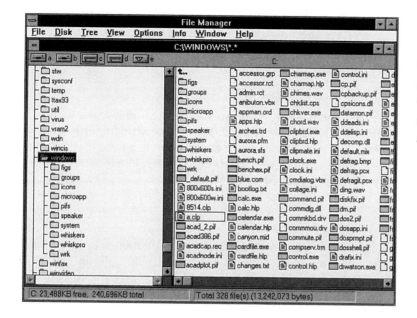

Figure 9.2

File Manager is a Windows program that makes it easier for you to find and manage all of the files on your disks.

File Manager is great for copying files, moving them around, and erasing them from a disk. It helps you find a file when you can't remember where you put it. It enables you to set up a new disk when you want to start using it to store stuff on. You can even start programs just by clicking on a file name in File Manager!

What File Manager is showing you...

At the top of the File Manager window is a typical Windows-style menu. File Manager's commands are located here. In the document area of File Manager's main window is a *document window* which shows the files that are on your current drive. Usually, this is drive C. Because it shows what's on a drive, we'll call it a *drive window*. Although you can have more than one drive window open at a time, let's concentrate on just one for now.

There's a drive bar...

At the top of each drive window is a *drive bar* that contains an icon, or symbol, that represents each of the disk drives that are connected to your computer.

The icon indicates the type of drive. Floppy disks, hard disks, CD-ROM disks, and network disks all have their own special icons. If you want to look at the files on a different disk, just click on its icon in the drive bar.

There's a directory window...

The left half of the document window shows some little folder icons with names beside them. This is the *directory window*. These little folder icons represent *directories*, and you'll learn more about them in a minute. For now, just know that they represent different areas on the disk, like different folders in which you can put your files.

And there's a files window...

The right half of the window shows some icons too, with names beside them. These are files. You also might see some folder icons in the right half of the window. And, the first item in the list at the right is an up-arrow with two dots beside it. That's for later. Be patient. This stuff takes time.

Why do some files have different pictures next to them?

File Manager uses different icons beside files because Windows recognizes them as being specific types of files.

If you see a file with an icon beside it that looks like a program window, that file is a program file of some kind.

If you see an icon that looks like a page with text on it, that's a document file, and Windows knows which program it belongs with.

If you see a blank-page icon beside a file, Windows is assuming that it is a document file, but it doesn't know with which program it belongs. Actually, Windows doesn't have a clue what the file is for—it's just using that icon because it doesn't know what else to do.

You Mean I Can Click on a File and It Opens?

When you install a Windows program, its installation program usually adds some settings to one or more Windows reference files. These settings *associate* the program's document file types with the program file.

When you double-click on a document file in File Manager, Windows checks in one of these reference files to see whether the file type you selected is associated with a program. If it is, Windows starts the program and loads the document file into it. If it doesn't find an association for the file, Windows gives you an error message in a dialog box (see fig. 9.3).

You also can launch your program from File Manager by double-clicking on its name.

TRICKS

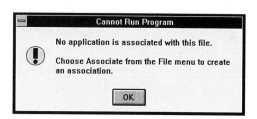

Figure 9.3

Oops! Your file is not associated with a program.

Why associate files and programs? (And how?)

If you like using File Manager to hunt for files, associating your documents with their respective programs makes sense. Then, you can just double-click on the document's file name when you want to open it for viewing or editing.

Usually, program associations are set up for you automatically when you install a program. If for some reason you need to do it manually, you use File Manager. Here's how:

1. In File Manager, find a document file of the type you want to associ-ate with a program, then select it (click on it once or select it with the cursor keys).

2. From File Manager's **F**ile menu, choose **A**ssociate. (Duh, that didn't take much brain power to figure out.) The Associate dialog box shown in figure 9.4 appears. Note that the file extension for the file you selected appears in the **F**iles with Extension text box.

Figure 9.4

This is the Associate dialog box. Use it to associate a document file type with a pro-gram.

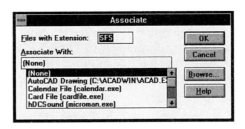

3. If the necessary program is already listed in the **A**ssociate With list, select it.

4. If the necessary program isn't in the list, choose the **B**rowse button. You'll see a Browse dialog box that looks suspiciously like the Open dialog box you read about earlier.

5. Use the Browse dialog box to locate the program file for the program with which you want to associate the document.

6. After you find the program file, double-click on it, or select it and press Enter. This takes you back to the Associate dialog box.

7. When everything is set, choose OK to form the file association.

I Can Drag Files Out of File Manager?

In addition to letting you start a program by clicking on its file, File Manager also supports drag-and-drop. That means you can drag a file name out of File Manager and drop it into a program window, onto a running program icon, or into a program group in Program Manager.

"Why?" you ask? Table 9.2 tells why.

Table 9.2
What a drag (and drop) it is

Drag-and-drop action	What happens
Drag-and-drop into a program window	When you drag a document file from File Manager and drop it into a program window, the document automatically loads into the program. Drag-and-drop a TXT file from File Manager into Notepad, for example, and the TXT file gets displayed in Notepad.
Drag-and-drop onto a program icon	When a program is running on the desktop as an icon, drag-and-drop a file onto the icon. You can, for example, drag-and-drop a document onto Print Manager to automatically print your document.
Drag-and-drop into a program group	If you drag a file from File Manager to a program group, Program Manager creates a program item from the file.

STOP!

> The drag-and-drop technique doesn't work with all programs. You can drop a document onto some programs and that document just sits there and looks stupid. A program has to support drag-and-drop for this to work.

I Need Organization (Directories)

Remember those little folder icons that show up in the directory window in File Manager? Those represent *directories*. What are directories? They're just different areas of a disk in which you can store information.

Directories are just like manila folders

If you have a filing system for your memos, letters, and other scraps of paper that have a habit of piling up, you probably keep them separated in manila folders. Computer directories are kind of like manila folders on disk.

NERDY
DETAILS

Have you ever wondered why manila folders are called *manila* folders? They're called that because they used to be made from manila paper, which was made from manila hemp. Manila hemp comes from the fiber of a banana plant's leaf stalk. The banana plants grew in the Philippines, wherein lies the city of Manila. My question is this: which came first, the city or the hemp?

You can separate a disk into different directory areas. Each directory has a name. When you store a file on a disk, you can put it in a specific directory.

You can put any kind of file in any directory, but they're really useful for separating different types of documents into different storage areas. You might keep all of your letters in one directory, all of your spreadsheets in another, and all of your checkbook stuff in a third.

You can put one directory inside another

Each disk has a main directory called the *root* directory. Directories are *hierarchical*, meaning you can put one directory inside another. A directory inside another directory is called a *subdirectory*. Figure 9.5 illustrates subdirectories. In the figure, C:\ is the root, or uppermost, directory. There are lots of subdirectories under the root, one of which is named APPSWIN. The APPSWIN directory contains six subdirectories of its own.

Here's an analogy: think of each disk as a big box in which you can store files. This main box is the root directory.

You also can put other medium-sized boxes inside the "root box." These other boxes are subdirectories. You can open one of these boxes and put a file in it. That's like storing a file in a subdirectory. You can keep doing this until you have everything organized the way you want it.

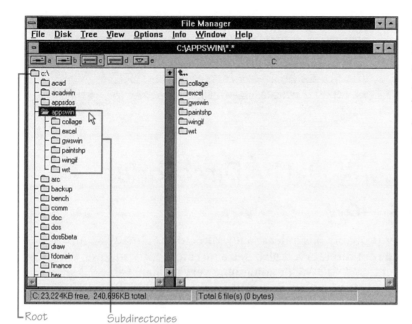

Figure 9.5

Here, C:\ is the root directory. APPSWIN is a subdirectory under the root. APPSWIN also has six of its own subdirectories.

Root directory

Subdirectories

A path tells you how to get to a file

With all these directories and subdirectories, how can you find anything? Directories are represented by their names. The root directory doesn't have a name, but it is represented by a backslash (\). The root directory of drive C, for example, is c:\.

If, for example, you want to find a file called AGNES.TXT that you stored in the root directory, you'd specify where it's located and its file name. That's called a *path*, and here's an example:

C:\AGNES.TXT

No problem. Now, what if the file was buried a couple of subdirectories deep? It's the same concept: you just specify each of the subdirectories down through the "stack" until you get to the file:

C:\MYDOCS\LETTERS\FAMILY\AGNES.TXT

NERDY
DETAILS

In the previous example, AGNES.TXT is inside a subdirectory called FAMILY.

FAMILY is a subdirectory of LETTERS. LETTERS is a subdirectory of MYDOCS, and MYDOCS is a subdirectory of the root.

A Quick Look at the Directories You Have Now

Your computer probably has at least a few directories already set up. It definitely has a root directory. It also has a directory for Windows, which is probably called C:\WINDOWS, or something very similar. Table 9.3 shows some directories you might have on your computer.

Table 9.3
Some Common Directories You Might Have

Directory	What's in It
C:\	System startup files like AUTOEXEC.BAT and CONFIG.SYS.
C:\DOS	DOS operating system files. Yuck!
C:\WINDOWS	Most of the Windows files, including Write, Notepad and Paintbrush.
C:\WINDOWS\SYSTEM	A subdirectory of the Windows directory. This has special files that you usually don't need to mess with.
C:\TEMP	Where Windows stores temporary files.

Okay, Now Do
Some File Things

C hapter 9 explained what files are, and gave you a little bit of information about File Manager. Now, it's time to put File Manager to work. This chapter is all about using File Manager to do all kinds of useful stuff to your disks, directories, and files. You'll learn how to:

🛖 Select files

🛖 Copy, move, delete, and change the name of files

🛖 Bring back that file you accidentally deleted (oops)

🛖 Find that letter you were writing to crazy Aunt Agnes

🛖 Change the way File Manager looks and works

🛖 Start using that new box of floppies you just bought

First Things First

File Manager is in your Main program group. Go start it up (see fig. 10.1). Then you'll be ready to learn how to select files.

Figure 10.1

This is File Manager. Remember it? Click on a disk icon to change to that disk. Everything is labeled for you.

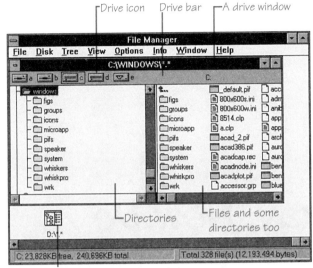

Drive icon   Drive bar   A drive window

Directories

Files and some directories too

A drive window minimized to an icon

Just click on it (the file, that is)

The easiest way to select a file in File Manager is to click on it once with the screen pointer. If you want to select a different file, just click on *it*. You also can use the cursor keys to select a file. Just press the Tab key on your keyboard until you get into the files window. Then, use the up and down arrow cursor keys to select the file you want.

Use the Select command

If you don't have the patience to hunt for the file you need, and you know the name of the file, you can use one of File Manager's commands to select the file.

1. Select the directory in which the file is located.

2. From File Manager's File menu, choose Select Files.

3. Choose Deselect to deselect any file that's currently selected.

4. In the File(s) text box, type the name of the file you want to select.

5. Choose the Select button, then choose Close to get out of the dialog box.

TRICKS

The **S**elect Files command is really useful for selecting a lot of files at once.

Doing Stuff to a File

Normally, when you save a document with a program you'll put it where you want it to be on the disk in the first place. But, you'll eventually want to move some files around to different directories. You also might want to make a duplicate of a file or remove a file from a disk or directory. You can do all of these things and more with File Manager.

Set those confirmation options right now!

Before you start messing around with your files, you should make File Manager as safe as possible to use. You can set File Manager up so that whenever you do something that will affect a file, File Manager will ask, "Are you really, absolutely, completely sure you want to do that?"

Well, maybe not in those words, but it will let you *confirm* the action it's about to take. That will give you the option of telling File Manager not to go on with what it is going to do. You can *cancel* the action instead of confirm it.

Here's how to set up File Manager to be safe to use:

1. In File Manager, choose the **O**ptions menu.

2. Choose the **C**onfirmation command.

3. When the Confirmation dialog box pops up, make sure all of the check boxes are *checked* (they should have Xs in them). If some of them are not checked, click on them to check them.

4. When all of the check boxes are filled in, choose OK.

Make a Duplicate of a File (Copy)

Okay, now you're *reasonably* safe. It's time to start doing some file stuff. The most common task you'll probably perform with File Manager is to make a duplicate of a file in another directory or on another disk. That's called *copying* a file.

 When you make a copy of a file, the original file stays where it is and a *duplicate* of the file is created. The duplicate is identical in every way, except it is in a different place (or you may give it a different name).

 This is what you'll do when you want to make a copy of a file for someone else or make a copy to keep in case something happens to the original (like you suddenly go brain-dead and erase it).

You can drag a file to copy it

You can copy a file to a different directory or to a different disk by dragging its file name around.

 Copy to another directory. Find the file you want to copy in the files window. If necessary, scroll in the directory window so you can see the icon for the directory where you want the file to go. Now, hold the Ctrl key down and drag the file name from the file window into the directory window. Drop it on top of the directory to which you want it to be copied.

STOP!

Important point: if you don't hold down the Ctrl key when you drag and drop the file, the file will be *moved* from the original directory to the new one. The original copy won't exist anymore.

 Copy to another disk. This one is really easy. Just locate the file in the files list, then drag it onto one of the disk icons in the drive bar. That's the bar with all the drive icons at the top of the drive window. You don't have to hold the Ctrl key down for this one.

The Confirm Mouse Action dialog box pops up when you do either one of the actions described above. (If it doesn't, you didn't set those Confirmation options like I told you to.) When the Confirm Mouse Action dialog box pops up, click on **Y**es if you want to go through with the copy, or click on **N**o if you're not sure.

**SAVE
THE DAY!**

Remember that you have to hold down the Ctrl key when dragging a file onto a directory to copy it. You don't have to hold down the Ctrl key when you drag a file onto a disk icon if you want to copy the file.

Another way to copy a file...

If you don't like dragging the file, you can use the Copy command to copy it. Here's how to do it:

1.   Select the file.

2.   From the File Manager **F**ile menu, choose **C**opy (you also can just press the F8 function key). This pops up the Copy dialog box.

3.   In the **T**o edit box, type the name of the directory where you want the file to go, like **C:\FRED**. That'll copy the file to a directory named FRED (yes, use your *own* directory names, and not FRED).

4.   Press Enter or choose OK.

TRICKS

You can copy a file to a different disk when you use the **C**opy command. Let's say you have a file on your hard drive (drive C) and you want to put it on a floppy drive (let's say in drive A). In the **T**o text box, include the disk ID (in this case A:\) where you want the file to go. If you want to change the name or put it in a specific directory, include the directory and new file name after the drive ID.

Another cool thing to do is to change the name of the file while you are copying it. Just type the new name that you want to use in the **T**o text box. The file is copied and it will have a different name. This is what you have to do, by the way, if you want a duplicate of a file in the same directory as the original. Windows won't let two copies of the same file live in the same directory.

Destroy a File (Delete)

If you went to all the trouble to create a file, why in the world would you want to delete it? Well, maybe it's an old file and you don't need it anymore. Or, maybe your program creates *backup* files each time you resave a document, and you want to get rid of some of those extra backup files to save some disk space. Maybe you've decided there is a program on your computer that you really don't need anymore.

Whatever the reason, to delete a file, do this:

1. Select the file you want to delete.

2. Press the Del key, or from File Manager's **F**ile menu, choose **D**el. This brings up a Delete dialog box you can use to confirm that you really want to delete the file.

3. When the Delete dialog box pops up (see fig. 10.2), make sure you have the right file listed in the De**l**ete text box, then choose OK.

4. A Confirm File Delete dialog box pops up. Choose **Y**es if you want to delete the file, or choose **N**o or Cancel if you don't want to delete it.

Figure 10.2

This is the Delete
dialog box.

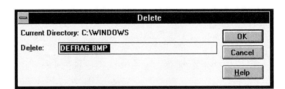

If you want to delete a different file, just change the name in the De**l**ete text box when the Delete dialog box shows up.

SAVE
THE DAY!

When you delete a file, it's gone. Adios! If you suddenly realize that you screwed up and deleted a file that you shouldn't have deleted, go immediately to the Undelete command (it's covered next). If you do anything else before going to the Undelete command, you risk losing the file for good. Boo hoo...

Oops...I need that file back (Undelete)

So, you're reading this because you didn't pay attention to those confirmation dialog boxes, aye? I guess you learned your lesson, didn't you?

Quit crying. Maybe all is not lost after all—try doing this stuff:

1. Exit Windows.

2. You'll end up at a DOS prompt. Use the CD command to change to the directory where the file used to be. For example, to change to the WINDOWS directory, type **CD \WINDOWS** and press Enter.

3. To undelete one file, type **UNDELETE** *filename*, where *filename* is the name of the file that you deleted. Then, press Enter. Or,

4. If you deleted a bunch of files and want to bring them back, type **UNDELETE** and press Enter. The UNDELETE command gives you a chance to undelete all of the deleted files that are in the directory. You might see a bunch of deleted files you didn't know were there.

5. Answer with a Y for Yes or N for No when the UNDELETE command asks you if you want to undelete the file.

6. When the UNDELETE command is finished, type **WIN** and press Enter. This returns you to Windows.

The chances are good that you can undelete a file as long as you use the UNDELETE command right after you delete the file(s). The more things you do in between, the greater the chances are that you'll lose some of the files.

GEEK

UNDELETE will not recover the first letter of the file name. You have to fill this in. You don't want it to be too easy, do you?

NERDY
DETAILS

Change a File's Name (Rename)

You can change the name of a file. Maybe you want to change just the extension, or maybe you want to change the whole name. It's easy to do, and it's called *renaming a file*.

To rename the file, you must do this:

1. Select the file in File Manager.

2. From File Manager's **F**ile menu, choose **R**ename. This opens the Rename dialog box.

3. In the **T**o text box, type the new name for the file (include the file extension, too).

4. Choose OK to rename the file.

I Want This File Over There (Move)

Earlier you read that you can copy a file, which duplicates it. You also can *move* a file to a different directory or to a different disk. When you move a file, the original file is relocated to the new disk or directory.

Drag that file over there

Do you remember how you copied a file by dragging it onto a directory or disk icon? You can move a file in much the same way:

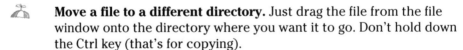

Move a file to a different directory. Just drag the file from the file window onto the directory where you want it to go. Don't hold down the Ctrl key (that's for copying).

Move a file to a different disk. Hold down the Shift key, then drag the file from the file window and drop it on one of the drive icons in the drive bar.

A confirmation dialog box pops up to ask you if you really want to move the file. Click on Yes if it is the right directory; click on No if it is not the right directory.

You can use the Move command

This is a lot like using the Copy command. Just select the file, then from File Manager's **F**ile menu, choose **M**ove (or you can press the F7 function key). You'll see a Move dialog box.

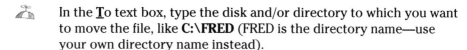

> In the **T**o text box, type the disk and/or directory to which you want to move the file, like **C:\FRED** (FRED is the directory name—use your own directory name instead).

> If you want to change the name, add a new name after the directory name, like **C:\FRED\NEWFILE.DOC**.

> If you specify a new name and don't specify a different disk or directory, all you'll do is rename the file. It won't be moved to a different directory, but its name will change.

Work with a Bunch of Files at Once

All of the previous examples only dealt with one file at a time. You can copy, move, delete, and rename a bunch of files at once. The first step is to select all of the files you want to work with.

> You can use the mouse to select more than one file, or you can use one of File Manager's commands.

> If you want to select a lot of files that have different file extensions, it's easiest to use the mouse.

Use the mouse to select a bunch of files

Each time you click on a file in File Manager, it gets selected. If there are any other files selected, they get deselected.

TRICKS

If you hold down the Ctrl key while clicking on files, you can select more than one file. This technique is good for selecting files that aren't right above or below each other in the list.

When you click on a file name with the Shift key down, all of the files in the list between the newly selected file and the last one you selected are highlighted (which means that they are selected).

Use the Select Files command

When you want to select a bunch of files that have the same file extension or have the same name, it's easiest to use the Select Files command (see fig. 10.3).

Figure 10.3

This is the Select Files dialog box. Use it to select a bunch of different files at one time.

Here are the steps you need to follow when selecting a group of files with the Select Files dialog box:

1. From File Manager's File menu, choose Select Files.

2. To select all of the files having a certain file extension, type ***.*ext*** in the Files text box, where *ext* is the type of file you want to select. To select all TXT files, for example, type ***.TXT**.

3. Choose Select or press Enter to select the files.

4. Repeat steps 2 and 3 to select any additional files.

5. When you've selected all the files you want, choose Close.

NERDY
DETAILS

What was that funky * thing in step 2? It's called a wild card and it specifies the files that you want to select.

If you want to select a bunch of files based on their file names—such as "select all file names that start with the letter Z"—you can use a wild card (it would be Z*.* and you read as "zee star dot star.")

Copying, moving, and deleting a bunch of files

After you select a bunch of files, you can do things like copy, move, and delete all of those files at once. The process is almost identical in each case to what you would do if you were monkeying around with only one file.

If you need a refresher course on copying, moving, or deleting files, turn back a few pages and read those sections again.

 One of the only things you might notice different when you use your mouse to copy and move more than one file is the icon that "sticks" to your pointer. You get what's called a "multiple document icon," which simply means the icon looks like three pieces of paper instead of two.

SAVE THE DAY!

If you delete a bunch of files at once, make sure you read the Delete confirmation dialog box and the files you have selected before you click on the Yes button.

Are you really brave? Are you sure you want to delete all of the files you select? If so, you can choose the Yes to <u>A</u>ll button. This deletes all of the files without letting you confirm them one-by-one. Again, read everything twice to make sure you're doing something you really want to do. You don't want to wipe out a bunch of your work because of a happy mouse finger.

What Can I Do with Directories?

You can do a lot with directories in File Manager. You can copy, move, delete, and rename a directory, just like you can a file. Here's what happens in each case:

 Copy a directory. If you copy a directory, all of the files in the directory get copied, too.

 Move a directory. If you move a directory, all of the files in the directory get moved, too.

 Delete a directory. If you delete a directory, all the files in that directory get deleted (ouch!). What's worse, any subdirectories in the directory, and any files in those subdirectories, also get deleted.

 Rename a directory. This one is pretty safe. All you're doing is changing the name of the directory. Nothing bad can happen. (Unless you have a program item that wants to use the directory by its old name. Then, you have to change the program item to point to the new directory name.)

STOP!

Please, don't ever, ever, ever try to delete the root directory of a hard disk. That's the directory that has the C:\ next to it. You'll wipe out *everything* on the disk. That means not only all of your programs and documents, but Windows and DOS, too. The computer will be absolutely useless. **If you turn it off, you might not be able to start it up again without reinstalling DOS!**

Now that you are scared to death to even get near your computer, read the next Save the Day note. It might help you breath easier.

SAVE
THE DAY!

If all of your synapses quit firing at once and you actually deleted all the files on your hard disk, you'd better hope you have a backup of your entire hard disk and a bootable DOS diskette. Later in this chapter you find a section that explains backups. If you already deleted the files without a backup, it's too late. Don't touch anything else. Go directly to Chapter 19 and find out who to call (don't call *me*). Beg for mercy. Offer large bribes. Prostrate yourself. Pray.

Copying, moving, renaming, and deleting directories

The only difference between doing these operations on a directory as opposed to doing them on a file is that you select a directory instead of a file.

In the directory window, click on the directory you want to work with. Then, drag the directory to another directory or disk, or use the appropriate command in the **F**ile menu. Remember, Ctrl is for copying and Shift is for moving.

Create Your Own Directories

It's really easy to create your own directories. The main thing to remember is that when you create a directory, that new directory is always created as a subdirectory of the currently selected directory.

If you want to create a subdirectory in your Windows directory, for example, select the WINDOWS directory, then create your own directory. If you want to create a directory at the highest level possible, select the root directory (C:\) when you create the directory.

1. In File Manager, select the directory in which you want to create the subdirectory.

2. From File Manager's **F**ile menu, choose Cr**e**ate Directory. This opens the Create Directory dialog box.

3. In the **N**ame text box, enter a name for the directory. It's just like a file name—eight characters and limited to the same types of characters. You don't need to include an extension for the name.

4. When you have the name entered, choose OK or press Enter.

That's all there is to it!

Where Did I Put That Letter?

You just can't find that letter to Aunt Agnes anywhere? Maybe it slid off the disk and it's lying inside the disk drive case in a pile of magnetic domains. Maybe the evil data fairy wiped it out last night while you were tossing in your sleep. Maybe...maybe...maybe you just can't remember where you put it.

Searching for files

When you can't find a file, just open up File Manager's **F**ile menu and choose the Sear**ch** command. The Search dialog box pops up (see fig. 10.4).

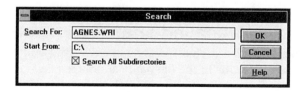

Figure 10.4

This is the Search dialog box. You can use it to find files that you have misplaced.

Here's what all the boxes and stuff in the Search dialog box signify:

 Search For. In this box, type the name of the file you're looking for, including its extension.

 Start From. Type the path of the directory in which you want to start the search. If you want to search through the whole disk, enter the root directory (like **C:**).

 Search All Subdirectories. Do you just want to search through the directory you specified in Start **F**rom, or do you want to search all of the subdirectories in it too? If you want to search all of the subdirectories, check this box.

When you have all the information ready in all the boxes, choose OK. File Manager hunts for the file and displays a window with a list of matching files, if it finds any (see fig. 10.5).

Figure 10.5

File Manager with the results of a file search. The window lists the files that match your search criteria.

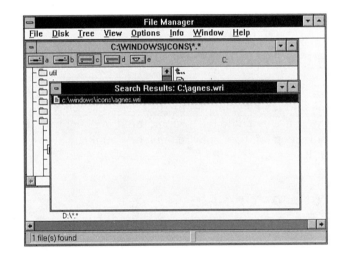

I can't remember what I called that file

Maybe you can't remember *exactly* what the file name was, but you have a vague idea. You can use *wild cards* in the file name and have File Manager find all the files that *sort of* match the file specification you give it.

Wild cards are characters that stand for something else, just like jokers can stand for other cards in poker. The two wild-card characters you can use are the asterisk (*****) and the question mark (**?**).

* This means "replace this with any number of characters."

 ? This means "replace this with just *one* character."

Table 10.1 shows some examples and some possible matches you'll get.

Table 10.1
Wild Cards and How They Work

File specification	File names that match
.	Matches all files (having *any* name and *any* extension)
*.TXT	Matches all files that have the file extension TXT. Examples: FRED.TXT and BARNEY.TXT.
*.DOC	Matches all files that have the file extension DOC, such as WHATSUP.DOC, WHEN.DOC, and IGIVEUP.DOC.
AGNES.*	Matches all files that have the name AGNES, and any extension (AGNES.TXT, AGNES.DOC, AGNES.XYZ).
ABC*.*	Matches all files that start with ABC, regardless of their extension. Examples: ABC123.TXT, ABC.DOC, ABC941AZ.QRZ.
ABC*.DOC	Matches all files that start with ABC and have a DOC extension, including. ABC123.DOC, ABC.DOC, and ABC-XYZ.DOC.
AGNES.?OC	Everything has to match except the character replaced by the ?. Such as AGNES.DOC, AGNES.LOC, AGNES.2OC, and AGNES.9OC.
?GNES.DOC	Everything still has to match except the ?. Examples: AGNES.DOC, BGNES.DOC, CGNES.DOC, 8GNES.DOC, 3GNES.DOC.
*.?	Matches any file that just has one character in the extension. Examples: BONEHEAD.1, HOSE.A, HOSE.B, FERGY.8, MALCOM.Z.

STOP!

You can't use a wild card when you save a file. In other words, a wild card can't actually *be* a part of a file name.

I Don't Like How File Manager Looks and Works

File Manager has some options and commands you can use to change the way it looks and how it works.

Look at more than one drive window

There are three main ways to open a new window in File Manager. The first is to use a command to do so. From the **W**indow menu, choose **N**ew Window. File Manager opens another window just like the current window, which shows the same drive and directory (see fig. 10.6). To view a different directory or drive, just select it in the new window.

Figure 10.6

When you choose the New Window command, File Manager opens another window just like the current one. It shows the same disk and directory.

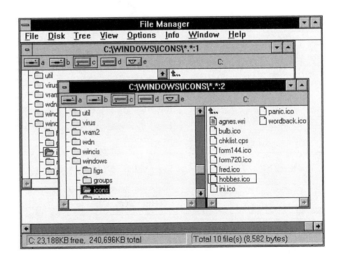

After the new window opens, just select a different directory or drive in the new window to change what it shows you.

Just double-click on a drive icon

If you double-click on a drive icon instead of single-click on it, File Manager opens a new window and displays the contents of the disk.

TRICKS

If you hold down the Shift key while double-clicking on a directory in any directory window, File Manager opens a new window and displays only the contents of that directory in the new window. (It's a regular drive window—the directory part of the window is just squashed all the way over to the left. You can drag it back open with the mouse if you want to.)

The tree of (file management) life

One of the best ways to think about how directories are related to each other is to imagine your hard drive as being an upside-down tree, with the root directory (C:\) at the top. In fact, the relationship between all directories is called the *directory tree*.

 Each of the subdirectories is a *branch*.

 When the directory window shows a directory and all of its subdirectories, it is shown *expanded*.

 If you just see the directory and none of the subdirectories, it is *collapsed*.

If you want to change how the tree looks...

The commands in the **T**ree menu in File Manager let you change the way the directory tree is displayed.

 Ex**p**and One Level. This command shows the selected directory to show any subdirectory directly under it.

 Expand One Branch. Use this one to show the whole branch (all subdirectories under the directory).

 Expand All. *All* directory branches are shown with this command. If you have a lot of directories, you may have to wait a few seconds.

 Collapse Branch. This "collapses" the selected branch so you don't see the subdirectories in it.

Indicate Expandable Branches. If this is checked, File Manager puts a plus sign (+) on the icons of directories that have subdirectories in them (see fig. 10.7). If you can see the subdirectories, File Manager puts a minus sign (–) on the icon instead.

Figure 10.7

This figure shows some branches expanded and others collapsed.

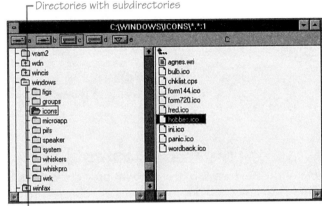

But I don't want to see everything

Three commands in the **V**iew menu control how the File Manager window looks:

 Tree and Directory. This is the normal view. It shows the directory window on the left and the files window on the right.

 Tree Only. If you want to see only the directory window, select this option. You don't see the files window.

 Directory Only. This shows only the files window. It doesn't show the directory window.

NERDY
DETAILS

> Okay, the directory window on the left is really called the *tree window*, and the files window is really called the *directory window*. I think it's easier to remember it the other way.

Change the type of information that shows

The operating system (that's DOS) stores some information about each file. This information includes the file's name; the date and time it was last changed; its size (how much space it takes on the disk); and some other letters that tell whether the file is a special system file, a hidden file, read only (can't be changed), or archive (whether it has been backed up).

The commands in the **V**iew menu let you control how much of that information File Manager displays.

TRICKS

If you want to change what information you see about your files, use these three commands in the **V**iew menu:

 Name. Shows just the file name.

 All File Details. Shows everything about the file.

 Partial Details. Lets you pick which items of information to display about your files.

Sorting all of those file names

The **V**iew menu also includes a few commands that let you sort the file names in the files window in different ways:

 Sort by Name. Sort by the name of the file.

 Sort by Type. Sort files by what kind they are; that is, what their extensions are (such as .BAK, .WRI, etc.).

 Sort by Size. Sort from biggest to smallest.

 Sort by Date. Sort by newest to oldest.

NERDY
DETAILS

The By File **T**ype command in the **V**iew menu really gives you a lot of control of how the files are displayed in the files window. Choosing that command opens the By File Type dialog box where you can pick different types of files to add to the view, use wild cards to specify files by their names, and make File Manager show you any hidden or system files.

Now That I Bought This New Box of Floppies...

Sooner or later you will have to buy some floppy disks for your computer. Floppy disks are real handy for when you want to send files to another person or to make extra copies of your files for backup reasons.

First, you have to prepare your floppies

Before you can use a new disk, it has to be *formatted*. That means Windows has to do some magic on the disk so that it can put your files on it. File Manager enables you to do this in a fairly easy and safe way. You usually have to format a disk only once.

In the **D**isk menu, choose **F**ormat Disk. That pops up the Format Disk dialog box.

The **D**isk In drop-down list lets you pick either drive A or drive B, depending on which drive you want to use to format the disk. Just click on it and pick the appropriate drive.

The **C**apacity drop-down list box lets you specify the capacity of the disk (that is, how much information it will hold). Table 10.2 shows the different disk sizes, possible capacities, and which type of disk you need for each capacity.

When you have all the options set and you're ready to format that disk, choose OK. File Manager will remind you that formatting a disk wipes out any information that might be on it. If that's okay, choose Yes. If you're not sure, choose No.

Table 10.2
Disk Sizes and Disk Capacities

Disk Size	Disk Capacity	*Disk Type To Use
5 1/4"	360K	DS/DD
5 1/4"	1.2M	DS/HD
3 1/2"	720K	DS/DD

Disk Size	Disk Capacity	*Disk Type To Use
3 1/2"	1.44M	DS/HD

*DS/DD stands for "Double-Sided/Double Density" and DS/HD stands for "Double-Sided/High Density." Look on the disk box for those letters.

You can format a high-density disk as a low-density disk, but you're wasting disk space and money. If you can format a disk as high density (1.2M or 1.44M), that's what you should do.

TRICKS

Make a system disk

A *system disk* is one that has some special files on it. It lets you boot the operating system from the floppy disk.

Do not delay! Do this right now! Don't wait until it's too late! HEY!!! Are you listening?

Okay, I got your attention. Now that you've opened up your first box of disks, you should make a system disk by putting a disk in drive A, selecting the **M**ake System Disk option in the Format Disk dialog box, and clicking on the OK button.

Copy all of the following files from your DOS directory to your new system disk: BACKUP.EXE, COMMAND.COM, FDISK.EXE, FORMAT.COM, MSD.EXE, RECOVER.EXE, RESTORE,EXE, UNDELETE.EXE, and XCOPY.EXE. Make sure you *copy* them instead of *move* them.

SAVE
THE DAY!

What is it good for? If something happens to your hard disk (like it goes belly-up and dies), you'll still be able to start your computer by using the system disk. The system disk is useful if you succeed in somehow deleting all of the files on your hard disk. And, it will be useful if you're fiddling around with your CONFIG.SYS and AUTOEXEC.BAT files and mess something up.

Oh yeah, make sure you put your system disk in a safe place where you can find it easily and quickly. When the time comes when you need it, you will not be in a mind-set to search all over the office to find it. You'll be in the mind-set to throw your computer out the window.

What the &%@#$! Is on This Floppy?

Unless you're psychic, you won't know what's on a disk unless you put some kind of label on it. You can put two kinds of labels on a disk—an electronic one and a sticky one.

Label command stuff

In the Format Disk dialog box is the **L**abel text box. If you put something in this box, File Manager stores that on the disk as an electronic label.

Where does that label show up? The most obvious place is in the Open dialog box, which displays when you want to open a file to work on. In figure 10.8, I labeled my hard disk C as "hi-there!"

Figure 10.8

The Open dialog box showing you what an electronic disk label looks like. You can add a label to a disk with File Manager.

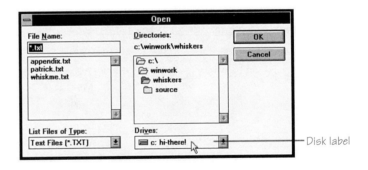

Disk label

TRICKS

If you choose the **L**abel command from File Manager's **D**isk menu, you can label a disk after it has been formatted. This process is the same as labeling a disk when you format it— it just lets you do it after the fact. Do you want to change a label on a disk? Use the **L**abel command in the **D**isk menu.

Those sticky disk labels

Okay, those electronic labels are fine when you're looking at the Open dialog box, but what about when you're looking at a three-foot-high stack of disks sitting on your desk?

Look in the box that your new disks came in and you should find some sticky-back paper labels. When you format a new disk and put some files on it, you should write a description of the files on one of those labels and then stick it on the disk. You'll be glad you did.

Panic Insurance: Doing Backups

Did your brain slip into neutral and you accidentally deleted some files that you just have to have back again? Did something bad happen to your hard disk and you can't find some files? Or do you just want to move some of your old files from the hard disk onto a floppy in case you need them some day twenty years from now? Make a backup.

NERDY
DETAILS

A backup is just an extra copy of a file that you put on a floppy to use in case the original file gets toasted somehow. A complete backup is a backup of all of the files on your hard disk. A partial backup is a backup of all of the files in one or more directories—or just a backup of one or more files.

Here's how to create a backup

It's really a lot easier to make a complete backup if your computer has a *tape drive* installed. If you're really paranoid about losing some of your files, consider spending the money to put a tape drive in your computer. You'll be able to back up the whole disk and recover files with the least amount of fuss.

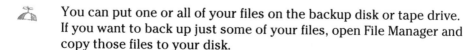

You can put one or all of your files on the backup disk or tape drive. If you want to back up just some of your files, open File Manager and copy those files to your disk.

You also can use floppies for making backups. There's nothing wrong with that. It just takes a bunch of floppies.

If you're going to make a backup of your whole disk, find out how much space the files on it are taking up (how many megabytes are used on the disk). Then, divide that number by 2. Divide that number by the capacity of the disk type you'll be using (1.2M or 1.44M). That's *roughly* the number of disks you'll need. Add a few extra disks as a fudge factor.

TRICKS

If you want to make a complete backup of all the files on your computer, open your DOS manual and read up on the BACKUP and RESTORE commands. Follow the directions in the manual to use the BACKUP command to back up your hard disk. Do the same if you just want to back up some directories. If you realize it's going to take 50 or 60 floppy disks to back up your hard disk, you should think about buying a tape drive.

What to do with a backup

Take the backups and put them in a safe place where you can find them. If you have some super-important files that absolutely have to be safe, consider making *two* backups. Put one in a fire-resistant safe and store the other copy somewhere else. If you're at the office, store a copy at home, or vice versa. Send a copy to Uncle Ned for safekeeping.

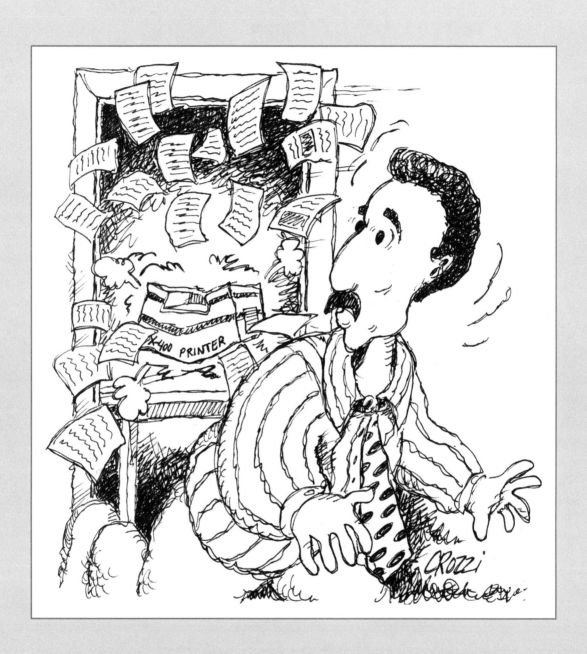

How Do I Get My $#@(%! Printer To Work?

P rinters used to be about the lowest-tech item in a computer system, but they always tended to cause the most problems. If we can put a man on the moon and make two-ply toilet paper, you'd think we could come up with a fool-proof printer. Ha! Fat chance. We're the species that used to buy pet rocks, remember?

This chapter will help you get that $#@(%! printer to work. This is what you'll learn about:

- Printing from a Windows program
- Printing from a DOS program
- Setting printing options to do really cool stuff with your printer
- Working with Print Manager, which lets you keep working while the printer prints
- Figuring out why the $#@(%! printer quit working and how to get it going again

Why Do I Need To Print Something?

Why use the printer? Maybe you need to send a letter or a memo to some-one. Maybe you want to print a grocery list (don't forget the toilet paper...). Maybe you want to print the doodle that your six-year-old made for Grandma with Paintbrush. Forget the paperless office! Let's use up some trees! They'll grow back...

NERDY
DETAILS

I'll assume that your printer is already hooked up and you think everything is set right. You just want some help figuring out how to send something to the printer. Great! Read the next section. If you're printer isn't set up or working yet, jump to the section that tells you how to hook it up, then come back here.

Print Something from a Windows Program

It's really easy to print a document from a Windows program. It doesn't really matter much what the program is—all Windows programs let you print in pretty much the same way. Regardless of the type of document you have created, you can probably print it.

Can't wait? Try this:

1.   Start the program and load the document you want to print.

2.   In the program's **F**ile menu, choose **P**rint.

3.   If the program pops up a dialog box asking you to set some printer options, just click on OK. Worry about that other stuff later.

Did it work? Great! If not, you may have to tell the program which printer to use.

Tell the program which printer to use

Sometimes your printer doesn't do anything because you haven't told the program which printer to use. Here's how to tell your program which printer to use:

1. From the program's **F**ile menu, choose P**r**int Setup. It may be worded a little differently, but it should be close. A Print Setup dialog box pops up (see fig. 11.1).

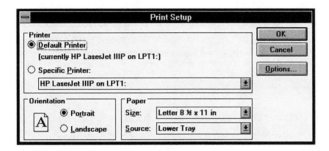

Figure 11.1

This is the Print Setup dialog box. Use it to pick the printer you want to use.

2. In the Printer group box there is a radio button labeled **D**efault Printer. If the printer it lists sounds like the one you have hooked up to your computer, it shows print unless you have some kind of problem.

3. If the printer listed by **D**efault Printer is different from what you want to use, click on the Specific **P**rinter drop-down list box. Find the printer you want to use and click on it. The printers you see in the list depend on how your Windows software has been set up.

That's all you have to do to tell the program which printer to use. Press Enter or click on OK and your printer is set up.

How the printer works

So, you don't like the way your printer prints your stuff? That means you need to change the *printer options*. The Print Setup dialog box usually shows you some basic options, including Orientation and Paper. These options change depending on the type of printer you select. Figure 11.1, for example, shows the options for an HP LaserJet IIIP printer. Yours might be different.

If you must know everything about everything, here's a little more about the printer options. Portrait is like you'd print text on a piece of paper for a letter. Landscape is like printing the text sideways on the paper.

NERDY
DETAILS

When you're using a dot-matrix printer, the Paper options probably are Tractor, Auto sheet feed, and Manual. Pick Tractor if you're using that paper that has perforated edges, like a roll of paper towels. Pick Manual to stick the paper in one page at a time. Pick Auto sheet feed if your printer is fed individual sheets of paper. If you're using a laser printer, you'll see "trays" mentioned in the list. These are the different cartridges that hold paper in the printer. Pick the one that you want to use.

If that's all you want to set, you can choose OK to go back to the program and choose the **P**rint command. You also can set some other options. Usually you won't have to, but if you want to see what you can change, choose the **O**ptions button. The Options dialog box pops up.

What you see in the Options dialog box depends completely on which printer you have selected. Figure 11.2 shows some common Options dialog boxes for different printer selections.

TRICKS

Because the options vary according to the printer, it's tough to cover all of the different possibilities in this book. If you need help with some of the options or want to know what they are, choose the **H**elp button. (Chapter 12 explains what Help is all about.)

Time to print!

When you have set up your options, it's time to print. If your default printer is the one you want and its normal options are the ones you normally use (they probably are), you don't have to mess with the Print **S**etup command at all. When you're ready to print, just open the program's **F**ile menu and choose **P**rint.

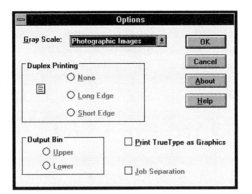

Figure 11.2

This Options dialog box is for an HP LaserJet IIIP printer. It's pretty typical of the options for a laser printer.

NERDY DETAILS

If the **P**rint command doesn't have an ellipsis after it (like **P**rint...), the program starts sending the document to the printer right away. If the program's print command *does* look like **P**rint..., that means the program is going to ask you for some more options before it starts printing. Figure 11.3 shows a Print dialog box that pops up for the HP LaserJet IIIP when I print to it from Write.

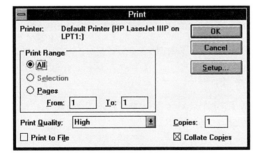

Figure 11.3

The Print dialog box is used to set some printer options just before you send the document to the printer.

The options you see in the Print dialog box change according to which printer you are using. Usually, the Print dialog box lets you set things such as which pages to print, print quality, number of copies to print, and so on.

If all is set up and working right, click on OK. The printer should start to make some irritating noises, and you should see some paper start to spit out of the printer in a few seconds. If nothing happens, check out the section later in the chapter on setting up a printer. Chill out. It's probably something really simple to fix.

Print Something from a DOS Program

All Windows programs work in pretty much the same way when it comes to printing. DOS programs don't. Most DOS programs are about as different from one another as a fist fight and a limited nuclear exchange.

NERDY DETAILS

(What the #$%@! is a *limited* nuclear exchange, anyway?) Why am I telling you this? I'm telling you that you're on your own when it comes to printing from a DOS program. I'm going to assume you've been using the DOS program for a while before you got Windows and you already know what buttons to push in the program to make it print.

Assuming you know how to print from the DOS program, here's how to print from the DOS program when you run it under Windows:

1. Start the program and load the document you want to print.

2. Make sure there aren't any Windows programs that are trying to print. DOS programs just take over the printer whether something else is trying to use it or not.

3. Tell the program which printer to use. You'll have to do the brainwork on this one.

4. Set any printing options that are necessary.

5. Push whatever button you have to press in the program to make the program print.

SAVE THE DAY!

The main thing to remember about printing from a DOS program in Windows is that the DOS program doesn't know any other programs exist. If you have a Windows program printing, the DOS program will take over the printer. The Windows print job won't get finished, and the DOS print job may end up screwy, too.

Isn't That Printer Done Yet?

I used to work in the engineering department at a shipyard, and one of the things I did was plot drawings that I'd done on the computer. (A *plotter* is a big thing like a printer, only it uses pens and actually draws the drawing like you have on your screen.) At first, the computer would be tied up when I plotted, and I couldn't do any work until it was done. I thought that was a real drag. Then we got some new software that let us keep working while the plotter plotted the drawing. What did I do? Why, I stood and watched the plotter plot, of course!

The point of that moderately droll story is that the plotter was working in the *background*.

NERDY DETAILS

What does background mean?

When a program or device works in the background, it means it can keep working without tying up your computer. Windows lets you start printing something then return to working with the computer. You can do something else with the computer while the printer prints your document. So, Windows lets you print in the background. It does that with a program called Print Manager (which comes free with Windows).

Okay, here's Print Manager

When you start printing from a Windows program, the program tells Windows that it wants to print. Windows starts up a program called Print Manager. The program spits out the document, and Windows sends it to

Print Manager. Print Manager then takes over the boring task of sending the document to the printer. You and your program are then free to go on with something else.

 Usually, you don't see Print Manager. It normally runs as an icon on the desktop. When it finishes sending everything to the printer, it usually goes away. Before it goes, however, you can use Print Manager to control how and when your documents are sent to the printer.

 If Print Manager is running as an icon on the desktop, double-click on it to open it to a window. If it is nowhere to be seen, look in your Main program group. That's where Print Manager lives when it has some free time. Figure 11.4 shows what Print Manager looks like.

Figure 11.4

This is Print Manager. It doesn't look like much when nothing is being printed, so this one shows some print jobs waiting to be printed. It is labeled for your viewing pleasure.

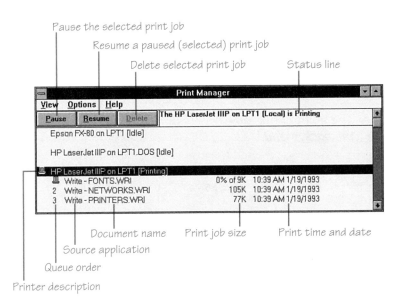

What is that stupid printer doing?

You can send lots of documents to the printer. You don't have to wait until one finishes printing before you send the next one. A document that is waiting to be printed is called a *print job*. Print Manager sets them up in a *queue* to be printed in turn. A queue (pronounced "q") is just a stack of print jobs waiting their turn at the printer. You can use Print Manager to view all of the jobs that are waiting to be printed. Figure 11.4 gives you an example.

Wait...I want to print this next!

You're looking at all of those jobs waiting to be printed and you decide that maybe one of the ones in the middle or at the bottom of the queue needs to be printed next. No problem! Print Manager lets you change the job's position in the queue.

 To move a print job either up or down in the queue, just click on it and drag it to the place in the queue you want it to be. Then release the mouse button. Print Manager rearranges the queue for you.

 That's great, but what if you haven't even sent the document from the program yet but you need it to print next? Just print the document from the program, which places it in the queue. Then, open Print Manager and move it from the bottom of the queue to the top of the queue.

Forget it...I don't want that printed

Did you suddenly decide that you don't want to print that 300-page letter of complaint to the boss after all? Just click on it in the queue, then choose the **D**elete button. Print Manager asks you if you really want to delete the print job from the queue. If that's what you want to do, choose **Y**es.

SAVE THE DAY!

What happens if all of the document has been sent to the printer and you want to cancel the print job, but the printer hasn't finished printing all of the pages yet? You can't delete the print job from Print Manager, because as far as Print Manager is concerned, its done its job. It's time to go over to the printer and do one of two things: press the Reset button if it has such a thing, or turn it off. Either one will stop the print job and clear it out of the printer's memory. Whew! You really didn't want to tell the boss all that stuff anyway, did you?

You can do other stuff with Print Manager

You can do many other things with Print Manager, especially if your computer is on a network. If that's the case, you probably can even pause and resume a single print job. The average user never messes much with Print

Manager, though, so that's all we're going to cover about it. If you're interested in fooling with Print Manager until your buttons fall off, check the Windows manual or pick up a copy of *Maximizing Windows 3.1*.

Let's Hook Up That Printer of Yours...

Have you been mumbling to yourself as you read the first part of this chapter? "I don't have it hooked up yet! When are you going to tell me how to do that? I can't do any of that other stuff until it's hooked up and humming, right?"

Right, so I'll tell you how to hook it up.

It would be a good start to take it out of the box. Make sure that there aren't any foam wedgies stuck down in the printer anywhere. Read through the printer manual to see if there are any packing materials or any special things you have to undo inside the printer after you unpack it.

TRICKS

If the people you bought the printer from are ecology-oriented, they either used popcorn for packing or those new water-soluble packing "peanuts." Feed the popcorn to the birds. Wash the others down the sink or toss them out in the rain. You're not sure if they're water-soluble? Spit on one. If it dissolves to a pile of goo, either it's water-soluble or you've been eating way too many jalapeños. If you got foam packing peanuts, box them up and send them back. Maybe they'll get the idea.

Cables, anyone?

Next, you need a cable to connect the printer to the computer. Your data (that is, the stuff you want to print) won't get to the printer by osmosis. Usually, the cable comes with the printer, but sometimes you have to buy it separately.

Now, how about that power cord? The printer has to be plugged into an outlet, because it needs electricity to make it go. It doesn't run off of the computer's juice.

NERDY
DETAILS

Most printers use the computer's *parallel port* to connect to
the computer. A few use a *serial port*. (These port-things are
in the back of your computer and you can read more about
them in Chapter 2.) Check your printer manual to see which one
it uses. Then find the right cable. If the cable didn't come with
the printer, you can probably pick one up at Sears, Wal-Mart,
K-mart, or any other place that sells computers or computer
gadgets. You won't have any trouble hooking up the cable
between the computer and printer—it only fits one way.

Time for a smoke test...

Turn on the printer. Does it smoke or make nasty noises? I hope not. I hate it
when that happens.

If you don't see any lights or hear any noises at all, the printer might be
dead. Check over everything again and make sure it's plugged in and getting
juice.

Set it up in Windows

When you hook up a new printer to your computer, you have to tell Windows about it. Windows has to install a *printer driver*, which is some software
that enables Windows to talk to the printer. You do this with the Windows
Control Panel. You also use the Control Panel to change options for a printer
that is already set up in Windows.

The Control Panel is located in your Main program group. Double-click on
the Control Panel icon, then double-click on the Printers icon. You'll see the
Printers dialog box shown in figure 11.5.

Install a driver? Huh?

In the Installed **P**rinters list, check to see whether your printer is listed. If it
isn't listed, you need to install a printer driver for it. It's really easy to do—
trust me. Do this:

1.   Choose the **A**dd>> button. This makes the dialog box bigger and
     gives you a list of printers you can install.

Figure 11.5

The Printers dialog
box, which you get to
from the Control
Panel, is what you
use to set up a new
printer in Windows.

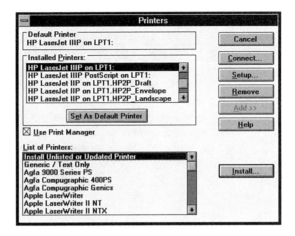

2. Hunt through the list until you find your printer, then select it.

3. Choose the **I**nstall button.

4. Windows probably will prompt you to insert one of your Windows disks. Insert the one it asks for, then choose OK. It may do this a couple of times.

That's all there is to it. You just installed a printer driver. Now you need to set it up to work properly.

Specify some options for the driver

First, you need to tell Windows how the printer is connected to the computer. Here are the steps:

1. In the Installed **P**rinters list box, select the printer driver that you just installed.

2. Choose the **C**onnect button. This opens the Connect dialog box.

3. Select the *port* to which your printer is connected. If it is your only printer, it probably is connected to LPT1. (If it is a *serial* printer, it is probably connected to either COM1 or COM2.)

4. Choose OK (you could monkey around with some other settings, but why spoil a good thing?).

5. I assume this is your only printer, so you probably want to set it up as the default printer. Make sure it is still selected in the Installed **P**rinters dialog box, then choose the S**e**t As Default Printer button.

6. Ready to start using the printer? Choose Close.

Fascinating! Why Did It Quit Working?

"Don't ask me, Spock! I'm a doctor, not a..." Sorry...Star Trek flashback.

Why didn't it print? Why did it start and then stop? It could be something really simple. It could be that you forgot to pay the electric bill. Are the lights still on? Good. Maybe it's the printer after all.

Table 11.1 lists some common printer problems and their solutions.

Table 11.1
Common printer screwups and their solutions

Symptom	What to do
No lights or sounds from the printer at all. The printer is on but it isn't doing anything.	Make sure it's plugged in and getting electricity. Check the cable between the computer and the printer. Is it secure? Is it connected to the correct port in the back of the computer? Did you remember that you have to issue the Print command in the program?
It still doesn't work.	Are there any error lights on the printer? See if there is a problem with the paper (like a jammed sheet or no more paper).
Come on! It *still* doesn't work!	Open up Print Manager and see if it is giving you any error messages about the printer. Open up Control Panel and make sure that you have the printer driver set up properly.

continues

Table 11.1
Continued

Symptom	What to do
It printed part of a page and then stopped.	The computer may be busy doing something else. Wait a minute or two to see if it starts up again. If you're printing something with lots of graphics or different fonts on a laser printer, it may be that the computer is still sending a new batch of information to the printer. It takes a while.
It still hasn't started up.	Check for error lights on the printer again. Then, check for loose cables.

CHAPTER 12

Argh! I Need Help!

Y ou're working along in your program, as happy as an alligator farmer in steel-toed waders, when you suddenly realize you don't know everything there is to know about the program. A dialog box that makes absolutely no sense peels itself off of the screen and slaps you in the face. Or, maybe all that coffee you've been drinking has torqued your brain two turns too tight, and you've just forgotten how to do something.

You need help. This chapter explains how you can get help with your program right in Windows without having to hunt down the program's manual.

What's in this chapter...

- What is Windows Help?
- How do I figure out how to do something in a program?
- How do I find out what this word over here means?
- This is important. How do I print it and stick it on the wall?
- Can I get help on a program I'm not using right now?

Forget the Manual!

Do you even know where the manuals are for your programs? Okay, maybe you know where they are, but you just can't bring yourself to open one up and hunt for the page that tells you how to do whatever it is you've forgotten how to do. Come on...that would be too much like reading the directions.

It's okay. You don't have to hunt down the manual. Take a look at the program's menu. Do you see an item called **H**elp? Ah, that's it! Just select that menu.

This is Help...

You almost always can get help right in Windows with the program that you are using. You don't have to thumb through a manual to find out how to do something or learn what a word means. Instead, you can view a sort of electronic manual for the program right on the screen. This electronic manual is stored in a *Help file* on disk. What's different about that than just thumbing through the paper manual? Usually, it's a lot easier to find what you're looking for. Most of all, you don't have to get up and hunt for the manual. The information you need is right on your computer.

You get to a program's electronic manual by choosing its **H**elp menu. Usually, the **H**elp menu in a program includes at least three items that are labeled something like this:

 Contents. This gives you a Table of Contents of all of the topics that are in the Help file.

 Search For Help On. This lets you search for help on a particular topic by providing a word that describes what you're trying to find.

 About. This item just gives you some general information about the program, like what the serial number is, who wrote the program, and so on.

TRICKS

> Do you want an easier way to open up a program's Help file? Okay, just press the F1 function key. That opens the program's Help file for you.

Pick what you want to learn about

If you want to see a list of all of the topics that a program's Help file covers, choose the **C**ontents command. This command opens a program called Help, which displays a Table of Contents for the current program's Help file. Figure 12.1 shows the Help program with the Contents page for Program Manager's Help file.

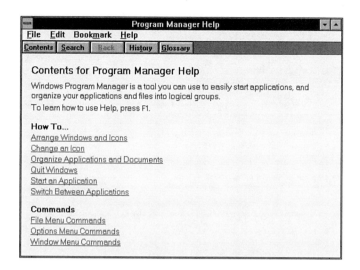

Figure 12.1

This is the Help program showing the Contents page of Program Manager's Help file. If you want to view it on your computer, choose the Contents command from Program Manager's Help menu.

The Contents pages for most programs have topics arranged by category or function. The topics are listed as underlined green text. Don't ask me why they chose green...I think it's hard to read.

TRICKS

You can change the color that Windows uses for the underlined topics by adding a setting to your WIN.INI file (WIN.INI is in your Windows directory). Open Notepad and load WIN.INI into it. Hunt for a section with the label [Windows Help]. Add a setting in that section that reads **JumpColor=0 0 0**, then save the file again.

The three numbers represent red, green, and blue. A setting of three zeros makes the underlined text black. You can get different colors by mixing the three colors together. If you want blue-green, for example, use **JumpColor=0 128 128**, which mixes equal parts of blue and green without any red. You can use numbers from 0 to 255. Play around with it until you get the color you want.

You can click on each topic to see a *topic page* that gives you information about that topic. If you click on the topic Arrange Windows and Icons in the Program Manager Help Contents page, for example, you see the topic page shown in figure 12.2. It explains the way you can arrange windows and icons.

Figure 12.2

This is a typical topic page from a Help file. Notice that in the first paragraph, the words "title bar" are underlined with a dashed line.

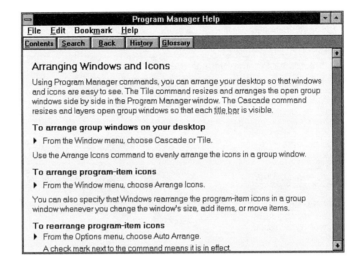

NERDY
DETAILS

The topic page gives you information about the selected topic. It also might list some other, related topics that you can view. Words appearing with a solid underline are topics. Just click on them to view a page of information about the topic.

What's that green word?

Did you notice the words "title bar" in the first paragraph in figure 12.2? That's called a *popup*, and it has a dotted line under it. If you click on a dotted underlined word, a little box pops up that contains a definition of the word. Figure 12.3 shows an example.

When you finish reading the definition, click anywhere to close it. If you are one of the poor, unfortunate souls who uses the keyboard instead of a mouse, you still can view popup definitions. Just press the Tab key until the word you want to see defined is highlighted. Then press Enter. After you read the definition, press Esc.

Wait...What did I read a minute ago?

You can wander through a program's Help file by picking topic after topic in whatever order you want. But what if you decide you want to go back to something you read a couple of pages ago? Do you have to start all over from the beginning? Nope! Just press the **B**ack button.

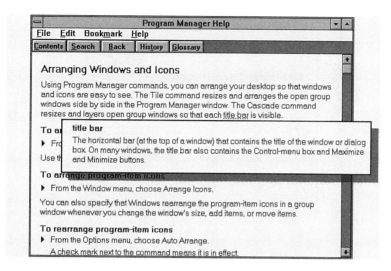

Figure 12.3

If you click on a word with a dotted underline, you see a definition of the word.

 As you view different topics, Help keeps track of which topics you have viewed and in what order.

 Each time you press the **B**ack button, Help flips back one topic page in the reverse order in which you've been viewing.

 If you choose a topic only to find out that it isn't the topic you wanted, just click on the **B**ack button to take you back to the topic page from which you came.

Okay, I still can't find what I want

Maybe you've been stumbling around in the Help file for a few minutes and still can't find what you need to know. This is as bad as thumbing through the manual! If only it had an index. Well, it does, sort of. It's called the **S**earch command.

When you want to find a particular topic but you're not sure what it's called, choose the **S**earch button. Help opens a Search dialog box (see fig. 12.4) with *keywords* listed in alphabetical order. You can scroll through the list or type a word. When you type a word, Help looks through the list of keywords to find one that matches. Then you can click on the **S**how Topics button to list all of the topics related to that keyword. In the topic window at the bottom of the dialog box, click on the topic you want to read and then choose **G**o To.

Figure 12.4

The Search dialog box lets you hunt for topics based on a list of keywords. You can type your own word to search for topics that relate to it.

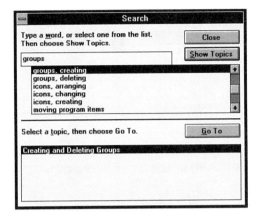

I want to fold this page so that I can find it again

When you're thumbing through a manual and find a page that looks like it might be interesting for future reading, you can fold the corner down ("dog-ear" it) or slip a bookmark in the book at that page. You can do a similar thing with a program's Help file.

If you want to mark a topic page, choose the Book**m**ark menu, then choose **D**efine. Help opens up the Bookmark Define dialog box (see fig. 12.5), which you can use to mark the page. Help puts the name of the topic in the **B**ookmark Name box, but you can type a name that makes sense to you. Instead of using something like "Saving a file," you can use something like "Keeping stuff on the computer."

Figure 12.5

This is the Bookmark Define dialog box. Use it to mark a topic page in a Help file to make it easy to find again.

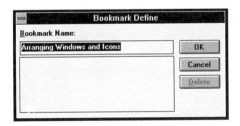

If you want to delete a bookmark, choose the **D**efine command in the Book**m**ark menu. In the Bookmark Define dialog box, click on the bookmark you want to delete, then click on the **D**elete button.

SAVE
THE DAY!

Now, how do you use the bookmark when you want to go back to that topic? Just open the Book**m**ark menu. In addition to the **D**efine command, the menu lists any previously defined bookmarks for the Help file you are currently viewing. Just click on the bookmark entry you want in the menu.

I want to paperclip a note on this page

Let's say you read a topic page and it actually makes some sense. Maybe you want to put a note on the page to remind you of some little extra step you need to do. Or, maybe you want to put a note on the page that says, "Don't ever use this command again!" Either way, just open Help's **E**dit menu and choose **A**nnotate. That pops up the Annotate dialog box shown in figure 12.6.

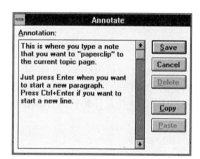

Figure 12.6

This is the Annotate dialog box. You can type a note about a topic and then "paperclip" the note onto the topic page.

Type whatever you want in the note, then choose the **S**ave button. Help saves your note and puts a little paperclip icon next to the topic title on the topic page. You can click on the paperclip to read the note, or you can open the **E**dit menu and choose **A**nnotate.

 The **D**elete button in the Annotate dialog box lets you delete the note (and its paperclip).

 The **C**opy and **P**aste buttons let you move the note in and out of the Clipboard. The Clipboard is covered in Chapter 15.

TRICKS

While you're working with a program's Help file, you might want to stop for a minute and look at a list of everything you've read. That's what the His**t**ory button is for. When you click on it, Help opens a window that lists all of the topics you have viewed. Just double-click on a topic in the list to view the topic. Help even keeps track of topics you viewed in other programs, so you can use the His**t**ory button to quickly look up something you read about a different program earlier in the day.

I need to know what a word means

If you click on the **G**lossary button, Help opens up a window that contains a long list of words. Just click on a word to view a definition of the word. If you don't have a mouse, use Tab to select a word and press Enter to view its definition.

I give up...I want to start over

After you've spent 20 minutes hunting for something in a Help file, you might decide you'd like to go back to the Contents page again and start the hunt all over again. This one's easy; just choose the **C**ontents button. Help switches back to the Contents page.

Okay, I want to paste this one on the wall

You've found a topic page that tells you exactly what you want to know. Now, you would really like to print it out and stick it on the wall where you won't lose it. No problem. You can do that.

With the topic page showing, just choose **F**ile, and then choose **P**rint Topic. Help sends the current topic page to the printer.

I Don't Want To Hunt All Over!

You'd think that a program would be smart enough to know that when you're trying to use the **F**ramistat command and you hit F1 or open up the Help menu, you probably want help with framistats. Come on; we're not asking the program to compute the size of the known Universe or anything...just to take a look at what you're doing and help you out. That's called *context sensitive help.*

NERDY
DETAILS

Context sensitive help means that when you tell your program you want help, it looks at what you're doing and automatically figures out what it is you need help with. To tell a program you want context sensitive help, press Shift-F1 instead of just F1 (which just starts Help). What happens next depends on the program and what you're doing with the program at the time.

What if no command is active when you press Shift-F1?

If there isn't a particular command or dialog box active when you press Shift-F1, the program usually can't tell what you're trying to do in the program. So, it changes the screen pointer to an arrow with a question mark beside it (see fig. 12.7).

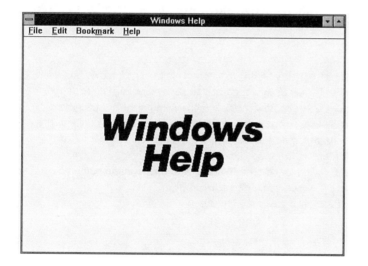

Figure 12.7

Here, I've pressed Shift-F1 in Excel. Now, Excel wants me to click on whatever it is I want help with.

 When the screen pointer changes to a question mark, the program is telling you to "Point to what you want help with."

 When you need this kind of help, use the pointer to click on a command button, select an item from a menu, or click on a gadget on the screen. The program tells the Help program to open the appropriate Help file and take you right to the topic page for the thing you selected.

I need help with a dialog box or a specific command

If you're in the middle of a command, or a dialog box is active on the screen, the program probably won't change the pointer and make you click on something to get help. Instead, the program says to itself, "Okay, the Implode the Universe dialog box is open, so I guess you want help imploding the Universe." The program starts the Help program and tells it to go to the Implode the Universe topic page.

Go implode to your heart's content.

But wait a minute!

You say you just pressed Shift-F1 and nothing happened? You don't see any cute question-mark pointer or anything? You still don't know anything about imploding the Universe? Sorry, but the active program doesn't include context sensitive help. You'll have to slog through the Help file the "old" way.

STOP!

Context sensitive help isn't something that Windows handles. Instead, each program has to be developed to include support for context sensitive help. The programmer or programmers who developed the program didn't go the extra few milli-bleeps necessary to add smart help to the program. You can't do much about it, except next time you call their technical support line, ask them, "When are you boneheads going to add context sensitive help to this program?" No, really; they'll be happy to help you out after that.

Not.

PART 4

Running Windows and DOS Programs in Windows

CHAPTER 13

Using Windows Programs

D o you have some Windows programs you want to start using, but you're a little unsure how to use them? You don't want to screw something up? Don't worry: the polar ice caps won't melt if you push the wrong button—as long as you read this chapter.

This chapter helps you work with those Windows programs you salivate over. Here's what you learn:

- How to install a Windows program
- Common Windows program menus and what to use them for
- How to open and save a file in a Windows program
- How to do some really cool stuff with the program
- How to balance a seal on the tip of your nose and not end up smelling like fish or falling in love with the seal

I Want This Program on My Computer

If you already have your new Windows program on your computer, you're home free. Otherwise, the first thing you must do is *install* the program. Install is just a fancy way of saying *put it on the computer so you can use it.* Fortunately, almost all Windows programs work in virtually the same way when it comes to installing them.

Rather than go through the entire process for installing a typical Windows program, the following tips should help you get your program installed with no problems. If you have a problem, break down and read the section about installation in the manual that came with the program.

 Look for a SETUP.EXE or INSTALL.EXE program. Almost all Windows programs use an *installation program* that automatically installs the program for you. Look on the first program disk for a file named INSTALL.EXE or SETUP.EXE. Run that program by selecting the **F**ile build, unleash, menu and **R**un command in Program Manager and follow the instructions it displays on the screen. Trust me—it's easy.

 Put the program in its own directory. One of the things the installation program asks is in which directory you want to put the new program. Put it in its own directory. If the directory you give the installation program doesn't exist, the installation program creates it for you.

 Set some installation options. Some of the more complex programs prompt you with questions during the installation process. These questions usually include specifying which optional parts of the program to install.

NERDY
DETAILS

With some programs, you must set some operating parameters before you can begin using the program. A fax program, for example, has to know how your fax-modem is hooked up to your computer. If the installation program doesn't prompt you to specify any operating parameters, chances are good that you can just start using the program.

With any luck (and a well-written installation program), your new program will be set up and ready to roll in less than ten minutes. After you install it, you will see that it looks much like most of your other Windows programs.

All Menus Are Created Equal

Virtually all Windows programs are built the same way. There are some differences in the way you do things with a program simply because it's used for a different function than your other programs. But the menus are relatively similar.

File

When you want to do something in the program with a file, you go to a Windows program's **F**ile menu (see fig. 13.1), which usually has the following commands:

  New. This menu item lets you start working on a new document, such as when a document is already in the program and you want to clear it from the program and start a new one.

  Save. This command lets you save the current document on your hard disk or floppy disk. If you never have saved the document (you just created it), choosing **S**ave brings up the Save As dialog box. If you choose **S**ave with a document that already has been saved on disk, the copy on disk is updated with whatever changes you have made to the document.

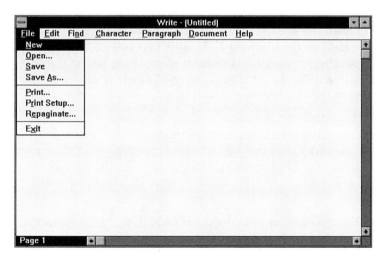

Figure 13.1

Use the **F**ile menu to get stuff (like documents) in and out of your program.

Save As. This command lets you specify a new name by which to save the document. Use this command when you want to keep the original file as it is and save the changed document to a different file or different directory.

Open. You use this command when you want to open a document you have saved sometime earlier on disk.

Print Setup. This command lets you specify which printer you want to use to print the document. It doesn't print the document, though.

Print. You use Print when you want to print your document.

Edit

The Edit menu has commands that let you move data around within a document, move some data from one document to a different one, or move something from a different document to the one you have open (see fig. 13.2).

Undo. This is the "Oops, I screwed up" command. If you do something you didn't want to do and you want to back up a step, look for Undo in the Edit menu.

Cut. After you select part of the document, this command removes, or *cuts*, that part of the document and puts the removed data into the Windows storage container, called the Clipboard (see Chapter 15 for more stuff on the Clipboard). Use it when you want to cut something from the document and move it somewhere else in the document (or to a different document) or use Cut when you just want to cut the part out and throw it away.

Copy. This command is similar to the Cut command, except that you don't remove the selected data from the document. Instead, the Copy command leaves the data where it is and places an identical twin of it into the Clipboard. You then can insert the data into the same document in a different place or insert it into a different document.

Paste. Paste inserts into the document any data that is in the Clipboard. Use this command when you want to insert something into the document from a different document or from a different place in the same document.

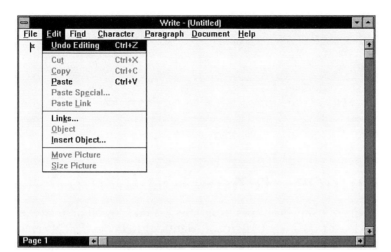

Figure 13.2

Use the Edit menu to cut and paste data from and to documents.

TRICKS

Chapter 15 provides more information about the Edit menu and the Clipboard.

Help

Help was discussed in Chapter 12, so you should already know what Help does. This list shows typical **H**elp menu items:

 Contents. Displays the Table of Contents for the program's Help file.

 Search for Help on. Displays the Search dialog box so that you can hunt for a topic by providing a keyword.

 How to Use Help. Opens the Help file for using Help.

 About *whatever.* Displays a dialog box that shows some general information about the selected program, including the serial number, the company that developed the program, and sometimes information about your system (such as the amount of available memory).

Help is your friend. Use it often.

NERDY
DETAILS

Geek

Underline{F}ile and Underline{E}dit are always the first two menus on the left side of a Windows program's menu bar. Underline{H}elp is always the last menu on the right side of the menu bar. The menus between Underline{F}ile and Underline{E}dit are anyone's guess. If the program has a Underline{V}iew menu, it usually appears immediately after the Underline{E}dit menu. Other menus that appear are specific to the program.

Some Common Things You Can Do

One of the benefits of using Windows programs is that they all behave the same way (or at least that's what Microsoft wants us to believe). This means that once you learn an action, such as saving a file, in one Windows program, you usually can use that same action in another Windows program.

TRICKS

Think of using Windows programs as you do driving a vehicle. Even though there are numerous types of cars and trucks on the road, if you know the basics of driving, you can apply that knowledge to virtually all motorized vehicles.

Open a file

When you want to work with a document that is already stored on your computer, whether you created it or someone else did, use the Underline{O}pen command in your program's Underline{F}ile menu. Here are the steps to open a file:

1. Choose Underline{F}ile and then choose Underline{O}pen. The Open dialog box appears.

2. In the Open dialog box, use the Dri Underline{v}es, Underline{D}irectories, and List Files of Underline{T}ype controls to locate the file you want to open. Double-click on the file name in the files list to open the file. Or, type the name of the file you want in the File Underline{N}ame text box , and then press Enter or choose OK. You can include a path to the file if it is not in the current directory.

NERDY
DETAILS

If your computer is on a network, you probably will see a button labeled Network. Click this button to locate a file stored somewhere else on the network.

Create a new document

Usually, you can begin creating a new document as soon as a program starts. You then can save what you have done or discard it. When you want to discard the current document (from memory only—not from disk), choose the **N**ew command.

When you choose **N**ew, nothing very interesting usually happens except that the document area of the window goes blank and gives you a "blank sheet" to start with.

With some programs, choosing the **N**ew command starts a new document but does not affect the current document. You can load one document and then use the **N**ew command to start a new one without removing the first document from memory. You can switch back and forth between the two (look in the **W**indow menu to find commands to switch between the documents on the screen).

Save what you have done

Two commands, **S**ave and Save **A**s, let you store your document on disk so that you can work with it later or send it to someone else. If you are working on a document you have not saved yet, choosing either the **S**ave or Save **A**s command has the same effect. It opens the Save As dialog box shown in figure 13.3.

Use the **S**ave command when you already have saved the document on your hard disk or floppy disk and want to save it again to record changes you have made. Use this command when you want to save the changes you have made to a document.

Figure 13.3

Use the Save As
dialog box to save your
document with a new
file name.

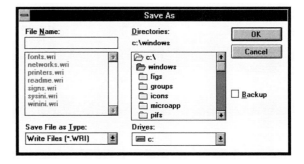

TRICKS

If you load a document and make some changes, and then you
want to save the modified document in a new file and keep the
original as it was, use Save **A**s. This command lets you specify
a new file name in which to store the file.

Make a hard copy of what is on-screen

Usually, the quickest way to make a paper copy of your document is to open
the program's **F**ile menu and choose **P**rint. Depending on the program, the
program either starts sending the document immediately to the printer or it
asks you for other information, such as how many copies you want to print.

P.S. Picking the **P**rint command from the **F**ile menu is the easy part. Getting
the printer set up and feeding paper to it is the hard part. If you want more
detail about printing than what is included here, see Chapter 11.

Do stuff to the program's windows

If a program lets you work with more than one document at a time, it almost
always has a **W**indow menu located near the **H**elp menu.

The **W**indow menu has commands that let you tile and cascade the windows,
arrange the icons of document windows that have been reduced to icons,
and select a window in which to work. You also can use the typical "drag the
borders around" method to change the size of the program's main and
document windows.

**SAVE
THE DAY!**

The main thing to keep in mind when you're learning to use a new program is not to worry about what the command is called: just remember what you can *do* with the program. Don't try to memorize all the commands your program offers. That would be intensely boring. If necessary, click them all open in turn until you find what you're looking for. If all else fails, make use of the <u>H</u>elp file.

Change the way the program works

In addition to *using* a program, you generally can *customize* it. That means that you can make it look different or function differently, like this stuff:

- Change the colors that show up on-screen.

- Change the way the letters and characters look on-screen (this is called the *font*).

- Turn on and off parts of the program's controls and menus.

- Add your own buttons to a button toolbar or change some of the buttons that are there.

- Set all sorts of options that control the way the program works.

- Convert the Universe to the metric system.

CHAPTER
14

Using DOS and DOS Programs

D OS is like a little green gremlin. It's bald, has pointed ears, little feet...
wait a minute. Maybe that's a bad analogy. Let's try that again. DOS is
like a meat cleaver. No, that's not it either. An aardvark with bad breath? No.
A three-toed sloth with a bad haircut? No, I guess that's not it either.

Oh, let's face it. DOS is *boring*. It's also necessary when you run windows.
DOS is like the old toilet plunger—you hate to have it laying around, but
you're glad it's there when you really need it. (I knew I'd find a fitting
analogy....)

This chapter is for those of you who are DOS junkies forced to live in a
Windows world. It's also for those of you who have invested too much
money in DOS programs to toss them out for Windows programs. This is
what the chapter covers:

- How to get to a DOS prompt in Windows

- Some common things that DOS is good for in Windows

- DOS things you should NEVER do in Windows

- How to run a DOS program in Windows

- How to create PIFs (Program Information Files)

I Can Use DOS Commands in Windows?

There are a lot of DOS commands you might find useful in Windows, if for no other reason than you are more comfortable using them than you are their Windows alternatives. To issue DOS commands in Windows, you have to get to a DOS prompt.

The MS-DOS Prompt

In the Main program group is a program item labeled MS-DOS Prompt. Double-click on that icon, and you'll see the familiar DOS prompt at which you can enter commands and run DOS programs. Figure 14.1 shows a DOS program running in Windows.

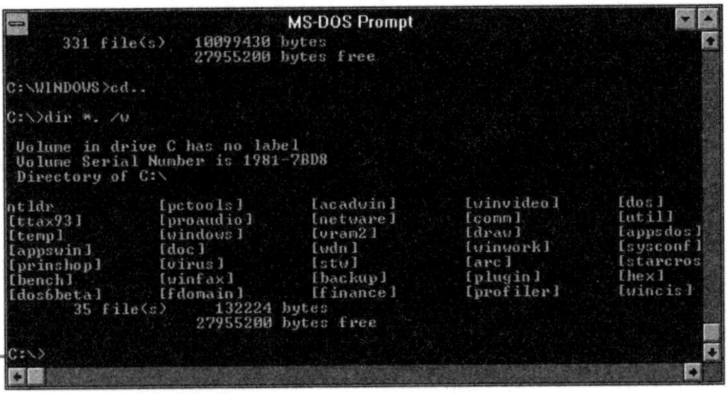

Figure 14.1

Yikes!!! The DOS prompt in Windows.

DOS prompt

When you get into a DOS prompt from Windows, you just type the DOS commands or execute programs as you do from the DOS environment outside of Windows. If you're running Windows 3.1, you can even run DOS graphics applications in a window, although they sometimes run very slowly.

Some common things to do (with DOS)

Here are some common tasks you might find useful to perform with DOS under Windows:

Copy and delete a few files. If you're just handling a few files, the DOS COPY and DELETE commands often are quicker than opening File Manager in Windows to perform the file operation. If you're dealing with lots of files or entire directories, File Manager is much better.

 Run DOS programs you can't do without. I use Microsoft Word for DOS simply because I've used it since version 1. I use Word for Windows also, but I do my day-to-day work with Word for DOS. I'm a Windows junkie, so I run it as a task under Windows. Don't drop out of Windows when you want to run your DOS programs—set them up to run under Windows.

 Format a disk. I generally use the DOS FORMAT command to format disks because I find it quicker than opening File Manager and using its Format dialog box. If you're not comfortable with the parameters of the FORMAT command, stick with File Manager.

Dangerous DOS! Don't do this!

Here are some DOS commands you should never use under Windows, or should use only under certain conditions:

 FDISK lets you change hard disk partitions and create logical drives in a partition. What this means is that you should never run it under Windows, and you should be *really* careful even when you run it from DOS. Don't run it if you don't know what it does.

 CHKDSK /F gives you information about your hard disk and lets you fix certain problems that can occur with the disk over time. You can run the CHKDSK command under windows as long as you don't use the /F parameter, but it's really not all that useful without the /F parameter, so why bother?

 RECOVER tries to recover data from a bad disk. Don't ever use it in Windows, and you might want to think twice before using it in DOS.

 FORMAT C ruins your whole day in Windows or in DOS. It wipes out all of the information on your hard disk.

Making DOS Programs Work in Windows

Windows is pretty tolerant of DOS programs. Most of the time you can just start a DOS program and it runs fine in Windows. To make sure that you're using your computer's resources, such as memory, to their best advantage, you need to tell Windows as much as you can about how the DOS program works and what it needs from Windows.

A PIF is what you need

You use a Program Information File, or PIF, (sounds like "jif")to give Windows all kinds of information about a DOS program. The PIF tells Windows how much memory the program needs, whether it should run in a window or full-screen, what its program file name is, and lots of other useful tidbits that Windows can use to make the DOS program run effectively.

SAVE
THE DAY!

> Some DOS programs (the nicer varieties) come with their own PIFs. The program developer was thoughtful enough to realize that you might want to run the program under Windows and took the time to set up a PIF for you. What nice people they are!

Let Setup do the dirty work for you

If your DOS program did not come with a PIF, you can use Windows Setup program to create one for you. Just find Setup in the Main program group and double-click on it. When it opens on the desktop, choose the **O**ptions menu, and then choose **S**et Up Applications. The Set Up Applications dialog box is displayed. Choose the radio button that reads Ask you to specify an application. Doing that opens the Set Up Applications dialog box.

Type the program's path and file name in the Application Path and Filename box. Then use the **A**dd to Program Group drop-down list to pick the group in which you want the new DOS program item to be placed. After everything is set, choose OK.

Windows probably knows about the DOS program you're trying to install because it keeps a list of DOS programs and what their settings should be when they run under Windows. If Setup isn't sure which program you're trying to install, it will pop up a dialog box like the one in figure 14.2.

Setup then creates a PIF for your program based on what it knows about the program. It also automatically adds the program item to the selected program group. You don't have to think at all. Just don't let your mouth hang open as you watch Setup do its thing.

Figure 14.2

Just pick your program from the list and choose OK.

The PIF Editor creates PIFs

Setup didn't recognize your program? Bummer! But all is not lost. You can create the PIF yourself and set up the program item. Just open up the PIF Editor. It's in your Main program group. Figure 14.3 shows what it looks like.

Setting stuff in the PIF

You can set up many settings in a PIF. Some of them are absolutely necessary and others you can usually ignore. The first four items in the PIF are the items you should set first. Here they are:

 Program Filename is the name of the program's executable file. This is usually a COM, BAT, or EXE file. Include the full path to the file, like **C:\APPSDOS\WORD\WORD.EXE**.

 Window Title is the name that you type that gets used in the program's title bar if you run it in a window.

Optional Parameters are any special *command line switches* you like to use with your program. In Word for DOS, for example, I use the /L parameter, which automatically makes Word load the last file I worked on when it starts up. Use a **?** on this line if you want Windows to prompt you for the command line parameters each time it starts the program.

 Start-up Directory is the directory you specify that becomes active when the program starts. You might want to specify the directory in which you keep the document files for the program.

TRICKS

There are a lot of ifs, ands, buts, and depends associated with these four settings. I'm not going to tell you about them because it would take forever. The main thing to remember is this: when you create a program item for a PIF or DOS program, some of the properties override the Window Title and Start-up Directory entries. Just make the settings in the PIF and the corresponding properties match, and you won't have any confusing behavior from the program.

Figure 14.3

This is the PIF Editor you see when Windows is in 386 Enhanced mode. If you click on the Advanced button, you see another dialog box with some advanced PIF options.

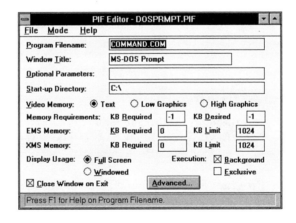

Set a few memory requirements

Next, set the memory requirements for the program. In the KB **R**equired box, specify the amount of RAM the program absolutely needs to run. Check the program's manual for that. If you can't find anything in the manual or on the program's box, try 256. In the KB **D**esired box, enter 640.

If the DOS program uses extended or expanded memory, check to see what the minimum is that it needs. In the appropriate KB Required setting, enter that amount. If you want the program to have as much as it wants, use -1. To prevent it from using extended or expanded memory, enter 0. For KB Limit for EMS and XMS memory, specify the maximum amount you want the program to have.

Do you want it in a window or full-screen?

If you want the DOS program to start up in a window when you're working in 386 Enhanced mode, choose the **W**indowed radio button. If you want the program to start up in full-screen mode, choose the F**u**ll Screen radio button. You can switch the program back and forth between the two modes by pressing Alt-Enter when the program is active.

SAVE
THE DAY!

Sometimes you'll experience problems with a DOS program and it will bomb out. Most of the time, it spits out some error messages that explain what happened. Usually, you can't read these because as soon as the program dies, it disappears from Windows. If you want the program to stay around even after it dies or you exit it, clear the **C**lose Window on Exit check box.

Background and exclusive, anyone?

If you want the program to run in the background (which lets it keep working as you use other programs), check the **B**ackground check box. This box is what lets you run lots of DOS programs at the same time (you can print from one and keep working in another, for example).

If you want a DOS program to have all of the CPU's attention when it runs, check the **E**xclusive check box. When the program is active, other programs can't run in the background.

Other stuff you can set

There are a lot of other settings you can set in a PIF, particularly when you choose the Advanced dialog box. For most DOS programs, you don't need to fiddle with these settings. If you want to know what they are, click on one and then press F1. The PIF Editor supports context sensitive help and will take you right to an explanation of what the selected control is for.

Here's How To Use That PIF...

Now that you have all of those settings just right, what do you do with the PIF? First, you save it. Just select the **F**ile menu and then choose Save **A**s (you also can use the **F**ile menu to open an existing PIF to tweak it, then choose **S**ave to resave it). There are a lot of ways to make the PIF work depending on what you name it. Here's the method you should use:

1. Name the PIF whatever you want, but use a name that roughly matches the DOS program name. That way it will be easier to find the PIF when you want to edit it.

2. Create a program item for the PIF. Close the PIF Editor and begin Program Manager. In the **C**ommand Line property, enter the name of the PIF and include the PIF extension, like **C:\WORD\JIM.PIF**.

As long as you directly specify the name of the PIF as the **C**ommand Line in the DOS program's item properties, it really doesn't matter what you name the PIF.

TRICKS

> How about the icon? I knew you'd ask that question. If you don't specify a particular icon, Program Manager uses a really boring icon that shows a little monitor with the words "MS DOS" on it. Snore... You can choose the Change **I**con button and use an icon from PROGMAN.EXE, MORICONS.DLL, an ICO file, or any other EXE or DLL file that contains icons. Just specify the icon as you do for a Windows program.

Resize DOS Programs

Most DOS programs let you customize the way they work or look. You also have a limited amount of control over how DOS programs look in Windows as long as they are running in a window.

If you want to make the DOS program window look bigger or smaller, you can change the font that Windows uses to display the program. Just open the DOS program's Control menu and choose the **F**onts command. Doing that opens the Font Selection dialog box shown in figure 14.4.

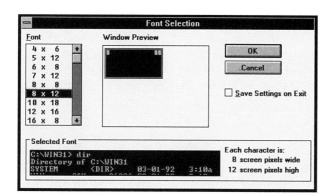

Figure 14.4

This is the Font Selection dialog box. It lets you change the font that Windows uses to display a DOS program in a window.

In the **F**ont list, choose the font size you want to use for the DOS program's window. When you pick a font, a couple of sample windows in the dialog box show you the results. If you want the change to be saved for the next time you use the program, check the **S**ave Settings on Exit check box. When everything is set, choose OK to change the program's font.

DOS Programs Can Really Screw Things Up

DOS programs are real snobs and computer hogs when it comes to working with other programs. Generally, they expect to have absolute control over the whole system. That can cause some problems now and then.

DOS stomps on the printer

DOS programs don't use the Print Manager to print. If Print Manager is sending some Windows print jobs to the printer and you start printing from a DOS program, the DOS program just takes over the printer. The currently printing Windows job gets garbled and you'll probably have to print it over again. The DOS print job might not print right either because Print Manager may have set up some options on the printer that don't apply to your DOS print job.

Your monitor just went black...

...when you tried to start a DOS program, and it stayed that way. The DOS program is hung up. If it is trying to start up full-screen, press Alt-Enter to see if you can get back to Windows so that you can kill the program. If you can't switch back to Windows, press Ctrl-Alt-Del. A window should pop up with instructions on how you can kill the DOS program and get back to windows.

The DOS window is just sitting there...

If you try to start a DOS program in a window and it hangs (you don't see anything but black in the window, for example), press Alt-Enter to switch the program to full-screen mode. Sometimes, certain Windows programs won't let a DOS program have any time to initialize. If switching to full-screen mode doesn't do the trick, switch back to Windows and kill the program.

Kill that DOS program and regain control

With the DOS program running in a window, open its Control menu. Pick the Settings command, and then choose the Terminate button. Follow the instructions in the dialog box about rebooting your system.

CHAPTER 15

I Want To Use This Stuff in This Other Program...

Y ou just finished this great drawing that you want to use in a letter to Uncle Ned, who's lounging on the beach in Jamaica. If you could just pull a page out of this document and put it over *here*. And how about that really cool picture of Jupiter...you'd like to stick that in the letter to Uncle Ned, too (he's a spacey kind of guy).

No problem! You can move stuff all over the place with Windows. Here's what's in this chapter:

- How and why to copy something between two Windows programs
- Copying stuff from Windows to DOS
- Copying stuff from DOS to Windows
- Changing stuff you copied to another program
- Making things change in a lot of places automatically
- Using OLE, DDE, and other useful acronyms

Moving Stuff Between Programs

Windows gives you a few different ways to take stuff that is in one document and put it in another document. You can copy the information to the new document and leave the original intact. Or, you can delete something from one document and move it to another one.

The documents don't even have to be created with the same program. You can create a spreadsheet with Excel, then copy it into a word processing program such as Word for Windows. Here are some examples of what I mean:

 Copy some text from a Word for Windows document to a Word for DOS document

 Cut out part of a picture in one program and insert the picture in a letter

 Cut out a bunch of text from one part of a document and move it somewhere else in the document

So? Why would I want to?

I'm basically a lazy person. I hate to do something twice, and if there is a way to automate it, I'll figure out how to make the computer do it for me. But that's just a part of it. I'm also really busy and don't have time to reinvent the wheel every day. So, I need some way to move and copy text, pictures, and other data between the different programs that I use.

NERDY
DETAILS

Besides saving a lot of time, moving and copying information between different documents and programs in Windows helps me make fewer mistakes. I don't have to worry about whether I copied down all the text or numbers right—whatever was in the original document is exactly duplicated in the second document.

In the case of data like digitized photographs (photos that have been scanned into a computer file), images of part of the screen, or complicated drawings, I wouldn't be able to re-create the data myself. Windows lets me use and copy the original information without needing the skills, special programs, or hardware that was necessary to create the images in the first place.

The Clipboard Lets You Do It

You can use something called the Windows Clipboard to move and copy data between different documents and programs. The Clipboard is an area in memory that Windows sets up automatically without any prodding from you.

The Clipboard acts as a common area in which all Windows programs can move data in and out. One program puts data in the Clipboard, and another pulls that data out of the Clipboard. It's a little like a real clipboard. You *cut* or *copy* something from one document, then stick it on the Clipboard. You open up another program or document, then pull the stuff off of the Clipboard and put it in your new document.

The Clipboard Viewer lets you see it

If you look in your Main program group you'll find an icon labeled Clipboard Viewer. This isn't the Clipboard itself—it represents a program called the Clipboard Viewer.

You don't need the Clipboard Viewer to move stuff between two documents. In fact, the standard Windows Clipboard Viewer really isn't all that useful, except for clearing out the Clipboard when you're done with it. You can use the Clipboard Viewer to look at what's in the Clipboard, but that's about it.

The Clipboard Viewer does help you understand how to use the Clipboard. To start it up, double-click on the Clipboard Viewer program icon.

For now, move it up to the top of your window, then open up Write and Notepad and position them the way they are in figure 15.1.

Copying stuff from one document to another

Here's how you copy some text from one Windows program to another. You can use just about any Windows program, but this example uses Notepad and Write:

1. Load into Notepad the file that has the text you want to put in the Write document.

2. Highlight the text—put the I-beam cursor at the beginning of the text, hold down the mouse button, and drag the cursor to the end of the text you want. Release the mouse button. The text now shows up in reversed colors.

Chapter 15: I Want To Use This Stuff in This Other Program...

260

3. In Notepad's **E**dit menu, choose **C**opy.

At this point, the text pops into the Clipboard Viewer window. You have just *copied* some text to the Clipboard. Write now can get at the text in the Clipboard.

4. Select the Write window, put the I-beam cursor where you want the text to be, and click the mouse button (if the Write file is empty, the cursor jumps to the beginning of the document).

5. From Write's **E**dit menu, choose **P**aste. The text shows up in the Write window (see fig. 15.2).

Figure 15.1

Notepad, Write, and Clipboard Viewer.

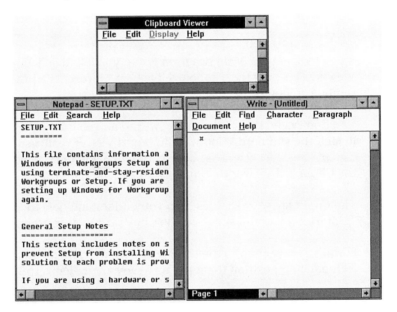

Moving stuff from one document to another

If you want to *remove* some text from one document and put it in another document, use the Cut command. Here's an example:

1. Highlight the text in Notepad.

2. In Notepad's **E**dit menu, choose Cu**t**. The text disappears from Notepad and goes to the Clipboard.

3. Select the Write window and place the cursor where the text will be inserted.

4. From Write's **E**dit menu, choose **C**opy. The text shows up in Write.

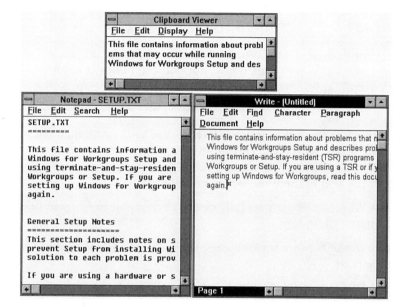

Figure 15.2

Text copied from Notepad to Write.

You can move text from one place in a document to another place in the same document—you don't have to move or copy it to a different program's document.

TRICKS

Moving drawings

The only thing that is different about moving or copying computer drawings versus moving or copying text is the way you select the drawings on your screen. With most Windows drawing programs (called *graphics programs*), you use the arrow cursor or a special cutting-tool cursor (like the scissors tool in Paintbrush) to select some graphics.

Depending on the program, you almost always can select a rectangular block of the graphics image. Some programs, like Paintbrush, let you select an irregular-shaped part of the image.

Chapter 15: I Want To Use This Stuff in This Other Program...

262

After you select the graphics, use the program's **C**opy or Cu**t** command to put the graphics in the Clipboard. Select the document in which you want to place the graphics, and then choose the **P**aste command.

Moving Stuff from Windows to DOS

You might not want to do it all that often, but you can move text from a Windows program to a DOS program. Sorry, but you can't copy graphics stuff (pictures) from Windows to DOS. But, maybe you want to copy some text from Notepad into Word for DOS or Wordperfect for DOS.

The process is a lot like the one you use with just Windows programs, but you use a different menu for the DOS program.

1. Highlight the text in the Windows document.

2. From the Windows program's **E**dit menu, choose Cu**t** or **C**opy to put the text in the Clipboard.

3. Switch to the DOS program and place the cursor where you want to insert the text.

4. Open the DOS program's Control menu.

SAVE
THE DAY!

Okay, maybe you need help with step 4. If the DOS program is running in a window, click the mouse button (once) with the mouse pointer in the upper-left corner of the window—that's the Control menu.

If the DOS program is running full-screen, press Alt-Tab as many times as you have to switch back to Program Manager. The DOS program shows up as an icon at the bottom of your desktop. Click on the DOS program's icon once to open its Control menu. Figure 15.3 shows a DOS program's Control menu.

With the Control menu open, you're ready to do some more steps.

5. Choose **E**dit (there's that **E**dit menu again...).

6. From the new menu that opens, choose **P**aste.

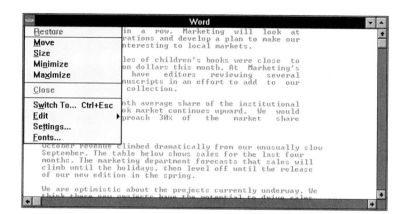

Figure 15.3

A DOS program's
Control menu.

If the DOS program is running in a window when you choose **P**aste, you'll see the text get typed into the program like magic. If the DOS program is running as an icon, the title under the icon changes to add the word "Paste" to the beginning of the title. When the paste is finished, the word "Paste" disappears from the title to let you know it's done. Wait until the paste operation is done before you do anything else.

Moving Stuff from DOS to Windows

This is a lot like the process you use to move stuff from one Windows program to another, but it gets a little more complicated. There are a lot of *depends on* and *ifs*. Here they are:

- You have to run the DOS program under Windows (but not necessarily in *a* window).

- If you're running Windows in Standard mode, you can copy only a full screen of text from the DOS program to the Windows Clipboard (because DOS programs can't run in a window in Standard mode).

- If you're running Windows in Standard mode, you can't copy graphics from DOS to Windows (nope, not at all—just text).

- If you're running Windows in 386-Enhanced mode and the DOS program is running full-screen, you can copy full-screen text or full-screen graphics to Windows.

- If you're running Windows in 386-Enhanced mode and the DOS program is running in a window, you can copy a selection of text or a selection of graphics from it to Windows. (You also can copy the whole DOS window to Windows.)

Copy stuff from DOS to Windows

1. Run the DOS program in a window (you have to run Windows in 386-Enhanced mode for this).

2. Open the DOS program's Control menu and choose **E**dit.

3. Choose the **M**ark command.

4. Use the mouse to highlight the text or graphics area you want from the DOS window.

5. When you have the data highlighted, press Enter.

6. Switch to the Windows program where the stuff is going and use its **P**aste command to bring the data in from the Clipboard.

OLE Is Another Way To Share Data

Using the Clipboard is just one of the ways you can copy and move data around in Windows. The cut-and-paste business using the Clipboard is usually the easiest way. But, there are two other methods—OLE and DDE— and there are times when each of these other two methods is the best. First, look at OLE.

This is OLE

OLE (pronounced "oh-lay") stands for Object Linking and Embedding. It's also something a matador says just before the bull tosses him on his butt and does a Mexican Hat Dance on his head.

Basically, OLE lets you *embed* a document or part of a document in another one. Let's say you just used Write to write a memo to someone that says something like, "Hey, here are the figures for the Wizbang Framistat project. Look them over. If you like them, give me a call. If you don't, go jump in a lake."

Now, you can paste the spreadsheet from your Excel spreadsheet program into your document and send it through e-mail (electronic mail), on a disk, or whatever.

But here's the problem with that: once you paste the spreadsheet stuff into Write, it's not spreadsheet stuff anymore. It's just a bunch of numbers and letters that *look* like spreadsheet stuff. What happens if the bozo on the receiving end of the memo wants to fiddle with the numbers and send them back to you? He'd have a hard time doing it.

SAVE
THE DAY!

Wouldn't it be really cool if you could just kind of wad the spreadsheet file into a little ball and glue it on the memo? Then, said bozo could pull it off of the memo, stick it in Excel (or whatever), and fiddle with the numbers to his heart's content.

That's just what OLE lets you do. It lets you stick (embed) all or part of a document in another one (see fig. 15.4).

	Write - [Untitled]	
File Edit Find Character Paragraph Document Help		

Direct Expenses		
YTD	$11,155.19	
Date	Description	Amount
12/7/92	CompuServe - Dec	167.76
1/3/92	Phone - Dec	134.62
1/25/92	10-Key Calculator	29.94
1/25/92	Calculator Paper	0.99
1/25/92	Windows Magazine	29.94
1/25/92	HD 3.5" Disks	11.91
1/25/92	DD 3.5" Disks	13.99
2/3/92	Phone - Jan	124.09
1/27/92	Postage	5.8

This is a packaged object

Page 1

Figure 15.4

Some objects embedded in a document.

NERDY
DETAILS

These embedded things are called *objects*. The embedded object shows up in one of two ways: it can appear in its "normal" format (look like spreadsheet data, for example), or it can be represented by a picture or icon. An object that is represented by an icon is called a *package* (just remember the word for now). You also can embed cool sounds in your documents.

Why would I use OLE?

Aside from doing cool but possibly useless things like embedding rude pig noises in a memo, OLE gives you a way to organize your documents. Instead of pasting data into a single document, you can embed objects in the document. The objects don't lose their identity—spreadsheet objects can still be used in your spreadsheet program; pictures can be loaded into a graphics program for viewing or editing; and useful sounds like comments about a contract can be included with the document.

Best of all, OLE gives you an easy way of working with *compound documents*. These are documents that are made up of data from a bunch of different programs. If you need to view or hear any particular object, you just double-click on it (or select it and press Enter). It gets displayed or played, depending on what it is.

TRICKS

To view or change the contents of an object, you have to have access to the program that created it. If someone sends you an Excel object, for example, you have to have Excel available to view or change the object.

Here's How To Use OLE

Jeez! This is another one of those things where there are forty zillion ways to do it, and a lot of *depends* and *ifs* like:

   Does the program support drag-and-drop (what the heck is that)?

   Do you want all of a document or just part of it?

Do you want to embed an icon to represent the object or embed the data itself?

 Are you embedding something that can only be represented by an icon (like a sound)?

Let's start with the easy ones first, using Write and Paintbrush as the sample programs. Before you start embedding stuff, take a minute to set up Paintbrush so it will work right for the next couple of examples.

STOP!

These steps set up Paintbrush to draw pictures that are 64 pixels square (*pixels are like dots*).

1. Start Paintbrush (it's in the Accessories group) and select the **O**ptions menu.

2. Choose **I**mage Attributes and select the pixels radio button.

3. Click in the **W**idth box and change the number there to 64.

4. Click in the **H**eight box and change the number there to 64.

5. Choose OK; then choose **F**ile, then E**x**it.

Embed part of something in a document

One of the easiest ways to embed an object in a document is to use the program's **E**dit menu. In Write, the **E**dit menu includes a command called **I**nsert Object. Try it out: start Write and choose **E**dit, then **I**nsert Object. You'll see an Insert Object dialog box like the one shown in figure 15.5.

GEEK

NERDY DETAILS

The number of object types that you see listed in the Insert Object dialog box depends on the programs that are installed or available on your computer. When you install a new program that uses OLE, it adds some settings to a couple of files so that its object types shows up in the Insert Object dialog box.

Figure 15.5

The Insert Object
dialog box.

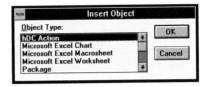

If you're through looking at the dialog box, choose Cancel. You're about to embed a Paintbrush picture in your Write document. Follow these steps:

1. Type a little bit of text in your Write document.

2. Choose **E**dit, and then **I**nsert Object.

3. Use the up/down scroll arrow to find Paintbrush Picture in the **O**bject Type list, and then select Paintbrush Picture.

4. Choose OK.

   Magically, Paintbrush appears on your desktop. Now, be creative.

5. Draw a few squiggles and jiggles in Paintbrush.

6. Choose **F**ile, and then choose E**x**it and Return to (Untitled).

7. A dialog box pops up asking if you want to update the embedded object. Choose **Y**es. Figure 15.6 shows the Paintbrush picture in the Write document.

Figure 15.6

A Paintbrush
picture embedded
in Write.

Embed a whole file in a document

Maybe you want to include a whole file in a document. Let's say you want to stick your tax-planning spreadsheet in a letter you're sending to your CPA (who also has Windows). Maybe you want to send a file of recipes in a letter to a friend. Or, maybe you want to stick a recording of little Melissa saying "Hi, Grandma!" in a letter you're sending to Grandma. You can embed the object in the letter as an icon. Here's how you do it:

1. Write the letter in Write or some other Windows word processor that can use OLE.

2. Put the cursor in the letter where you want the file to be inserted.

3. Open File Manager, find the file you want to embed, and select it (click on it once or use the cursor keys to select it).

4. From File Manager's **F**ile menu, choose **C**opy.

5. When the Copy dialog box pops up, choose the **C**opy to Clipboard radio button, then choose OK.

6. In the word processing program's **E**dit menu, choose **P**aste.

An icon for the file pops up in your letter. When the recipient reads the letter, he or she can double-click on the icon to view or hear the embedded object.

Linking? That's a new one...

In all of the examples so far, you have put a copy of some data in a file. If the original data changes, the copy that is embedded in the other document won't change. Bummer. Say you have a weekly memo you prepare that includes some sales figures or something. The sales figures always come from the same file. It would be nice if you didn't have to recopy the stuff every week.

Well, you don't have to. You can create a *link* to the data instead of actually embedding it in the document. The following are a couple of examples.

Link a whole file into a document

This is how you link a whole file into a document:

1. Open File Manager and locate the file you want to link into your document. Select the file.

2. From File Manager's **F**ile menu, choose **C**opy.

3. When the Copy dialog box pops up, choose the **C**opy to Clipboard radio button, then choose OK.

4. In your document program's **E**dit menu, choose Paste **L**ink.

If you don't see Paste **L**ink as an option in the program's **E**dit menu, it doesn't support linking (and it probably doesn't support OLE, either).

STOP!

Link part of a file into a document

This is how you link just part of a file into a document:

1. Open the program that you used to create the file you want to link into your document. If you're linking in part of a spreadsheet file, for example, open the spreadsheet program.

2. Highlight the data you want to link into the other document, then from the **E**dit menu, choose **C**opy.

3. In the other program (where the data will be linked), choose **E**dit, then choose Paste **L**ink or Paste **S**pecial.

4. If you had to use Paste **S**pecial in step 3, pick the data format you want to use from the dialog box that pops up, then choose the Paste **L**ink button.

What happens when I want to change it?

The really useful thing about linking is that if you make a change to the original document, you'll see the changes the next time you double-click on the object in any document where it's linked.

Let's say you link part of a spreadsheet into a memo. You print the memo to send it out. Then, you realize you need to fiddle with the numbers. Just open the spreadsheet program, fiddle with the numbers, and resave the spreadsheet file. When you look at your memo again, the numbers will be changed automatically.

Here are some things to think about with linking:

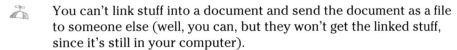

- You can't link stuff into a document and send the document as a file to someone else (well, you can, but they won't get the linked stuff, since it's still in your computer).

- If you do want to link stuff into a document that you send to someone, you need to *print* the document and send the printout to them (this still doesn't do any good if you embedded an icon of the data, instead of an *image* of the data—then, you just get a picture of the icon on the printout).

- If you want to put an object in a document that you're sending to someone else, embed it—don't link it.

- When you change the stuff in the file that contains the data you linked into a document, you'll see the change in the document the next time you open it up.

- If you change some data that is linked into a lot of documents, the change happens in *all* of those documents automatically.

- A package that contains linked data is always *embedded* in a document, even though it contains a *link*. You can't link a package in a document (the link has to be *in* the package...confusing, no?)

This Is DDE

If the programs you use don't do OLE, they might do something else called DDE, which stands for Dynamic Data Exchange. DDE is like antique OLE—DDE came first, and then Microsoft jazzed it up and called it OLE. OLE is more useful, so this chapter just covers some real basic stuff about DDE. If you want to know more about DDE, get a copy of *Maximizing Windows 3.1*, published by New Riders Publishing (and written by Jim Boyce, of course).

GEEK

NERDY
DETAILS

When you use DDE, you can establish a link between one document and another. That part is pretty much like OLE. You can copy something to the Clipboard, then use a program's Paste Link command to put the data in a document. When the original data changes, you will see the change happen in the document where the stuff was paste-linked in.

What's the difference from OLE?

With OLE, the objects that get pasted in retain some knowledge about the application that created them. When you double-click on an OLE object, that application opens so that you can view or edit the data.

With DDE, you just get a representation of the data. You can double-click on the data all you want and nothing happens. Is that bad? Not really. It just makes it a little harder to change stuff that you inserted in a document with DDE.

Here's how to use DDE

Most programs that use DDE all work about the same. Here's how you link something into a document with a program that does DDE:

 You still need the Clipboard. The data that you're going to link into the document has to be in the Clipboard. Open up the program that you use to create or view the data, select the part you want to put in the other document, then choose **C**opy from the program's **E**dit menu.

 Just use the Paste Link Command. Now, go over to the program you are using to create the document. From that program's **E**dit menu, choose Paste **L**ink. If there is a Paste **S**pecial command instead of (or in addition to) Paste **L**ink, choose that. The Paste **S**pecial command will give you a few options for the type of format you want to use for the stuff that's coming in from the Clipboard.

I want to change it everywhere

With DDE, you can make changes to data automatically. Let's say you have linked some tax spreadsheet data into a memo, a report, and another spreadsheet. Now, that tax information changes. No problem. Just open up the spreadsheet program and load the tax spreadsheet file. Make the changes and resave the file. When you open up the memo, report, or other spreadsheet, you'll see the new tax figures.

Check out your programs' manuals to see if and how they use DDE.

PART 5

You Mean I Have To Set Up More Stuff?

AGNES FARKLEBLATT SUFFERED FROM A TERRIBLE, INCESSANT NEED TO CUSTOMIZE HER SYSTEM.

CHAPTER
16

Tweaking, Fiddling, and Fooling Around

Y ou're just not satisfied, are you? You've got to rearrange the living room every month. That picture of Great Uncle Farkleblatt migrates from wall to wall like a herd of caribou. You've got *fiddleitis*. Well, you can fiddle to your heart's content with Windows. There is hardly a thing in Windows that you can't tweak, fiddle, or fool with.

This chapter explains how to change the way Windows looks and works. You learn about these exciting topics:

- Understanding the Control Panel
- Changing the time and date
- Changing those boring colors Windows uses for the desktop and window stuff
- Making your computer do weird things while you're away
- Making the computer squeal like a pig when you exit Windows
- Adding some new fonts or getting rid of some fonts

You Can Change Just About Everything

The Control Panel is what you use to tweak and fiddle in Windows. You find the Control Panel in your Main program group. When you open the Control Panel, you see a selection of icons. The number of icons you see depends on the Windows mode you are using and whether you're on a network. If you're running in 386 Enhanced mode or using Windows on a network, you see additional icons. Figure 16.1 shows the Control Panel.

Figure 16.1

This is the Control Panel. Just double-click on whichever item you want to change.

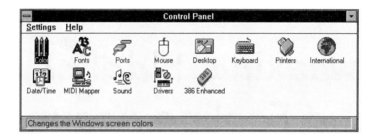

Change the Date and Time

The Date/Time icon displays the Date & Time dialog box shown in figure 16.2. Use this dialog box to set the date and time on your computer.

Figure 16.2

This is the Date & Time dialog box.

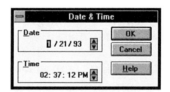

Just click on the up and down arrows to set the date and time, then choose OK. If your time doesn't stay right from day to day, the battery in your computer is bad. Check out Chapter 18 for help.

Change the Way Windows Looks

There are a lot of controls in the Control Panel that you can use to change the way just about every feature of Windows looks. Color is one of the biggies.

These colors are really boring

I think that the default colors Windows uses are boring. Fortunately, you can change them. Select the Color icon in the Control Panel to see the Color dialog box. You then select and view predefined color schemes for the way Windows looks on-screen. You also can save a color scheme by name.

NERDY
DETAILS

Windows includes 23 predefined color schemes from which to choose. Personally, I like Emerald City, Ocean, and Arizona. Some of the color schemes, such as Hotdog Stand and Fluorescent, are really gross, but if you have no taste, you're welcome to use them.

In addition to using predefined color schemes, you also can make up your own color schemes or change the color of just one item. Select the Color **P**alette button to set the color of individual display components and define custom colors (see fig. 16.3). Components is just a fancy word for buttons, windows, title bars, and stuff like that.

 With the expanded Color dialog box you can change 21 different components of Windows. Click on the Screen Element drop-down list box to change these 21 different areas. You should have fun and change different areas on your screen to see what colors you prefer.

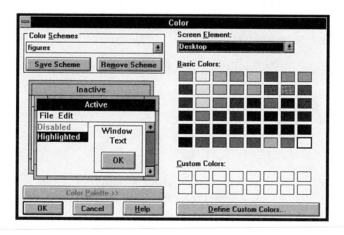

Figure 16.3

This is the expanded Color dialog box. Use it to change the color of a couple of interface components.

278

 If you want to be really artsy, you can create custom colors that aren't shown in the basic color chart by choosing the **D**efine Custom Colors button. This displays the Custom Color Selector dialog box shown in figure 16.4.

Figure 16.4

This is the Custom Color Selector dialog box. Use it to create your own colors and store them in the Custom Color boxes.

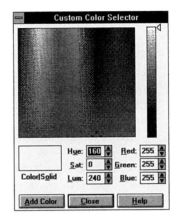

TRICKS

You can use the Custom Color Selector dialog box to quickly define custom colors to use for various Windows components. Just click in the big colored box to get close to the color you want, then use the increment controls to fine-tune it. I won't go into detail on what all those controls are—just fiddle with them, and you'll get the idea. When you have the color you want, choose the **A**dd Color button to place it in a **C**ustom Colors box.

I Thought Windows Was Supposed To Look Cool

The Desktop icon in Control Panel lets you change a bunch of things that control the way Windows looks. It also includes a few options for controlling the way that Windows works. Choosing the Desktop icon in the Control Panel displays the Desktop dialog box shown in figure 16.5.

Figure 16.5

The Desktop dialog box lets you change all sorts of things that control the way the desktop is set up.

Use a brick wall for your desktop

The Pattern group box enables you to specify a pattern to appear as the Windows desktop. The pattern appears behind any wallpaper you configure Windows to display. You can choose from several patterns so that you can redecorate your desktop as often as your spouse redecorates the living room.

Stick a picture of Bart on the desktop

The Wallpaper group box contains controls for specifying a wallpaper pattern. The wallpaper pattern is a computer picture (called a *bit map*) that appears on top of the desktop pattern, if any is selected. Figure 16.6 shows a bit map used as a wallpaper image.

Windows includes a selection of bit maps you can use for wallpaper. You also can use any Windows bit map file (BMP format) as a wallpaper image. Use this when you want to suck up to your boss—put a picture of the tyrant on your desktop.

TRICKS

The Applications group box contains the Fast "Alt-Tab" Switching check box. Pressing Alt-Tab makes the program icons pop up in a window. This check box turns that on and off.

Figure 16.6

A wallpaper bit map shows up behind all your windows but on top of the desktop pattern if you're using one.

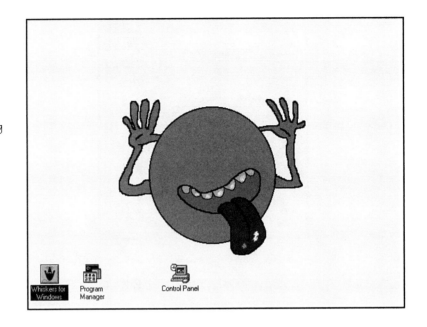

Make the computer do weird stuff while you're gone

The Screen Saver group box lets you choose and set up your Windows screen saver. If you use a screen saver, your screen goes blank after the time limit you specify and puts some kind of random pattern on the screen. Mainly, it keeps people from seeing what your computer is up to when you're not there. You can set it up so that you have to enter a password to get back to the normal Windows display.

SAVE
THE DAY!

If you forget your screen saver password and can't get back into Windows, reboot your computer by pressing Ctrl-Alt-Del (you might lose any changes to documents that haven't been saved). Start up Windows and open Notepad. Load the file SYSTEM.INI into it from your WINDOWS directory and look for the line that reads SCRNSAVE.EXE=whatever. Delete everything after the = sign, then resave the file. Go back into Control Panel and set up your screen saver again.

Make those windows line up

The Sizing Grid group box lets you control the way windows are positioned on the Windows desktop and specify the width of window borders. The **G**ranularity setting, if set to anything other than 0, makes your windows jump to an invisible grid on the screen. I don't like it, but you're welcome to use it.

The **B**order Width setting is a lot more useful. Use it to make the borders around all of your windows larger or smaller. Make them bigger if you have a hard time grabbing a border to drag it.

Change the distance between icons

The Icons group box lets you set the horizontal spacing between icons in program groups. It also controls whether or not icon descriptions display as one line or multiple lines.

NERDY
DETAILS

You can change the vertical spacing between icons also, by using the IconVerticalSpacing= setting in the [Desktop] section of WIN.INI. Use Notepad to open the WIN.INI file and add the setting to the section. Include some number with it, such as IconVerticalSpacing=60.

Make that little cursor blink like crazy

The Cursor Blink Rate group box lets you control the speed at which the cursor blinks. This controls the blink rate for Windows programs and for windowed DOS programs. I don't really know why you'd want to change it, but it's up to you.

Fonts Are What the Letters Look Like

The Fonts icon in Control Panel lets you view installed fonts, add new fonts, and remove fonts. *Fonts* are what the letters look like on your screen and on your printed page. Selecting the Fonts icon displays the Fonts dialog box shown in figure 16.7.

The Fonts dialog box includes a **T**rueType button that displays the TrueType dialog box that is also shown in figure 16.7. You use the TrueType dialog box to specify options for using TrueType fonts in Windows.

NERDY
DETAILS

Instead of going into a big deal about what TrueType fonts are, I'm just going to tell you that they are better than other fonts. TrueType fonts have a little icon (looks like "TT") next to them in the selection list whenever you're picking a font. That tells you they're TrueType fonts.

Figure 16.7

Here are the Fonts and TrueType dialog boxes. Use these to add new fonts, delete fonts, and set up the way TrueType fonts are used.

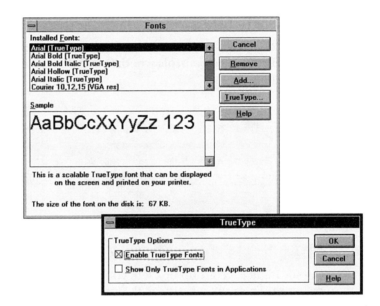

When you want to add or delete a font, use the **A**dd and **R**emove buttons in the Fonts dialog box. In the TrueType dialog box, check the **E**nable TrueType Fonts check box if you want to use TrueType fonts (which you should use). If you want to use *only* TrueType fonts, check the **S**how Only TrueType Fonts in Applications check box.

Change the Way That Windows Works

Most of the changes covered up to this point just change the way Windows looks. There are a lot of things you can do to change the way Windows and some of your computer hardware works.

Train your mouse

The Mouse icon in the Control Panel controls a few aspects of the way the mouse works. Choosing the Mouse icon displays the Mouse dialog box.

Here is an explanation of the controls in the Mouse dialog box:

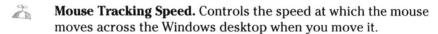 **Mouse Tracking Speed.** Controls the speed at which the mouse moves across the Windows desktop when you move it.

Double Click Speed. Sets the relative amount of time that must pass between two clicks of the mouse button for it to be recognized by Windows as a double-click. Slow this down if you can't get the hang of that double-click action.

Swap Left/Right Buttons. Swaps the function of the left and right mouse buttons. This is great if you are a "lefty."

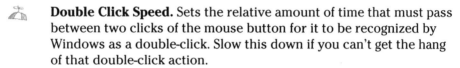 **Mouse Trails.** When checked, causes a ghost image to follow the mouse pointer on the display. This makes the cursor more visible on LCD displays.

What's a port?

A *port* is what is in the back of your computer where you hook up things like a movie or a modem. Use the Ports icon in Control Panel to set up your system's serial (COM) ports. You can set baud rate, number of data bits, parity, number of stop bits, and flow control method. Choosing the Ports icon displays the Ports dialog box, which enables you to select which port you want to set up: COM1, COM2, COM3, or COM4. Usually, the settings that already are there are OK for most users.

NERDY
DETAILS

In addition to setting these general parameters, you also can set the base I/O port address and Interrupt Request Line (IRQ) for each COM port. Choosing the **A**dvanced button in the

continues

continued

Settings for COMx dialog box displays the Advanced Settings for COMx dialog box shown in figure 16.8. Use this dialog box to specify the base I/O address and IRQ for the selected port.

You usually don't have to mess with the Ports dialog box. Programs that use the COM ports usually set up the COM ports when they use them.

Figure 16.8

The Advanced Settings for COMx dialog box.

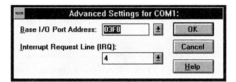

I can't get used to this keyboard

The Keyboard icon in Control Panel lets you control how fast a key repeats when you hold it down. It also lets you tell windows how long to wait before it starts repeating a key's character. Choosing the Keyboard icon displays the Keyboard dialog box .

TRICKS

I like a fast keyboard that repeats quickly, but I type fast. If you feel like you're all thumbs with the keyboard or you have "heavy fingers" and keep repeating characters when you don't want to, slow down the two settings in the Keyboard dialog box. Click in the **T**est box and press some keys to test your changes.

I want it to squeal like a pig (Sound)

The Sound icon in the Control Panel displays the Sound dialog box shown in figure 16.9. If your system contains a sound adapter, you can use the Sound dialog box to assign sounds to various Windows events (such as exiting Windows). When the event occurs, the sound plays on the sound adapter.

If your system doesn't include a sound adapter, the Sound dialog box just lets you turn on and off Windows' standard warning beep. This beep happens when you try to do something that doesn't compute.

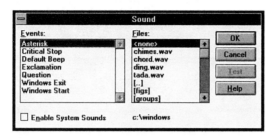

Figure 16.9

The Sound dialog box lets you assign sounds to Windows events.

TRICKS

> If you want to add limited sound capability to your system without adding a sound adapter, you can install a special software driver for your PC's speaker. You'll find the driver in the WINADV forum on CompuServe, the MSL library on CompuServe, and the Microsoft BBS. Look for a file called SPEAK.EXE, which contains the files you'll need. This driver enables the standard speaker in the PC to be used to play WAV files such as those you assign to various Windows events through the Sound dialog box. The speaker driver is kind of a dog, though, and you'll only be truly happy with a sound card.

Multitasking (386 Enhanced)

The 386 Enhanced icon displays the 386 Enhanced dialog box. This dialog box lets you set the way Windows works on a 386 or 486 system. It's mainly for setting the way Windows runs multiple programs at once.

Keep devices from fighting over the computer

The Device Contention group box controls the way Windows handles the way that applications attempt to access the same COM or LPT ports. For COM ports, you should probably use the **A**lways Warn setting. For LPT ports, the **I**dle setting is usually good. Use a setting of 60 seconds.

STOP!

The Scheduling group box controls priority values Windows uses for multitasking Windows and DOS programs. The priority valves control how much of the CPU's time your appplications receive. It also enables you to specify that Windows applications will have 100 percent of the CPU's time when any Windows program is active. The Minimum Timeslice control specifies the amount of time allocated to each process when multitasking. You probably don't need to mess with these settings, so I'm not going to tell you how.

Here's something to make Windows better

The **V**irtual Memory button displays the Virtual Memory dialog box shown in figure 16.10. This dialog box lets you change the type and size of swap file that Windows uses in 386 Enhanced mode. It also lets you enable and disable Windows' 32-bit disk access.

Figure 16.10

The Virtual Memory dialog box lets you alter your swap file.

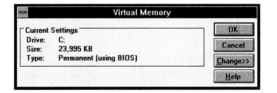

NERDY DETAILS

A swap file is a special file that Windows creates on your hard disk. Windows uses the swap file to store stuff when it starts to run low on memory (RAM). A permanent swap file of at least twice the size of your system's memory is best. If you have 8M of RAM, for example, you should use a 16M swap file. Before you change your swap file, you should defragment your disk drive. Chapter 17 explains what defragmenting is and how to do it.

Stuff You Use Once, If Ever

Some of the stuff in the Control Panel you might use once, if you ever use it at all. The MIDI Mapper, Drivers, and International icons are the ones you probably have little use for.

 MIDI Mapper. This item lets you configure a musical device, such as an electronic keyboard, that you have connected to your computer.

 Drivers. This item lets you add, configure, and remove various device drivers for multimedia equipment. Multimedia equipment includes sound boards, MIDI devices, and audio CD drivers.

 International. This one lets you change language, keyboard layout, date format, time format, currency format, number format, and other country-specific settings.

If you really think you need to use these icons, check out Control Panel's Help file.

Other Stuff in Control Panel

Depending on your computer, Control Panel may have a few other icons in it. Check out the Control Panel Help file for help with these other items. Check out Chapter 9 for help with the Printers icon.

Souping It Up and Changing Things

N ow that you've been through Chapter 16 and fiddled and fooled around with everything in Windows, you probably want *more*. More speed, more colors, more *everything*...grunt, grunt, grunt. Okay, there are some things you might want to think about doing to speed up your computer. That's what this chapter is about, and here's what's in it:

- Why would you want to mess with a good thing?
- What kinds of things can you do to make your system better?
- How, when, and why to change your video setup.
- What to do with the disk so Windows works better.
- What *not* to do with the disk in Windows.

It Works Just Fine, Thank You

Your computer probably gets you from point A to point B in your work just fine. Now that you're almost a Windows expert, there's nothing you can't do with your computer. So the question becomes "Why would I want to mess around with it?"

Why soup it up?

Windows is a real hog when it comes to certain resources in your computer. I'll tell you what "resources" are in a minute. The main thing is that the more resources you give Windows to play with, the faster it will be. The faster Windows can get its job done, the faster you get *your* job done.

TRICKS

The other side of the coin is making Windows more useful. That includes giving yourself more room on the screen for more windows, or fixing it so you can use a lot more colors in Windows. Either way, you'll probably enjoy using Windows more.

What kinds of things can I change?

You can change a lot of things in Windows, but the main three have to do with video, memory, and disk. Memory and disk space are *resources* (I told you I'd tell you...). You can add more memory to your system or do some things to the disk drive to make Windows operate faster.

You also can change your video adapter's *resolution* and *color capability*. Changing resolution gives you more space on the desktop for your programs. Changing color capability lets you use more colors in your programs.

TRICKS

This doesn't really soup up your computer but I'll throw it in anyway because you'll like it. To make Windows start automatically when you start your computer do the following:

1. In Windows, open Notepad and load the AUTOEXEC.BAT file from the root directory of drive C.

2. Add a new line that just reads **WIN** at the bottom of the file.

3. Save the file and exit Notepad.

The next time you reboot or restart your computer, Windows will start automatically.

Make the Desktop Bigger and Faster

Now do some real souping up. Take a look at video and see if you can give yourself more room to work with. First, you need to know what *resolution* means to a techno-weenie computer person.

A little bit about resolution

Your video adapter and monitor work together to display images on the computer screen. Without launching into a long-winded explanation, let's just say that these images are made of really small dots. Put a bunch of dots of different colors together, and you have a color image of something.

NERDY
DETAILS

What if you use big dots? The picture won't look as good as it could if you used small dots. Why? Think of it this way: say you're making a picture by arranging rocks in a pattern instead of dots. Picture the rock pattern in your mind.

Now, picture what the possibilities would be if you used grains of sand instead of rocks. The picture would be much finer and have a lot more detail. That's kind of what video resolution is all about. Big dots mean a poorer image; small dots mean a fine image with lots of detail.

Now, shake those rocks out of your head and pay attention.

How much resolution can you get?

The image you see on your computer screen is made up of *pixels*. Just think of pixels as being the dots that the picture is made of, and we're okay.

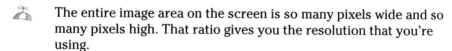 The entire image area on the screen is so many pixels wide and so many pixels high. That ratio gives you the resolution that you're using.

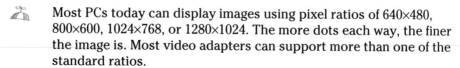 Most PCs today can display images using pixel ratios of 640×480, 800×600, 1024×768, or 1280×1024. The more dots each way, the finer the image is. Most video adapters can support more than one of the standard ratios.

STOP!

Your monitor and the video adapter in your computer have to work together. The monitor has to be able to handle the resolution that the video adapter sends it. So before you rush out and buy a new video adapter or start monkeying around with the one you have, check the manual for your monitor and see what its maximum supported resolution is.

How does resolution affect Windows?

Text, icons, and all other Windows gadgets and doodads are made up of pixels. If you increase the video resolution, things are going to get smaller. This means that you can fit more text into a window, which lets you see more of a document on the screen at one time. Or, you can work with the usual amount of the document and just put more windows on the screen. So, using a higher resolution makes it easier to use more programs at once.

GEEK

NERDY
DETAILS

Unless you're made of money, you probably have a 14" or 15" monitor. Personally, I think 800x600 is the highest you would want to go on these sizes of monitors. If you go with a higher resolution, your text and icons will be so small that you'll probably have trouble reading them. If you have a larger monitor, you probably will want to go with either 1024x768 or 1280x1024. Just remember that if you switch to a higher resolution and don't like it, you can always switch back.

The net effect of switching to a higher resolution is this: it gives you more room to work with in Windows.

Use the Setup icon to change video

After you figure out what your maximum resolution can be (the highest resolution that both the video adapter and monitor can support), it's time to run the Windows Setup program. You'll find it in your Main group. Double-click on it to start Setup.

When the Windows Setup dialog box pops up on your screen (see fig. 17.1), notice that it lists your system's current display resolution. It also shows you which keyboard and mouse you're using, and might also tell you what network you're using.

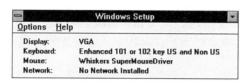

Figure 17.1

The Windows Setup dialog box.

 To change the display resolution, choose the **O**ptions menu, then choose **C**hange System Settings. The Change System Settings dialog box pops up.

 Click on the **D**isplay drop-down list, then hunt through the list to see if there is a higher resolution option for your video adapter. If you are currently using the VGA driver and you know that your video adapter and monitor will go up to 800×600, you probably can use the SuperVGA driver. That will give you 800×600 resolution in 16 colors.

SAVE THE DAY!

If you don't see an option that is obviously for your video adapter, check the disks that came with your video adapter. See if you have a disk for the video adapter that has Windows drivers on it. (If all else fails, read the manual for the video adapter to see if it has Windows drivers included with it.)

 If you have a disk like the one mentioned above, open the **D**isplay drop-down list box and scroll all the way to the bottom. Pick the option that reads "Other Display (Requires disk from OEM)..." Setup opens a dialog box asking you to insert a disk. Insert the disk that contains the Windows drivers for your video card, then choose OK.

At this point, Setup displays a list of the drivers that are on the disk. Select the one you want to use and choose OK. When you get back to the Change System Settings dialog box, choose OK. Setup gives you the option of restarting Windows or continuing. Restart Windows to start using the new video resolution.

Hey, what about color?

When you look at the list of video drivers in Setup, you'll notice that they tell you how many colors they support. The three common settings are monochrome (two colors), 16 colors, and 256 colors.

If you want to work with lots of colors, you'll probably want to go with a 256 color driver. If you're working with digitized pictures, you'll find that using a 256 color driver makes the pictures look better.

If You Don't Do Anything Else, Add Memory

If there is only one thing you ever do to soup up your computer, add more memory to it. More memory makes Windows run faster, lets you use more programs at one time, and lets you work with larger documents in your programs.

This is all you have to know about memory

Memory goes in your computer in one of three ways. First, your computer's motherboard (the big board inside the computer where all the electronic stuff lives) might have some sockets on it that are about 3" long.

Usually the motherboard has eight sockets, in four groups of two. The memory consists of some small circuit cards that go in each socket. Memory chips are mounted on each card. Those are called *SIMs* or *SIPs*, depending on what type of socket the computer uses. To add more memory to this type of system you just plug in more SIMs or SIPs.

NERDY
DETAILS

Memory can be horribly confusing to a novice, so I'll just say this: call the place where you bought the computer and tell them you want to add more memory to your system. Tell them how much is in it, and they can tell you what types of memory you need to bring it up to the total amount you want. Write down exactly what type, speed, and capacity they tell you you're going to need.

The other possibility is that there are lots of little sockets on the motherboard into which little memory chips go. These are called *DRAM* chips (which stands for Dynamic Random-Access Memory). To add more memory to this type of system, you plug in more DRAM chips.

The third possibility is that all of your computer's memory lives on an adapter card that plugs into the computer bus sockets, just like the video adapter and other adapters. These cards usually have DRAM chips on them. You add more memory by adding more DRAM chips.

TRICKS

Keep in mind that you may have to replace some of the memory with different memory, which means you might have some extra left over. Donate it to a worthy organization that uses computers or sell it to a friend.

How much is enough?

Although you need only 2M (M stands for *megabytes*) of memory to run Windows, the very *bare* minimum should be 4M. If you don't want to go crazy buying memory but want a really good system, try for 6M to 8M. If money is no object, stick in 12M to 16M or more.

Where can I get more memory?

Memory these days usually sells for $50 or less per megabyte. When you call the place where you bought the computer, ask them how much it would be per megabyte to add memory to your system. If they're not too unreasonable, buy it from them. If their price is outrageous, shop around. Pick up a copy of a computer magazine, such as *Windows Magazine*, *PC Magazine*, *Byte*, or *Computer Shopper*, and look through the ads.

SAVE
THE DAY!

If you bought your computer from a local store, they probably will be happy to install the memory for you. If they want to charge a few bucks to install it, there's nothing wrong with that. Just be willing to pay a little more to have someone install it for you.

Can I put it in myself?

Yes, you can, but you need to be careful. Do the obvious things like unplug the computer before you open it up. The other thing to be careful about is static electricity.

 A very small static charge can wipe out a memory chip (any kind of microchip is vulnerable).

 Before you even touch the chips, make sure you touch the metal part of the computer case to discharge any static build-up.

I'm not going to tell you how to actually install the memory. If you don't know how to do it and can't get someone to do it for you, buy the memory and then call the place where you bought the computer. Tell them you're adding some more memory and you'd like for them to step you through it over the phone.

Buy a 386 or 486 Computer

On the front of your computer somewhere there should be a sticker or something that tells you whether your computer is a 286, 386, or 486 system. If not, look in the manual that came with the computer to find out which number applies. Remember, the higher the number , the more powerful the computer is.

NERDY
DETAILS

There's nothing wrong with a 286 computer, but they just don't run Windows very well. They don't have the raw speed that Windows needs. A 386 system is a good choice for running Windows, and a 486 is even better.

Can I stick a 386 or 486 chip in this computer?

You can make your computer stronger and faster (what nerds call "upgrading") by putting in a new microprocessor. On older machines, however, you must replace the entire motherboard to add a new microprocessor.

Depending on which type of CPU you're going to put in the computer to upgrade it, doing so will cost anywhere from about $300 to $1200 or more. Bear in mind that you may also have to replace the memory because what you have may not be the same type as what your new motherboard needs.

TRICKS

I don't recommend changing motherboards unless you're upgrading from a 286 to one of the other two CPUs. If you want to upgrade your system at the least expense, see if your favorite computer dealer offers a bare-bones system. That's a computer case, motherboard, power supply, and sometimes memory. You use your old video card, disk drives, monitor, keyboard, and other gadgets. This usually is not much more expensive than just buying a new motherboard.

Your Disk Is a Real Dog

The other weak link in a Windows system is the hard disk. Windows beats the heck out of the hard disk, using up lots of space on it for its files and for a swap file (see Chapter 16 if you're not sure what a swap file is). With Windows using your disk that much, the faster the disk is, the faster Windows will be and the better it will perform overall.

Don't tell me I need a new hard disk!

No, you don't necessarily need a new hard disk (whew!). You probably can get by with the one you have. The only reason to buy a new disk is if you've completely run out of space on your old one. But, there are some alternatives to buying a new disk just because your old one is full.

No, the disk doesn't weigh more when it's full

It doesn't weigh any more, but Windows will work better with one that isn't full. Check your hard disk for files that you don't need anymore. If you can't bear to destroy them, put them on a floppy disk and tuck them away in the closet.

Erase files with a BAK extension (leave alone those BA*T* files). BAK files are backup files created by a program when you modify a document.

 Erase programs that you don't use anymore. Also, if you don't use wallpaper on your desktop, consider getting rid of the BMP files in your Windows directory.

STOP!

As you go through your directories looking for things to delete, you might think to yourself, "Can I get rid of some of these Windows files?"

The best way to remove Windows components is to let Setup do it for you. Run Setup in Windows and choose the Add/Remove Windows Components command from the Options menu. Follow the directions to remove any Windows components you don't need. Figure 17.2 shows the dialog box that helps you remove stuff you don't need.

Figure 17.2

This is the dialog box that pops up when you use Setup to remove Windows components that you don't need. You also can use it to add stuff back that you have deleted.

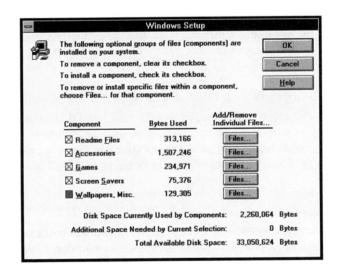

If you're running out of disk space, you may be able to compress (shrink) the files that are on your disk, giving you more space on the disk. Check with your favorite computer dealer or software dealer on this one. Ask if they sell any "on-the-fly disk compression software." They'll be impressed. They'll probably tell you about a product called Stacker. It's good, but there are other good ones, too.

Speed up the one you have

After you have freed up as much space as possible, another thing you can do to speed up the disk is to *defragment* it. As you store and delete files on a disk, the files tend to get scattered around on the disk. A single file might not be located all in one place on the disk. A part of it may be *here*, another part may be *there*, and the rest may be *over there*. The file is said to be *fragmented*.

- There's nothing wrong with a fragmented file—DOS and Windows can read them just fine. It just takes them longer to gather all the pieces together into a whole file.

- There are a lot of utility programs that let you defragment the disk. These programs move all of your files back into side-by-side places on the disk.

- Check with your favorite software dealer for "disk optimization" software. Disk optimization software also can do some other nifty things to make your disk work better, like put the files you use most in a place on the disk where Windows can get to them more quickly.

STOP!

Although optimizing a disk will make it work better, you shouldn't run disk optimizing programs in Windows. Most of these programs will tell you this in big letters somewhere. Believe them. Exit Windows and run the disk optimization software from DOS.

PART 6

I Really Need Help

GEEK

CHAPTER
18

Argh...I Screwed Up Again!

O kay, the chapter title says it all. You're here because you pressed a button and the computer imploded into a molten pile of goo. The disk drive light is floating on the surface of the goo, pulsing feebly like a Mayfly trapped in molasses. Oh, boy...you've really done it now. Don't bother to shoot it—you'd be wasting a good bullet.

This chapter won't coagulate that goo back into a computer again, but it will help you solve some of the common problems you'll run up against. Here are a few of the problems you'll find answers to and other nuggets of wisdom you'll get out of this chapter:

- The computer makes noises but nothing interesting happens

- You get really useless error messages when you try to start the computer

- Windows somehow went on vacation and you can't start it

- Programs won't start or won't stop

- The mouse slipped through a wormhole into another dimension

My Computer Doesn't Start!

You flicked the big red switch or punched the power button and expected the computer to hum to life like Frankenstein's monster. Instead, all you got was blissful but painful silence. There are no whirring sounds coming from the computer and the monitor is as black as the third black hole south of Andromeda. The first thing to check is:

Is the computer plugged into the wall?

This may sound stupid, but maybe your pet weasel pulled it out of the socket. Plug in a toaster and toast a bagel to figure out if the plug works. If it does, you can munch on it (the bagel, not the plug) while you figure out what else might be wrong. If the toaster doesn't work, check the breaker. If it still doesn't work, call an electrician.

The toaster works, but not the computer

If you're getting juice at the socket, try this:

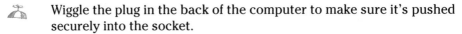 Wiggle the plug in the back of the computer to make sure it's pushed securely into the socket.

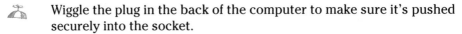 If you think you need a new cord, go to Sears, Wal-Mart, or a computer store and buy a new one. Take the old one along for comparison.

I hear noises but don't see anything

Your computer came on and is humming and whirring just like it always does. It may even have beeped and booped a few times. The only problem is that the screen is still black.

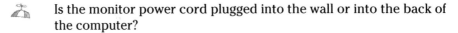 Is the monitor power cord plugged into the wall or into the back of the computer?

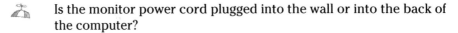 Did you turn on the monitor?

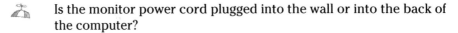 Did your three-year-old fiddle with the contrast and brightness knobs while you were out of the room?

Enough about the cord; it's good!

The cord is good and the power is on but you still have no picture? Try this:

 Make sure the cable that connects the monitor to the video card in the computer is securely attached to the adapter card *and* to the monitor.

If you still don't have a picture, call the place where you got the computer. There could be something wrong with either the video card or the monitor.

What Is a Non-System Disk?

Your computer is running and you're getting stuff on the screen, but you end up with a message on the screen that says something like this:

```
Non-System disk or disk error
Replace and press any key when ready
```

The most common cause of this problem is that you have left a floppy disk in drive A. The disk is not *bootable* (doesn't have the DOS system files on it), so the computer wants you to kindly remove it so it can get on with its business of finding some system files. Open the drive door by pushing the eject button or turning the drive door latch (depends on which type of drive you have). You don't have to actually remove the disk—just disengage it.

Next, press a key on the keyboard—pick a key; any key will do. The spacebar is nice, or the Enter key.

NERDY
DETAILS

> There is no such key as the Any key. Whenever you see a prompt to press any key when ready, just smack the spacebar, Enter key, or whatever is handy (not the weasel, please).

If you remove the disk from drive A and press Enter, or there *isn't* a disk in drive A, and you still can't get the computer to boot, you may have a problem with the system's hard disk. The next section covers that most unpleasant problem.

Still no joy

Everything seems to be okay and the computer will run, but you still can't seem to get DOS to load. I hope you made a bootable DOS floppy disk like I told you to do back in Chapter 10. It's possible that your hard disk has suffered some sort of unforeseen and unfortunate screwup, like maybe you accidentally erased all of the files from the root directory of your hard disk (ouch). Do you get this error message?:

```
Bad or Missing Command Interpreter
```

If so, your computer can't find a file called COMMAND.COM like it used to be able to do. Here's how to get around that problem:

1. Put the bootable DOS floppy disk in drive A and close the drive door.

2. Hold down the Ctrl key and the Alt key, then press the Delete (or Del) key. Let all of the keys up. This reboots the computer. (This is called Control Alt Delete, or the three-finger salute.)

3. The system should boot from your DOS disk and you should get a prompt that looks something like A:>.

4. Type **COPY A:\COMMAND.COM C:\DOS**.

5. Type **COPY A:\COMMAND.COM C:**.

Doing both of the last two steps makes sure that you have a copy of COMMAND.COM in one of the two places your computer is likely to look for it. It doesn't hurt to have more than one copy of COMMAND.COM (as long as they are identical, which in this case, they are).

6. Remove the disk from drive A, then reboot the computer using the Ctrl-Alt-Del keys the same way you did before.

SAVE
THE DAY!

But wait! You don't have a bootable DOS disk? Find someone else who has a DOS-type computer and make one. Do it right this minute! You're hosed without it.

It still won't go!

If you *don't* get the error message `Bad or Missing Command Interpreter`, and the computer still won't start, there is probably something wrong with the hard disk. Try putting the bootable DOS floppy disk in drive A and rebooting the computer with the Ctrl-Alt-Del keys. If DOS boots okay from drive A, at least you know the problem isn't the computer itself. It's probably still the hard disk. Call the place where you got the computer. They should be able to help.

Windows Doesn't Start

Your computer starts just fine, but when you type WIN and press Enter to start Windows, Windows doesn't start. One of these two things might happen, for example:

 The screen goes black after you type WIN and press Enter, and a black screen is all you get.

 The screen goes black, the Windows startup picture appears and disappears, and you get dumped back to the nasty DOS C:\> prompt.

You're missing a file somewhere that Windows needs, some piece of equipment isn't working right (unlikely), or you've been monkeying with some of the settings in the SYSTEM.INI file. The easiest solution to this one is to call Microsoft (see Chapter 19 on how to do this). Let them figure out what got screwed up.

The mouse took a hike

The computer starts and Windows starts, but the mouse doesn't work. Do these things:

 Check to make sure the mouse is plugged into the back of the computer.

 Reboot the computer by using the Ctrl-Alt-Del keys.

The mouse still is on vacation

If the mouse is plugged in and it still doesn't work right after you reboot the system, the program that drives the mouse is probably not getting loaded by Windows. If you're not running Windows, do these steps:

 Type **SETUP** to start the Windows Setup program.

 Follow the directions in the Setup program to select a mouse (see fig. 18.1).

Figure 18.1

The Windows Setup program in DOS.

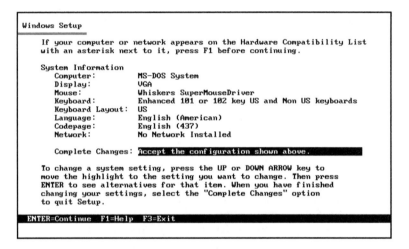

```
Windows Setup

   If your computer or network appears on the Hardware Compatibility List
   with an asterisk next to it, press F1 before continuing.

   System Information
      Computer:          MS-DOS System
      Display:           VGA
      Mouse:             Whiskers SuperMouseDriver
      Keyboard:          Enhanced 101 or 102 key US and Non US keyboards
      Keyboard Layout:   US
      Language:          English (American)
      Codepage:          English (437)
      Network:           No Network Installed

      Complete Changes: Accept the configuration shown above.

   To change a system setting, press the UP or DOWN ARROW key to
   move the highlight to the setting you want to change. Then press
   ENTER to see alternatives for that item. When you have finished
   changing your settings, select the "Complete Changes" option
   to quit Setup.

ENTER=Continue   F1=Help   F3=Exit
```

 If Setup tells you that you already have a driver on the system for your mouse, tell it to install a new one (Setup gives you the instructions for doing this).

 When you're through telling Setup to install the mouse driver program, it will do it and return you to the DOS prompt. Type **WIN** and press Enter to start Windows.

If you are in Windows and the mouse isn't working, exit Windows and run Setup. You also can run Setup from within Windows, but it'll be easier if you run it from DOS.

SAVE
THE DAY!

> If you still can't get the mouse to work, call Microsoft.

The Time and Date Keep Changing!

You've set the date and time on your computer, but it doesn't "stick"—the time and/or date keeps changing.

 Use the DATE and TIME commands from the DOS prompt. This method sets the date and time only for the current session—it doesn't save it for the next time you turn on the computer. Don't do it this way.

Use the Date/Time icon in the Windows Control Panel (see fig. 18.2).

Figure 18.2

The Date & Time dialog box.

STOP!

You also can get into the computer's CMOS setup program to change the date and time. On my system, I have to press Ctrl-Alt-Esc at the DOS prompt to get the CMOS setup program to run. (By the way, you pronounce CMOS like "sea moss.") You probably don't want to use this method, since you could potentially screw something up in your computer's internal configuration.

There are no batteries in there!

If your date and time doesn't stay set right, maybe the batteries are bad. All the batteries do is keep some information about the system's configuration from getting lost. Part of that information includes the current date and time.

STOP!

Static electricity in your body can zap electronic components into junk. Always touch the metal frame of your computer to discharge static before reaching into the computer's guts. Try not to touch anything you don't have to touch.

There are two types of batteries you'll find tucked into your computer. If you **unplug the computer** (that's a hint, folks) and open it up, you might see a battery pack in the computer somewhere that holds four AA batteries. If that's the case:

 Go down to the store and pick up four brand new AA alkaline batteries (get whatever batteries you need if your system uses a different type or number of batteries).

 Remove the old ones and put in the new ones, getting them into the holder in the same way the old ones came out.

 Make sure you don't disconnect anything or smack anything accidentally while you're monkeying around inside the computer.

 Close up the computer again, plug it in, and restart it.

 Start Windows and use the Date/Time icon to set the date and time.

You might have an enclosed battery pack in the computer instead of one that holds those AA cells. This is a *removable rechargeable* battery. Disconnect it and go down to the computer store to get another one.

Batteries are good, but weird stuff still happens

If your computer does weird things when you turn it on after replacing the batteries, and you can't get into Windows, you may have lost some of the system's configuration information (like what type of hard drive it uses). If that's the case, call the place where you got the computer and say:

 "I need help running the CMOS setup program on my computer. I had to replace the batteries and need to reset everything."

NERDY DETAILS

GEEK

If you're the adventurous sort, you can open up your computer manual and find the part where it tells you how to run the CMOS setup program, then do everything yourself. But what for? You can get the computer people to tell you how to do it and suffer through a lot less monkeying around.

Now, what happens if you look in the computer and there aren't any battery packs or batteries floating around in there? Well, you have *rechargeable* batteries built right onto your computer's motherboard. If that's what you have, the battery might be bad. You probably won't be able to replace it yourself, so you'll have to call the place where you bought the computer.

Hey! That Program Started By Itself

When you start Windows, at least one program—Program Manager— is going to start by itself. You need Program Manager, so this is okay. But, you might also have some other programs starting by themselves—they show up on the desktop after Program Manager starts, or they show up as icons at the bottom of the screen.

First place to look—the Startup group

Assuming you don't need or want these programs to start automatically, do this:

1.   Start Windows and open the Startup group window (see fig. 18.3).

Figure 18.3

The Startup group window.

2.   Click on the icon of the program that you don't want to start when Windows starts and press the Del key on your keyboard or move the icon to another group. This removes the program from your Startup so the program doesn't start with Windows. Don't worry. If you use the Del key, you don't delete the program from the hard drive. You just delete the icon.

3.   When Windows asks you if you really want to delete the icon, click on the **Y**es button to delete it. Click on the **N**o button if you've just changed your mind. Next time you start Windows, the programs you remove from the Startup group won't start automatically.

I Want That Program To Start

Most of the time, programs start just fine in Windows. But, what happens if:

   You double-click on a program icon and nothing happens at all.

Hmmm...this doesn't happen too often. I've only seen it a couple of times, and then it was with software that wasn't released to the public yet (it still was full of bugs). If this happens to you, call Microsoft and let *them* try to figure it out.

A program might be missing some parts

The next problem is much more likely:

 You try to start a program and get the message: "Cannot find file *your program here* (or one of its components). Check to ensure the path and filename are correct and that all required libraries are available." (See fig. 18.4.)

This means that, more than likely, something is wrong with the program icon's *properties*. The properties tell Windows how to start and run the program. To check and fix a program icon's properties, do this:

 If the error message is still being displayed, choose OK to get rid of the error message.

 Select the icon you're having problems with by clicking on it once.

Figure 18.4

Missing parts
dialog box.

 Hold down the Alt key and press Enter (if you want to use the menu instead, choose the **P**roperties command from Program Manager's **F**ile menu). This brings up the program icon's properties in a dialog box (see fig. 18.5).

Figure 18.5

The Program Item
Properties dialog box.

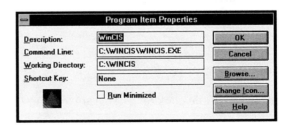

Check the **C**ommand Line property to make sure the name of the program file is right. You might need to add the full path to the file. For example, instead of just EXCEL.EXE, you might need to change the command line to C:\EXCEL\EXCEL.EXE (or whatever the correct path is to the file).

 A path consists of the drive letter, directory name, and file name that tells your program where a file is on a disk.

NERDY
DETAILS

 Check the **W**orking Directory property. Try setting it to the same directory where the program is installed. If the program file is in the directory C:\PROGRAMS\ZAPPO, make that the **W**orking Directory entry.

 When everything looks good, choose OK.

If you don't get any error messages when you choose OK, see if you can start the program.

My Icons Are All Screwed Up

All of a sudden, you realize that your icons have been toasted. They are scattered in groups where they don't belong, or they are just plain *gone*. Either you have been screwing around with your program icons, moving them and deleting them, or your pet weasel has been playing with the computer (okay, maybe it was your three-year-old). This is an inconvenience, but not bad enough to go ballistic about or burst a blood vessel.

The icons are scattered into groups where they don't belong. This one is pretty easy. Here's what to do:

1.   Open up the group window where the icons *are*, and also open the group window where they *should be*.

2. Use the mouse to drag the icons from where they are to where they should be. After you drag the icon into the right group, release the mouse button. This "drops" the icon into the group where it belongs.

3. Repeat that process until everything is back where it belongs.

Some of the icons are absolutely gone!

Now, what if some of those icons are just plain *gone*? Some of them are still there, but others are missing. If you're missing only one or two, do this:

🚰 Open and select the group window that the icon is supposed to be in.

🚰 From Program Manager's File menu, choose New.

🚰 Choose the Program Item radio button, then choose OK.

🚰 Set up the program item again. If you can't remember how to set up a program icon by filling in its properties, go back to Chapter 7 for a refresher.

They're all gone! Argh!

Let's say the weasel or the three-year-old (or you) succeeded in wiping out most or all of your icons in the Main, Accessories, or Games group. There is an easy way to fix this problem:

1. Start Windows. In Program Manager, choose File. Then choose Run.

2. When the Run dialog box shows up, type **SETUP /P** in the Command Line box. Then, press OK.

Setup should run automatically without any more fiddling from you. It will re-create your program groups if they are missing, and put all of the normal program icons back into each of the groups.

Here's how to fix the Applications group

The SETUP /P thing works only for the Main, Accessories, and Games groups (and maybe the Startup group)—not for the Applications group. If all of the icons in your Applications group are gone, do this:

1. In Program Manager, choose <u>F</u>ile then <u>R</u>un.

2. When the Run dialog box shows up, type **SETUP** in the <u>C</u>ommand Line box (just SETUP—don't add anything else). Then, press OK.

3. When the Windows Setup dialog box shows up, choose <u>O</u>ptions, then choose <u>S</u>et Up Applications.

4. When the Set Up Applications dialog box shows up, choose the Search for applications radio button, then choose OK.

Setup gives you a list that includes path and any hard disks on your system (not including any network drives you may be hooked up to). Pick the locations you want Setup to search for programs. You can choose more than one.

5. When you've selected where Setup should search, choose the <u>S</u>earch Now button. Setup may ask you a few times to identify a program if it can't decide which program it has found. Pick the one that applies and choose OK.

6. After Setup finds all of the programs, it shows you a list of all the ones it found (see fig. 18.6). Pick from the list all of the ones you want to put in the Applications group, then choose the <u>A</u>dd button.

7. When you're ready to add them to the group, choose OK.

The thing I need is past the edge of the display

This is an easy one. Maybe you have a group window that is only halfway on the screen. The rest is hiding past the edge of the screen. Unfortunately, the program icon you need is one of the ones that's hiding off-screen. Or, maybe a program you are using has somehow slipped past the edge of the screen. There are two things you can do:

 Use the mouse to drag the group window (or program window) back into view. To do that, put the tip of the arrow pointer on the window's title bar, press and hold the mouse button down, then drag the window back into place.

Figure 18.6

The Setup Applications
dialog box.

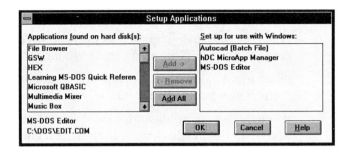

Setup Applications		
Applications found on hard disk[s]:		**Set up for use with Windows:**
File Browser		Autocad [Batch File]
GSW	Add ->	hDC MicroApp Manager
HEX		MS-DOS Editor
Learning MS-DOS Quick Referen	<- Remove	
Microsoft QBASIC		
Multimedia Mixer	Add All	
Music Box		

MS-DOS Editor
C:\DOS\EDIT.COM   OK   Cancel   Help

TRICKS

If the previous step doesn't work for some reason, you should
see a scroll bar at the bottom of Program Manager's window
(or the bottom of whatever program you're using). Use the
scroll bar to "slide" the window back into view.

I've Lost a Group!

There are two possibilities here (at least two that I can think of). First, the
group may just be hiding. Check these things:

 Is the missing group icon hiding behind one of the other group
windows? If so, just move or minimize the other group windows until
you find the one that's missing.

 Is it past the edge of the Program Manager desktop? If so, use the
scroll bars at the bottom and right side of Program Manager's
window to find the group icon that's missing. If there are no scroll
bars, there is nothing hiding past the edge of the Program Manager
window, which means the group icon has gone adios.

The second possibility is that someone or something (weasel) deleted the
program group. You'll have to re-create it and put the program icons back
into it. Read the section titled "My Icons Are All Screwed Up" to figure out
how to put the group back.

CHAPTER
19

Some Words You Should Know

T his chapter has some words and their definitions to help you understand the crazy world of Windows. If you need more specific information on these terms, turn to the Index or Table of Contents to find where they are discussed in greater detail.

active window. This is the area in Windows that you currently are working in. Although you can have several windows open on your desktop in Windows, you can have only one active window.

applet. The free programs that you get when you buy Windows, including Write, Paintbrush, and Terminal. If you get tired of these cluttering up your hard disk, you can take them off, although I recommend you keep Notepad for reading text files.

application. You might also hear this term referred to as *program*. Either way, an application is a set of instructions that tells your computer what to do so you can get something done. See also *Windows applications*.

associate. How Windows identifies an extension (such as .WRI) with an application (such as Write). You associate file name extensions with applications when you want that program to start automatically when you open the file (that is, double-clicking on it) in File Manager.

AUTOEXEC.BAT. This file tells your computer what to do when you first start it, such as automatically run Windows after your computer starts. If you get in the habit of customizing your system, you will need to get comfortable working with this file.

background. Area that is not the active window, including the desktop or any other icons or windows that are not active.

background application. Program that you currently aren't using, but you still have open on the desktop.

bit map. A picture that is created by using a series of dots (called *pixels*). You see this term a lot if you read about programs that help you create pretty computer pictures, such as Paintbrush. You can create pictures (*graphics*) in Paintbrush that have a .BMP file extension.

boot. What you get up the side of the head if you play Solitaire all day long and don't use your computer to get something important done. Actually, when you start your computer, it's called a *boot*.

cascading menu. A submenu that displays after you select a command from a menu. All commands do not have submenus—just those that can't make up their own minds.

cascading windows. What you see on your screen when you arrange the windows so that they overlap with their title bars showing.

check box. Those little square boxes you see in dialog boxes that either are blank inside or have an X inside of them. If there is an X inside the box, then that option is selected. No X means that the option is turned off.

click. That sound your mouse makes when you press once on its left button. This usually is referred to as an action, as in "Click the left mouse button to select the File menu."

Clipboard. An area of memory that Windows sets aside for you to store data when you want to transfer the data from one place to another. You use the Clipboard when you copy and paste something, for instance.

close. What Windows geeks say when they are "turning off" a program or application. You might also hear them say that they are "exiting" a program or application.

command. An order you give the computer to do something. You usually find commands in menus.

command button. In a dialog box, a button that orders the computer to do something.

CONFIG.SYS. A special file that your computer reads when you first start it. It tells the computer how you want it configured and what drivers you want to load.

control menu. Menu in the upper left corner of all Windows applications that has options that let you do things like minimize, maximize, and close the active window.

copy. Action you take to make a duplicate of your file so you can store it in another directory or on another disk, such as a floppy disk. You also can copy part or all of your document to the Windows Clipboard so that you can use it in another document or in another part of the same document.

cursor. Little blinking thing on your screen that tells you where you are.

cut. The art of moving data from an application to the Windows Clipboard. Most Windows programs give you a way to cut data from your document.

default. If you don't know what option or command to choose, Windows has one picked out for you already. This is called the default. You usually can change the default of most settings.

desktop. Area on which your windows and icons are displayed.

dialog box. Special boxes that display and let you set options and change configurations of your applications.

dimmed. Denotes when an option or command is not available.

directory. An index of the stuff that is on your hard disk or floppy disks. You can see this stuff by using the File Manager.

document. This is what you create with an application. A document can be a letter, a spreadsheet, a picture, or a sound bite. You store a document as a *file* on your hard disk or floppy disk.

document window. This is the window that you see when you are working in an application. You can have more than one document window open in most Windows applications.

double-click. Action that you usually take to start a program. When you double-click on something, you move your mouse until the pointer is on top of the object you want to start, then press the left mouse button twice, real fast.

drag. What you feel like doing to your computer when you can't figure out how to turn it on, as in "drag it back to the store and ask for your money back." It's the process of moving an object on your screen by using the mouse.

driver. Set of special instructions that tell your computer how to use the printer, mouse, and keyboard. Sometimes Windows asks you for these drivers when you add something new to your system.

Dynamic Data Exchange (DDE). A long-winded term that means "use this data from this program in that other program." You can, for example, use DDE to update your information automatically.

extension. A period and (usually) three-letter identifier at the end of a file name that tells what kind of file you have. If you have a file name with the extension .WRI, for example, you have a Windows Write file. Extensions help you sort your files when you have a ton of them on your disk.

file. What your computer stores your information in.

floppy disk. Those magnetic pieces of plastic that you slip into your disk drives that store important information for you.

font. The look of the printed letters. Windows 3.1 lets you use TrueType fonts.

foreground application. The active window.

format. What you must do to prepare your floppy disks for DOS and Windows files. Although you can format your hard disk, don't do it, unless you want to pay a computer geek a lot of money to fix your computer for you. Format also refers to the way in which you have your text set up on a page.

full-screen application. DOS application that takes up your entire screen, instead of just a small portion of it.

graphics. Term used by computer enthusiasts that means the same as "picture."

group. Set of programs that Program Manager sees as one unit. This helps you find your programs easier.

group icon. Icon that refers to a certain group in Program Manager. You see this when a particular group is minimized to an icon.

group window. In Program Manager, the window that stores your group icons.

hard disk. Area inside your computer that stores your programs, such as Windows and DOS, and your files, such as that mushy letter to your boyfriend or girlfriend. You can make more space on your hard disk by storing your files on floppy disks.

hardware. Computer equipment that computer nerds dream about. Hardware includes those things such as the system unit, monitor, keyboard, and mouse.

highlighted. Shows you what you have selected, usually by making it reverse video of what you have your system set at. A lot of times your highlighted item(s) is denoted with a blackened rectangle with white text inside of it. When you click once on an icon in Program Manager, for instance, the text below the icon becomes highlighted.

icon. Tiny picture that represents a program or file. Icons are those things you double-click on to start your programs.

inactive window. Any window that you have opened in Windows that you currently are not using.

initialization files. If you hear computer geeks talking about "INI" files, this is what they are talking about. These files contain very important information about the behavior of the Windows environment. You might read or hear about SYSTEM.INI and WIN.INI, two of the several initialization files that Windows and applications look at. If you ever have to go in and change something in these files, be sure to make a backup of your original file. This way if you screw something up, you can go back to your original file.

install. Action you take to put programs onto your hard disk. When you install programs in Windows, it prepares them so you can use them.

list box. Area in a dialog box where you are shown a collection of things from which you can choose.

macro. Set of actions that you record to automate repetitive, boring tasks. You can use the Windows Recorder program to create macros.

maximize. To enlarge your active window so that it covers your entire screen.

memory. Area on your computer where your data and programs are stored when you are using them.

menu. List of options or commands that you can choose from when you are using programs in Windows.

minimize. To reduce your active window so that it covers only a portion of your screen. This way you can see other windows that you have open.

modem. Piece of electronic hardware that lets you send computer data over phone lines to another computer. Computer nerds use modems as their means to socialize with the world.

monitor. The thing sitting on your desk that looks like a TV set.

mouse. That funny looking object connected to the back of your computer with a long, thin wire that lets you move objects on the computer screen. Try not to name your mouse, unless you want to be referred to as "that computer geek."

MS-DOS. An operating system that helps you control what your computer does. You need DOS to run Windows on your system.

multimedia. A buzzword associated with the capability to transfer information and data by using different computer media, including voice, animation, and video.

multitasking. Using more than one application at the same time. Much like a mother who has to work a full-time job, wash clothes, cook dinner, clean house, and make everyone's life run that much smoother (even when hers seems out of control!).

Object Linking and Embedding (OLE). Enables you to package a document into another document.

operating system. Set of really special instructions that manage and supervise your computer's resources.

path. Tells you where a file is in your directory.

PIF (program information file). Special file that tells Windows how to run a DOS program.

pointer. The arrow-shaped thing on your screen that moves when you move your mouse. The pointer changes shapes depending on what you are doing.

port. A sweet, fortified, usually red wine served before the main course. In computer lingo, it's a place on the back of your computer where you connect your other hardware devices, such as a printer, modem, and mouse.

printer. Piece of computer hardware that lets you make a hard copy of what you are working on.

program. Set of instructions that tells your computer what to do so you can get something done, even if it is just to play Solitaire. Sometimes referred to as an application.

program group. What Program Manager calls the collection of programs that you put together in one unit.

program item. The applications or documents that you use to make a group in Program Manager. These are what icons usually are used for.

prompt. Usually that dog-ugly thing that you see when you are stuck in DOS. Computer nerds test their manhood by using the DOS prompt more than the really cool things like icons and pretty colors offered by Windows.

random-access memory (RAM). The area in your computer where information is stored until you turn off your computer. This usually is just called *memory*.

read-only memory (ROM). Memory that cannot be erased or lost when your computer is turned off.

scroll bars. Bars that run on the right and/or bottom of your window when the contents of the window is too great to fit on the screen. You use the scroll bars to move the view of the window so you can see more of your document.

scroll box. In a scroll bar, a small box that shows you where you are in relation to the entire document.

shortcut key. Combinations of keystrokes that you press to make Windows or programs automatically do something. In some programs, you can assign your own shortcut keys.

subdirectory. Directory within another directory.

swap file. This is kind of techie, but still is important. A swap file is an area of your hard disk that Windows uses to transfer information from your memory to your hard disk. This frees up your memory so that you can have more programs running at the same time.

system unit. That big, heavy box that makes a bunch of noise when you turn it on in the morning (no, not your lazy husband). It's sometimes referred to as the "computer," but it's just the system unit and it houses the hard disk, central processing unit (the "chip"), and some other important parts of your computer system.

thumb box. In a scroll box, the tiny box that lets you move the view of the window.

tiled window. Window that is next to another window on-screen, but is not overlapping it.

title bar. Place at the top of a window where the name of the program and sometimes the name of the open file resides. If you say this term three times real fast, it sounds kind of cool.

TrueType fonts. Some really cool typefaces that let you see on your hard copy printout exactly what you see on your screen. This is a new technology that is available to Windows 3.1 users.

volume label. ID of a disk that appears in the title bar of a directory window in File Manager. You can set the volume label of floppy disks when you format them.

wallpaper. Smooth looking picture that you can put on your desktop. Ask around the office for wallpaper files. You might find a really cool one, like a Calvin and Hobbes or a Ren and Stimpy cartoon.

window. Rectangular area on your screen that your document or program resides in when you are in Windows. You can move, resize, close, or open windows.

Windows applications. These are programs specially designed to run under Windows. All Windows applications share similar features, such as menu bars, windows, dialog boxes, and sometimes toolbars. If you have Windows and you want to buy a new program, get a Windows application instead of a DOS application. You'll be happier that you did.

INDEX

C

K

T

X-Z

Windows Crossword, by Terry Hall

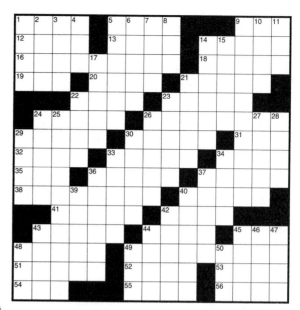

ACROSS

1 Mouse's move?
5 Capture screen
9 Menu and title are two
12 Big bus
13 Database units, in brief
14 Borland's information manager
16 Copy/cut transfer site
18 Diamonds: slang
19 Before carte or mode
20 Enticement
21 Microsoft's "5-in-1" tool
22 Object-oriented programming system
23 Circuit board tine
24 Windows' foundation
26 Application's startup directory, e.g.
29 Monitors are inter___ or not
30 Jogs
31 PC Tools' home state
32 Goes astray
33 Cover with cloth
34 Control Panel colors
35 Hubbub
36 Mouse-catchers' sounds
37 Professional principle
38 Data pic to double-click: 2 wds.
40 Whom this book is not for
41 Alpha joiners of K and Q
42 Solitaire or Minesweeper
43 Lustrous black
44 Slow trickle
45 Sixteenth President: infor.
48 Greek philosopher
49 Buttons in a border: 2 wds.
51 Turn in or out
52 Neck back
53 "Scuzzy" (peripheral connection)
54 Part of Fall Comdex city
55 Diskette format
56 Computer-___ instruction: abbr.

DOWN

1 Ten prefix
2 Small spring
3 Pacific Rim
4 Inter-frame space
5 Program Manager units
6 Brings up
7 God's ___ (burial ground)
8 Berkeley System Distribution (UNIX)
9 Where Windows wallpaper hangs
10 Requests
11 Monitor detail meas.
14 Withers
15 Carried
17 Goes with sweat and tears
21 Done in Windows Write
22 Keats and Shelley poems, e.g.
23 Supports
24 ___ Gras
25 Window's right and bottom edge ribbons
26 Shrimp
27 File Manager's directory branches
28 Day before, in brief
29 Page
30 Girl Scout unit
33 Trojan Horse, e.g.
34 This point
36 Goldfish is one
37 Digitized sound rate
39 Gush
40 Fixed in position
42 Data picture
43 Evangelical Lutheran Church in America
44 Cape of Good Hope navigator
45 Basic Windows skills, for example
46 Supervisor
47 Close Windows
48 Public (software) Library
49 Popular computer adventures, for short
50 Fed's Windows buyer

Puzzles are designed by Terry Hall, Media Ministies, Wheaton, IL

Windows Wordsearch, by Terry Hall

Find these Windows words hidden in the puzzle above. Words may be hidden diagonally, horizontally, vertically, backwards, or forwards. Hint: Spaces and hyphens are not used.

```
R A H X O B B M U H T H W V T L U A F E D
W O D N I W P U O R G P W A G E S G D O M
G R M U N E M L O R T N O C L S L N N N E
A D Y R Z R W T F S M J D T O L U P C C M
R R E Q K E B I T M A P N C K O P A P X O
D A K S I T P T O O B E I Y R S S A O A R
N O T R S N H A B B Z A W G P C E B P M Y
U B U A W I N S D I T D E C A O L D U E P
O P C B F O M K M E X R V D A L C Z O T R
R I T L L P D I R O O V I C O A M A R I A
G L R L T E X N B F Q N T R S Z W U G M B
K C O O I A C G I T G I C C B O E R M A E
C H H R M L O L F W V S A M D T O S A R L
A E S C O L I O I E T D N N Y U E W R G T
B C V S A S S N W C I N I P P Z M A G O I
W K E I T O D I U N K W E I I O J P O R T
O B D B R O N T G C D F C M U T H F R P V
D O O C W D J M I E O O I S U U I I P N Y
N X I S O F E L L N N N E E R C S L L U F
I M Q W E N C I T I I D X V O S O E O Q K
W G H J U A T S Z M D O N N S W O D N I W
```

active window
applet
associate
background
bit map
boot
cascading menu
cascading windows
check box
click
Clipboard
close
control menu
copy
cut
DDE
default
desktop
dialog box
document window
double-click
drag
foreground
full-screen
group
group icon
group window
icon

inactive window
list box
maximize
memory
Microsoft
minimize
mouse
multitasking
PIF
pointer
port
program group
program item
RAM

ROM
scroll bars
scroll box
shortcut key

swap file
thumb box
tiled window
title bar

TrueType fonts
wallpaper
window
Windows

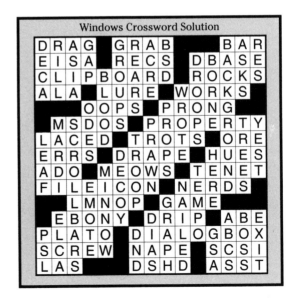

Windows Crossword Solution

D	R	A	G		G	R	A	B				B	A	R
E	I	S	A		R	E	C	S		D	B	A	S	E
C	L	I	P	B	O	A	R	D		R	O	C	K	S
A	L	A		L	U	R	E		W	O	R	K	S	
			O	O	P	S		P	R	O	N	G		
	M	S	D	O	S		P	R	O	P	E	R	T	Y
L	A	C	E	D		T	R	O	T	S		O	R	E
E	R	R	S		D	R	A	P	E		H	U	E	S
A	D	O		M	E	O	W	S		T	E	N	E	T
F	I	L	E	I	C	O	N		N	E	R	D	S	
	L	M	N	O	P		G	A	M	E				
	E	B	O	N	Y		D	R	I	P		A	B	E
P	L	A	T	O		D	I	A	L	O	G	B	O	X
S	C	R	E	W		N	A	P	E		S	C	S	I
L	A	S				D	S	H	D		A	S	S	T

This is to certify that

_____

is a graduate of the Non-Nerds School of Windows,
and has successfully completed all training, testing, and
behavior modification counseling necessary for this
course. But that doesn't mean much.

_Awarded this _____ day of _____, Nineteen-hundred-ninety-_____

_____
Chief Executive Non-Nerd

NRP
NEW RIDERS
PUBLISHING